DUST

DU

MORE LIVES OF THE POETS (WITH GUITARS)

ST

RAY ROBERTSON

BIBLIOASIS
WINDSOR, ONTARIO

FIRST EDITION
10 9 8 7 6 5 4 3 2 1

Library and Archives Canada Cataloguing in Publication

Title: Dust : more lives of the poets (with guitars) / Ray Robertson.
Other titles: More lives of the poets (with guitars)
Names: Robertson, Ray, 1966– author.
Identifiers: Canadiana (print) 20250191393 | Canadiana (ebook) 20250195968
ISBN 9781771966559 (softcover) | ISBN 9781771966566 (EPUB)
Subjects: LCSH: Musicians—Biography. | LCGFT: Biographies.
Classification: LCC ML385 .R562 2025 | DDC 780.92/2—dc23

Edited by Daniel Wells
Copyedited by Martin Ainsley
Designed and typeset by Ingrid Paulson

Published with the generous assistance of the Canada Council for the Arts, which last year invested $153 million to bring the arts to Canadians throughout the country, and the financial support of the Government of Canada. Biblioasis also acknowledges the support of the Ontario Arts Council (OAC), an agency of the Government of Ontario, which last year funded 1,709 individual artists and 1,078 organizations in 204 communities across Ontario, for a total of $52.1 million, and the contribution of the Government of Ontario through the Ontario Book Publishing Tax Credit and Ontario Creates.

PRINTED AND BOUND IN CANADA

To Mara

And now you're here
Brighten my northern sky

And A. J., Graham, and Bubba
and Danny, again.

Music above all, and for this
Choose the irregular
–Paul Verlaine, "Art Poétique"

CONTENTS

INTRODUCTION

Second verse same as the first...

With one main difference: there won't be a third. I couldn't stop writing about music if I wanted to—and why would I?—but *Dust: More Lives of the Poets (with Guitars)* is both a sequel to its predecessor and the last of its kind, at least as written by me. In V. S. Pritchett's *The Living Novel*, one of his many collections of indispensable literary essays, he baldly admits to being "too idle and specific in my enquiry to call myself a critic," maintaining instead that he is merely "an ordinary reader who has some private axe to grind." Me, too, but as an ordinary listener.

I've always been a not-so-secret proselytizer for whatever has given me those too-rare glimpses of joy, profundity, and occasional transcendence that make human existence more than the sum of its oftentimes puzzling parts. If my musical appreciations have been predicated on any critical theory, it is simply this: If I believe something is uncommonly good or interesting, I'm going to try to help the reader hear and see what I hear and see in the hope they'll listen for themselves and think so too. Granted, it's not much of an aesthetic, but that's how much of the criticism I gravitate toward operates—experientially. Besides, I'd rather be myself and wrong than correct and somebody else.

It may be that, as Swift (about whom Samuel Johnson, in his pioneering *Lives of the Poets*, wrote so superbly) said, "To endeavour to work upon the vulgar with fine sense is like attempting to hew blocks with a razor," but a lifetime of reading about music certainly inspired me to try my own hand at music criticism (or, if you prefer, musical cheerleading). The best of these writers—Lillian Roxon, Nick Tosches, Lester Bangs, Nick Kent—dependably delivered the goods regarding what music is worth obsessing over, but they did so in styles demonstrably their own and in the context of the life and times of the musician or musicians under consideration. They weren't writing minibiographies (lacking the inclination, aptitude, and energy of the biographer, neither am I), but they did highlight, when appropriate, aspects of the musicians' lives to help the reader better understand their music and their careers.

Every one of the artists in this book has been, and continues to be, important to me—and not just musically. The music is where the fascination began, but it's not where it ended. Alex Chilton's ongoing tussle with commercial success; the relationship between unhappiness and creativity in the music of James Booker; Nico's intrepid, if doomed, self-reinvention; the gap between aesthetic bliss and worldly consequence in the Staple Singers' story; Captain Beefheart's dogged, dictatorial individualism; Handsome Ned and the lure of the local; Duane Allman and the dictates of fate; Lee Mavers's paralyzing perfectionism; the alternately injurious and inspiring Manichaeism of Duster Bennett; the supernova-like artistic extinction of Danny Kirwan; Nick Drake and the vagaries of fame; Muddy Waters and the exhaustion of form: each of these stories is grounded in great music but also imbued with tragedies and trials and quandaries and paradoxes often typical of the artist's life—in some cases, quandaries and paradoxes as absorbing and enriching as the music itself.

And when the subject is music and the tools of your trade are black squiggles on a white page, metaphors, similes, and analogies are some of your best friends, especially when, like me, the writer in question isn't also a musician with a head full of technical terminology. Every musician is a potential Orpheus, charming the beasts and setting the stones dancing, but short of the sound itself, we have, for instance, Sam Phillips' observation that the first time he heard Howlin' Wolf's voice, he thought, "This is where the soul of man never dies." Writing about music might be like dancing about architecture, but so what? Dancing is rarely ever a bad idea.

And speaking of words, a few quick ones about the words "poets" and "poetry." Songwriters use words much as a painter employs colour—rhythm, sound, and strategic word placement conveying a song's "meaning" more than any limp literalism. The best Muddy Waters music *is* poetic, but the lyrics to "I Can't Be Satisfied" or "I've Got My Mojo Working" all on their own aren't poetry. There's more poetry in the five-second, introductory *Oh, yeah, Oh, yeah* growl and giddy-up of "Mannish Boy" than there is in any Bob Dylan or Joni Mitchell lyric. Every one of the musicians in this book *is* an electric poet—not because of the words they sing, but because of how those words are sung and because of the music that makes those words so memorable. Poems come with their own built-in melody, meter, and structure. Song lyrics require the magic of music to sparkle and inspire and swing. And whether it's words on the page or music in our ears, swinging is what we're after.

Even though most of the musicians celebrated in this book and in its predecessor are dead. Despite the fact that the conditions—economic, social, technological—that helped make their music possible have changed almost beyond recognition. The title of this book is taken from a Danny Kirwan song, the lyrics of which were written several decades earlier by the English poet and sailor Rupert Brooke, who died of blood poisoning in World War I. It's sad, it's beautiful, it is what art can do that life all on its own cannot: praise. "When we are dust, when we are dust!" Yes. Undoubtedly. But listen to how Danny so sacredly sings it. Marvel at how a dead man's words are wedded to a young man's music and the world becomes a different place. Who said dust can't dance?

I had a nightmare once: an LP was playing on a record player, over and over and over, the tone arm of the turntable automatically returning to the beginning of the record as soon as the side was done. Eventually, the record literally ran its grooves out and was unlistenable, useless, dead black plastic. And the entire time, no one was listening.

Does a tree fall in the forest if no one hears it? I wouldn't know. I was listening to my records.

ALEX CHILTON

Where honour or where conscience does not bind,
No other law shall shackle me
–Cowley

Everybody wants to be cool—it's how you get to heaven when you don't believe in God—but there's cool, and then there's *cool*. Alex Chilton is *cool*. Not that he would have cared that I or anyone else thought as much, but of course, that's just another reason why he's cool. Because the key to being cool is not caring about what's not worth caring about, like what other people think or what you're expected to do or not do. But outsider cool comes with a cost. If it didn't, it wouldn't qualify as cool. Sometimes independence of thought and action and principled integrity can look a lot like wilful self-sabotage. Such are the wages of cool.

He was born in Memphis, Tennessee, in 1950, the son of a Day-Brite Lighting salesman and amateur musician and a mother who shared her husband's love of jazz and icy cocktails consumed on warm Memphis evenings. Financially comfortable, cultured, and extremely liberal, Alex's parents provided him and his two brothers and sister with as enlightened an upbringing as any kid growing up in the deep south in the 1950s could hope for. Elvis cut his first records for Memphis-based producer and disc jockey Sam Phillips in 1953, and Alex grew to love the burgeoning sounds of rock and roll while absorbing the omnipresent R&B and blues music that his hometown was already renowned for.

Alex's parents' carpe diem approach to living—his mother opened an art gallery in their house, and his father frequently invited like-minded musicians over to drink and jam—sometimes bled over into their parenting philosophy. The salon-like atmosphere may have made the Chilton residence the preferred destination for many Memphis artists, musicians, and iconoclastic thinkers (the photographer William Eggleston had a darkroom in the backyard), but a house habitually full of raving, pissed-up musicians and artists didn't make for a regular supper hour or an enforced bedtime. In the documentary *Big Star: Nothing Can Hurt Me,* producer, musician, and Memphis man-about-town Jim Dickinson recalls his initial impression of the young Alex:

> The first time I saw Alex Chilton I guess he was eleven or twelve years old. Now, Alex is what I call an 'art brat.' The mother ran an art gallery. His father was a hobbyist clarinet player. Bill Eggleston, the Memphis art photographer, had given him peyote and he was running around with his eyes spinning like that, you know, his hair sticking out. And I thought, 'Well, this kid is going to have a unique life'.

In addition to keeping up with what was happening in rock and roll (by the early 1960s, not much), Alex had access to his father's enormous collection of jazz records. In Robert Gordon's book *It Came from Memphis,* Alex remembered discovering Ray Charles, Charles Mingus, and Cannonball Adderley and tells Gordon about how Chet Baker became a favourite vocalist, inspiring him to sing for the first time. During a period when real rock and roll had been eclipsed by assembly-line schmaltz, Alex was able to dip his toe into other, more-vibrant musical waters. And even though his parents were primarily jazz listeners, they had always encouraged their children to do, say, and feel whatever they wanted, so when the Beatles appeared on *The Ed Sullivan Show* in 1964 and saved rock and roll, they never discouraged their son's growing infatuation with all things moptop (like growing out his hair).

Alex inevitably joined a local garage band, the Moondogs, when he was around thirteen, playing hits by the better British Invasion bands alongside popular R&B and Motown tunes. Even though the group members had barely entered their teens and weren't much more than a slapdash jukebox, Alex (primarily a vocalist at this time) was clearly the leader. Friend Michael O'Brien told Alex's biographer Holly George-Warren (*A Man Called Destruction*):

> Alex was nothing like my other friends. He had a well-defined sense of himself and was already a bit defiant. He knew who he was, what he wanted to do, and what he wouldn't tolerate. And that never changed as long as I knew him. Hanging out with Alex involved listening to music

that he wanted you to hear. It was like a class, with Alex as teacher and us—his friends—as his students. Alex would pick, say, one of his dad's Ray Charles records and point out a certain vocal phrasing and play it again and again and again—while smiling approvingly.

Another, more established band (one that actually got paid to play) heard Alex's group performing at his high school talent show and were impressed enough by the teenage singer's surprisingly deep, gravelly voice to invite him to join their group, the Devilles, when their lead singer quit. Despite not caring much for the handful of imitation British Invasion singles the band had previously cut, Alex was game. High school was a drag, he'd get a chance to sing in front of people and meet lots of girls, and who knew what it might lead to? It led to the biggest commercial success of Alex's forty-four-year musical career. He was sixteen years old.

~

The Box Tops (once they cut their first single with Alex as lead singer, management decided a name change was in order) were the Memphis Monkees, a group of very young men eager for success and willing to do almost anything to get it. That included recording whatever songs they were told to record and often not even doing that, Alex's voice frequently the only authentically Box Tops thing on much of their music. In the beginning, however, was "The Letter," an infectious little pop gem written by veteran songwriter Wayne Carson and souped up in the studio by writer and producer Dan Penn (the sound of the jet taking off at the end of "The Letter" was his idea, as was the MOR string section). The song sat on the shelf for a while before the small Bell label eventually issued it on its even smaller Mala imprint. The tune immediately hit number one on the singles chart and eventually sold four million copies. Penn (and his sometimes songwriting companion Spooner Oldham) had authored such hardcore rhythm and blues classics as "Do Right Woman" and "Dark End of the Street," but the sound he gave the Box Tops was a new kind of R&B—rhythm and bubble gum—the combination of Alex's engagingly raspy voice (the song initially got played on many Black stations because the singer sounded African American) and the driving, drum- and bass-heavy arrangement making it irresistible to AM-radio listeners in the fall of 1967.

The band set off in the matching coats and shirts that their manager insisted they wear to play for their many new fans—who often didn't believe that this collection of skinny white kids was the group who sang their favourite new song, until Alex opened his mouth, at which point the fanatical screaming would commence. It didn't hurt, either, that Alex was slim and good looking and had a sneering, sideways grin and long hair that often fell over his eyes. Bands like the Box Tops were expected to relentlessly promote the company's latest product, and this the group did, once performing three concerts over the course of the same night in three different Pennsylvanian cities. Mostly it was the usual one-hit-wonder grind: boredom, booze, exhaustion, and intraband hostilities dominating, when they weren't on stage having a ball recreating their lone hit and cranking out the usual selection of cover songs to pad out their short sets. The screaming girls and increasingly available illicit substances aside, however, touring conditions were, predictably, lousy. Townes Van Zandt once said that being a folksinger is ninety percent driving, ten percent playing. If the music is great and the concerts transformative (for performer and audience both), those are pretty decent percentages. If not, not so much.

An album (*The Letter/Neon Rainbow*) to go along with the big single; another tasty hit ("Cry Like a Baby," although not a number one) and eponymous album (*Cry Like a Baby*), fleshed out with more Penn–Oldham Memphis-pop confections and predictable covers; a third, then a fourth and final album (*Nonstop* and *Dimensions*), which were more of the same, but without that most important of pop things—another popular single; and enough one-nighters to fill a lifetime. The Box Tops did get to open for some of Alex's musical heroes—the Beach Boys, among them—but it wasn't only the incessant touring or the substandard performing conditions that were depressing: Alex simply didn't feel that they were good enough (or willing to *get* good enough) on their instruments and that they weren't nearly as proficient as the other bands they encountered on the road. Plus, the label was resistant to Alex's efforts to get his own songs on Box Tops albums. There were also the usual ubiquitous questions from band members about management and where all the money had gone. After a two-week tour of England in late 1969 was cancelled once the band discovered that the equipment that management had procured for them was broken and essentially unusable, Alex and the Box Tops were no more.

~

While not exactly flush after the dissolution of the Box Tops, Alex could afford to write some songs and practice the guitar and even record several demos with Ardent Studios engineer Terry Manning. Ardent was a small Memphis recording studio that had developed a reputation for making wonderful-sounding records, both because of its state-of-the-art equipment and because of owner-operator John Fry's unmatched skills behind the mixing board. Fry was also a very generous man, who held sound-engineering classes for whoever was interested. One such student was Alex's future Big Star bandmate Chris Bell, but Bell wasn't the only scuffling musician Fry would entrust with a key to the studio for late-night recording sessions.

Not released until two and a half decades later (as the album *1970*, the year of their origin), the songs Alex recorded together with Manning (behind the board and adding bass and keyboards) and drummer Richard Rosebrough might not make for a cohesive album, but they do provide an interesting auditory X-ray of Alex's musically schizophrenic state of mind at the time. Having rejected the R&B-tinged, Top 40 pop craft of the Box Tops, Alex experimented with country rock (the giddy, self-explanatory "Free Again" and "The Happy Song"), near-parodic blues rock ("All I Want Is Money"), *Sunflower*-era Beach Boys ("Every Day As We Grow Closer"), quirky covers (a slowed-down, surprisingly catchy version of the Stones' "Jumpin' Jack Flash"), and even indulged his nascent musical eccentricity with a medley combining that most bubble gum of all bubble gum tunes, the Archies' "Sugar, Sugar," with "There Was a Time" by soul-and-funk god James Brown. He also experimented with his voice, for the most part eschewing his signature, croaky Box Tops vocal style for a much more relaxed, honest approach that could be tenderly vulnerable one minute, scorchingly acerbic the next. Not surprisingly, the demos didn't create much label interest, and Alex moved to New York and continued to write, practice, and play the occasional solo acoustic set on open mic nights in Greenwich Village. Folk was dead, but performing his own songs, his own way, by himself, was enough. As 1970 turned into 1971, Alex ended up back in Memphis.

Alex had known Chris Bell from around town, and when he returned from New York he caught a performance by the latter's band, Icewater. He enjoyed the British Invasion–inspired, melodically rich mix of hard-rocking originals and tasteful covers, and it wasn't long before he was hanging out at Ardent after-hours with Bell and his bandmates, bassist Andy Hummel and drummer Jody Stephens. After the smorgasbord of styles sampled during his initial post–Box Top recording sessions and his time folking around in New York, Bell's musical Anglophilia provided Alex with a fresh-but-familiar foundation for the new songs he was writing. Inspiration can come from anywhere—even a guy from your own hometown. Soon Alex was the fourth member of the group.

All but two of the twelve tracks on Big Star's first album are Bell–Chilton compositions. (Alex and the ex-Icewater guys had been inspired to adopt the "Big Star" moniker by the Memphis grocery-store chain of that name.) The writing method the two employed usually involved one of them bringing something into the studio, where the other would add to it, either harmonically, instrumentally, or lyrically. Alex was Lennon to Bell's McCartney. Alex would write something sour, Bell would add something sweet, and the result was usually gently sautéed sweet-and-sour perfection. The influence worked the other way as well. In the liner notes to Omnivore's posthumous compilation of Bell's mostly previously unreleased solo tracks, *I Am the Cosmos*, Fry notes that Bell liked to swathe his voice in reverb, but that in their Big Star days together Chilton would encourage him to record his vocals raw. Bell and Alex made for such a mutually advantageous writing team partially because they were so different. Bell was still living at home and taking classes part-time at a local college when the new band recorded its first album. He was also plagued by what was probably a deeply repressed homosexuality; in *Nothing Can Hurt Me*, Bell's brother David described how Chris once told him that he should take drugs because they killed one's sex drive. Chilton, on the other hand, already had a number-one single; had been briefly married, had a child, and divorced; and was never lacking for female companionship.

Fry did a considerable amount of production work at Ardent for Stax and was approached by the soul label's head, Al Bell, who wanted to expand into the pop (i.e., white) market, to ask Fry if he was interested in Ardent becoming Stax's subsidiary rock-and-roll label. Fry immediately said yes, and Big Star suddenly had the promise of a record deal. And just how easy was that? Most bands had to bash it out, live, night after night, sometimes for years; *then*—maybe—they scored that elusive record deal and entered the studio. Big Star was born in the studio. They never played a note of music live until *after* their first LP was released.

#1 Record—such an unassuming title (it's their first record); such a bold boast (it's number-one-in-the-charts worthy); such a retrospectively oxymoronic encapsulation of Big Star's complicated relationship with artistic success and commercial failure—was released in late summer, 1972. Although a cowrite with Alex, lead track "Feel" is pure Chris Bell at his larynx-shredding shrillest—it and "Don't Lie to Me," examples of Bell's

love of Led Zeppelin's more bombastic side. Both songs throb with energy, though, and they *sound* great—as does the whole record—Bell's ceaseless pursuit of the right sonic colours to adorn each of the band's tunes is evidence that those engineering classes with Fry had paid off.

"The Ballad of El Goodo" is Alex's *#1 Record* debut, and it is everything that makes Big Star the quintessential power-pop band. "Power pop" may have been coined by Pete Townshend to describe concise, energetic, guitar-based, and melodically distinctive rock songs that exhibit a minimum of soloing and are usually about nothing weightier than romantic relationships; but no one—not the early Who, not Badfinger, not the Raspberries, not Dwight Twilley—ever came close to Big Star's perfection of the form and their simultaneous ability to transcend it. "The Ballad of El Goodo" is everything power pop is supposed to be: it is melodically gorgeous, with just the right amount of background-vocal sweetening; it is driven by a rich mix of sparkling acoustic and electric guitars; it brims with passion and conviction—but, contra power pop's minimalist credo, it is an ode to hard-earned individualism, as opposed to adolescent dating rituals, and it is also two songs in one: the ballad-like verses morphing into the anthemic choruses.

"In the Street" is probably Big Star's best-known tune (it was covered by Cheap Trick and used as the theme song for Fox TV's *That '70s Show*, a quarter of a century after *#1 Record* was relegated to the discount bin). Once again, we're treated to one of Bell's balls-to-the-wall vocal performances, and it works perfectly—the subject matter, this time, not romantic disillusionment but adolescent agitation and ennui, the song's initial bravado dissolving into the loneliness, boredom, and longing of suburban youth. The music mirrors the song's voices, the electric guitars chugging along in tandem until the yearning chorus is accented by Bell's and Alex's equally yearning instruments. "Thirteen" successfully mines the same territory, but in an entirely different way, the gentle, finger-picked acoustic guitars providing the feathery foundation for Alex's melancholic evocation of first love. Bassist Hummel's "The India Song" is chiefly notable for being the only cut on the album that neither Alex nor Bell had a hand in writing.

Because power pop is all about the song—there isn't any instrumental virtuosity to distract because there isn't any—even the best bands working in the genre tend to produce great singles but only so-so albums. Not Big Star. Side 2 (of the original vinyl release of *#1 Record*) opens with "When My Baby's Beside Me," a terrific, stirring rocker that only the most miserable sort of person could resist dancing to (or at least playing air guitar along with). Here and elsewhere one can hear the influence of the three *B*'s on *#1 Record*—the Beatles, the Byrds, and the Beach Boys—the triadic template of so much good pop music. But what you don't hear is what most people who learn that the band was from Memphis might have expected: there's virtually no blues, R&B, or soul influences on the album's sound. This is a Southern band that knows its indigenous musical lineage (Alex and the Box Tops regularly opened for Sam and Dave and the Staple Singers) but is true to what genuinely inspires them. And for Bell, that was the Beatles, his "My Life Is Right" (a track originally written and recorded with a previous band of his, Rock City) the most Beatlesque of *#1 Record*'s twelve cuts. A bouncy, upbeat tune, its background-vocal exclamations on the chorus, while delightful, are perhaps a tad too derivative of the same at the end of the Beatles' "Rain."

The album's remaining four tracks are all primarily acoustic, a conspicuously anticlimactic and iconoclastic way to conclude a rock-and-roll album, and further evidence that Big Star, while inspired by the past, didn't feel beholden to it. "Give Me Another Chance" sounds like Bell is singing lead, but it's actually Alex at the absolute upper end of his vocal register. After the pleasant "Try Again," another Rock City leftover, *#1 Record* concludes (except for the brief, Bell-sung, barely there "ST 100/6") with Alex's surprisingly sanguine "Watch the Sunrise." Although the same melody was used by Bell for his Rock City tune "Country Morn," the new lyrics, Alex's buoyant vocal, and the luscious background vocals make for a much better song.

Speaking of the Beatles: in a way, this was all their fault. If they could be both undeniably great and massively popular, why, fans like Chris Bell wondered, couldn't Big Star? The simple answer is: because. Because nine times out of ten it doesn't work that way. For every Beatles, Shakespeare, or *The Sopranos*—lasting art (pop or otherwise) that almost everybody loves—there's a Big Star, whom the right people respect but most people don't know or care about. The Beatles were not only among the very best at what they did *and* enormously successful, they were also constantly evolving as artists who took their listeners happily along with them. Big Star didn't set out to be a cool underground band that only the with-it people knew about and loved: they wanted—and thought they could achieve—at least enough popularity to ensure that they could play music for a living.

All of Big Star's members came of musical age in the mid-1960s, when you could flip on your car's AM radio and hear not only the Fab Four, but also the Mamas and the Papas, James Brown, Bob Dylan, the Supremes, the Beach Boys, the Byrds, Marvin Gaye, the Animals, Otis Redding, the Rolling Stones, et cetera. No artistically restrictive musical labels, no major-label monopoly of the marketplace and the means of distribution, no corporate-dictated radio playlists, no big-budget marketing strategies. Good music was good music and that was good enough. Sure, there were also people like Herman's Hermits and Eddy Arnold clogging up the Top 40, but the point is that the best pop music was also quite frequently the most popular. Corporate America soon took care of that (just like it had previously taken care of the nation's railways, ensuring that every American needed their own automobile), as soon as they figured out that there was real money to be made with what used to be considered nickel-and-dime kid's music.

Alex and Big Star were about five years ahead of their time—were one of the godfathers of the subsequent power-pop, jangle-rock, and alternative-rock movements—because they were about five years behind the times, emphasizing smart, guitar-driven, melody-rich rock and roll and tender-but-never-soppy acoustic songs at a time when progressive rock, hard rock, glam, and singer-songwriters were what most mattered in the marketplace. Alex et al. possessed the courage to be aesthetically passé, which elevated them to the avant-garde, which meant that *#1 Record*'s reception upon its appearance was predictable: rock critics with ears loved it, while radio (except for a handful of college stations) ignored it. Worse, the few people who wanted to hear it had a difficult time finding it in their local record store, Stax's distribution not what Fry and everyone else at Ardent expected it to be (perhaps because they were still primarily known as an R&B and soul label, and record stores were not particularly interested in stocking product from the label's new, lesser-known rock brand). Even then, FM radio, where most "serious" rock was played now—AM becoming home to talk, soft rock, and other make-your-workday-go-by-quicker pabulum—was enamoured of what Alex derisively described to interviewer Bruce Eaton (author of the essential *Big Star's "Radio City,"* volume 65 in the 33 ⅓ series) as "heavy music."

Reviews of the LP were frequently dazzling. I own a faded copy of the February 1, 1973, issue of *Rolling Stone* containing Bud Scoppa's take, in which he marvels at how "even the prettiest tunes have tension and subtle energy to them, and the rockers reverberate with power." It is the kind of laudatory, thoughtful review that every artist fantasizes about. Unfortunately for band morale, the focus of most reviews was usually Alex. Not surprising, perhaps, considering he was the only member that the musical world had heard of—and the last time they had, it was as the croaky-throated kid with teeny-bopper sensation the Box Tops—but that didn't make Bell feel any less marginalized. It was his band (and his initial vision) that Alex had joined, not the other way around.

Lacking a presence on the radio, the only other way to get their music in people's ears was to tour, tour, tour, one lousy, under-attended gig at a time, just like other trailblazing bands such as the Ramones dutifully did, hopefully picking up a few new converts along the way. The shows were poorly attended, all right, but instead of feeding off the indifference and becoming even more determined, the band, and Bell in particular, chafed at the lack of sleep and the crappy food and the tedium of spending too much time with the same three guys in the back of a van and, most of all, the typically indifferent audiences. For Alex, the rock-and-roll veteran at age twenty-two who'd already achieved both top-ten success and commercial irrelevancy with the Box Tops, as well as having already endured thousands of hours of highway drudgery, it was disappointing. For the far-less worldly-wise Bell, it was devastating. Bad things weren't supposed to happen to good rock-and-roll bands.

Bell began to argue with the venerable Fry, perhaps the band's biggest supporter, blaming him personally for Stax's poor distribution and *#1 Record*'s lack of commercial success. Deeply depressed, and after failing to convince the other members of Big Star that the band's problems could be traced back to Fry and Ardent and that they should move to another label, Bell quit the band. He also vandalized Fry's car in the Ardent parking lot, tried to destroy the master tapes of *#1 Record*, and attempted to kill himself. The remainder of Bell's short life—he would die in a car accident in 1978 at age twenty-seven—was dominated by further musical frustrations, depression and drug problems, a conversion to evangelical Christianity, and the sole solo record released during his lifetime, the stupendous single "I Am the Cosmos" b/w "You and Your Sister."

The band, now a three-piece, played a few hometown gigs that weren't much better attended than those undertaken out of town, and they continued to mess around at Ardent after-hours, recording demos of some of Alex's new songs (several co-composed with Hummel) and a handful of tunes cowritten with Bell, before his departure. Bell might have been in charge during the recording of *#1 Record*, but Big Star was now Alex's band. Which meant he set both the musical and the social agenda. "Alex really loved his cocktails" (and Quaaludes), John King, who had been brought into the Ardent fold to help with promotion, recalled, "especially if someone else was buying. He loved it that I had a company credit card. We'd get really drunk at Ardent, and then Fry would come in the next morning, and we'd be huddled under the drum blankets."

Drink and drugs were part of what was going on in the studio, but not why the band was there. What Alex and Hummel and Stephens (and a handful of like-minded Memphis musicians, including drummer Richard Rosebrough, who'd played on the unreleased *1970* material) were doing was piecing together, whether they knew it for not, Big Star's second album. Not that anyone called it that. Not that anyone was even sure there *was* a band. How could they when the group's founder had quit and their first LP had been commercially stillborn? But songwriters write songs and musicians play music, and the tunes Alex was demoing, whether with the Big Star guys or whomever else was hanging around Ardent, were as good as or better than the material on the first album. They were also much looser, in every possible way. Bassist Danny Jones, a frequent late-night Ardent attendee: "[Alex] wanted it to be so spontaneous and so free and loose. That's why he came up with some really cool recording techniques. That's just what he lived and breathed: You don't want to overproduce anything. Alex ran the board, and everything was one take—Alex wouldn't do more than one take."

What was the source of this new attitude toward recording? Feeling liberated from Bell's obsessive studio perfectionism? Resentment bordering on spite, toward a public that had rejected the band's finely crafted first album? An evolving reevaluation of the role of spontaneity and first-take feel in the recording process? Alcohol- and drug-abetted indifference? An argument can be made for all or some of the above, although the audio evidence is obvious: the bulk of Alex's new songs were less glorious pop confections and more jagged slices of rock-and-roll splendour.

Things were changing on the business front, as well. Stax (and therefore Ardent) had a new and presumably much better distributor in industry heavyweight Columbia. And, attempting to capitalize on the wonderful reviews *#1 Record* had received, John King (with Stax's generous backing) organized something called the Rock Writers Convention. The ruse was to gather scribes like Greg Shaw, Cameron Crowe, Richard Meltzer, Lenny Kaye, Nick Tosches, Jaan Uhelszki, Lester Bangs, Ben Edmonds, and Pete Frame in Memphis, at Stax's expense, to organize themselves as a union to get rock writers everywhere a fairer shake from magazines and newspapers, though the real reason Stax dropped such a large chunk of change on a bunch of freeloading rock critics was to showcase several of Ardent's new bands, Big Star included.

The writers never got themselves unionized, but Ardent employee Steve Rhea remembered Big Star's set as "one of the most exciting nights of my entire Ardent experience. They played all the songs from *#1 Record* and some from [the yet-to-be released] *Radio City*. There were all sorts of punk guys [among the writers] who were into all the obscure British bands, everything we had been into. It was the perfect audience." The band was buoyed by the rapturous response, a rarity in their brief performing career. If there had been any doubts before about whether Big Star would record and release a second album, they were now extinguished.

Radio City (so named, according to drummer Stephens, because "We all thought this was a radio-friendly album"—these guys obviously didn't worry much about jinxing themselves with audacious album titles) opens with "O, My Soul." The difference between Big Star 1 and Big Star 2 is immediately evinced by the nearly minute-long lead up to the first line of lyric. Also, at five minutes, forty seconds, it is nearly a minute and a half longer than the lengthiest cut on *#1 Record*. It's still bright-and-bouncy power pop—sort of—but the herky-jerky rhythm, what sounds like organ swells (but is probably a Mellotron), the funky *chunka chunka chunka chunka* guitar breaks, the frantic tom-tom fills, and the absence of background vocals and a second guitar make it something else too. Some people—myself among them—favour the generally roomier, more eclectic sound of *Radio City*, and "O, My Soul" (although it sounds like it was mixed in mono) is a good example why. The gorgeously melancholic "Life Is White" is another boy-girl song that again features only Alex on vocal, and whose most distinctive characteristic is the wheezing harmonica. It's odd, it shouldn't work, it does. Composed entirely by Hummel and sung by Stephens, "Way Out West" is one of the tunes on *Radio City* that most recalls the band's first LP. The words aren't much more than boy-misses-girl, but Stephens' vulnerable vocal and Alex's help on the chorus's high parts is deeply affecting. "What's Goin' Ahn" is one of three album cuts where Alex is the only Big Star member present, Rosebrough and Jones helping out on drums and bass, respectively. It is also another sign of Alex's own growth as a songwriter and arranger. The softer, more introspective material on *#1 Record* tended to manifest itself in either ballads or straight-out acoustic exercises, but while "What's Going Ahn" is *Radio City*'s most ruminative track, its lovely, hesitant melody is coaxed out with the aid of a gorgeous blend of acoustic and electric guitars, as well as drums and bass. If one had to give it a label, "Nervous Folk-Rock" would probably be the least misleading. The last track on side 1, "You Get What You Deserve," is nothing special, either melodically or lyrically, but that is what's so special about it. If this is what passes for filler on the album—an agreeable, mid-tempo rocker, adorned with bright piano and more of Alex's increasingly inventive electric guitar playing—then this must be a very special LP.

Side 2 opener "Mod Lang" is the bluesiest thing Big Star ever recorded (although it's actually the Chilton–Rosebrough–Jones lineup again), but because one of the things that made the band so special was its allergy to clichés, Alex fashioned the lyrics out of lines from several different old blues songs, then named the whole thing after a local university's modern-languages building. Blues purists, they weren't. "Back of a Car" was one of the numbers Bell ceded to the band when he departed. The adolescent uncertainty and anxiety of the lyrics and the verse-chorus-verse classicism of its structure certainly do convey Bell's influence, but the swagger in the vocals and the short, rude guitar solo are all Alex Chilton, each helping keep the song from sounding twee or self-consciously naïve. (On a demo of one of the songs Bell kept for himself, and later recorded on his own, "There Was a Light," Alex sings lead, and it's another example of how Bell benefited from Alex's collaborative influence. The Big Star demo version sounds tragic; Bell's later version, while still an undeniably beautiful song at its core, veers uncomfortably close to whiny.)

"Daisy Glaze" is slow-fast-slow-fast, equal parts gauzy and brawny, the quieter parts sung in Alex's anti–Box Tops falsetto, the louder, faster sections redolent of his snotty, rocker side (ask someone else what the title means; to me, it says that, in spite of their "radio city" ambitions, the band was being piloted by an increasingly commercially sceptical insurgent, who wasn't averse to getting some of his kicks throwing listeners a compositional curveball). The final artifact of the Chilton–Rosebrough–Jones late-night sessions to be included on *Radio City* is "She's a Mover," a chugging paean to a particularly captivating wild woman (although the reference to "Catholic school" leads one to wonder whether "woman" is the right word). If the band had survived to become a regular touring group, it would have made a terrific mid-set rocker.

"September Gurls" is simply one of the greatest pop songs ever written, post-1970, right up there with Todd Rundgren's "Couldn't We Just Discuss It," the Undertones' "Teenage Kicks," the La's' "There She Goes," or—feel free to pick your own favourite ditty. It is the culmination of everything that *#1 Record* had been about—a symphony of chiming electric guitars, sweet-but-never-syrupy background vocals (particularly those gorgeous "ooh's" just before Alex's succinct-but-soaring guitar solo), simple love/lust lyrics sung with obvious conviction, powerful-but-never-show-offy drumming, and a melody that simply negates the possibility of one ever forgetting it. Alex would never write another song so perfectly power pop. After the pretty piano-and-vocal fragment "Morpha Too" (1:27), the charming solo-acoustic "I'm In Love with a Girl" (itself only 1:48) brings the album to a delicate, ghostly close. Better play it again: this is one of the last times listeners would ever hear Alex Chilton this emotionally unguarded.

More rave reviews and minimal sales when the record was released in 1974; more bad business news (Columbia had fired Clive Davis, the man who'd negotiated the new distribution deal with Stax, which basically went kaput with Davis' ouster); a successful media showcase in New York, followed by another band defection (Hummel this time, headed back to university, because working a straight job was better than being a penniless big star); a new bass player, John Lightman; and touring like they meant it this time, although the results, unfortunately, were often the same. Roadie John Dando remembered one gig where "there was absolutely nobody in the club. Not one single person." On another tour stop, Dando recalled Alex "eating... fried mushrooms onstage while he was trying to play and he couldn't sing because his mouth was so full.... That was just the way he was. [By this point, Alex] really didn't care much about getting to an audience—he was just playing for himself."

Alex's dejection and increasing cynicism are understandable. And refusing to make music that other people, like record buyers and radio programmers, want you to make is admirable—and very cool. Disrespecting your audience isn't. Even if it is smaller than you'd like and less appreciative than is ideal. Not caring about the oblivious and the indifferent is righteous; not caring about the people who *are* listening and *do* care isn't. It's also dangerous. Not caring can become habit-forming.

"If the fool would persist in his folly he would become wise," William Blake wrote. It is easier to attempt foolish things in the pursuit of wisdom, however, when one has allies. To make his masterpiece, Alex had Jim Dickinson and Lesa Aldridge. Alex had known the burly, charismatic Dickinson since he was a kid, and he had followed the latter's varied career (something Alex couldn't be bothered to do with too many people) as session man, producer, solo artist, and all-around rock-and-roll raconteur. Maybe just as importantly, the two shared a twisted sense of humour (a collection of Dickinson's posthumous writings was published under the title *I'm Just Dead, I'm Not Gone*) and enjoyed each other's conversation. Despite Big Star being whittled down to only Alex and Stephens, and no one talking about making another Big Star album, Alex had written and demoed with acoustic guitar several new songs, and he asked Dickinson if he would be interested in producing. Ardent, the business operation, might not have had what it took to make Big Star a profitable proposition, but John Fry remained sufficiently enamoured of Alex's artistry to continue to allow him virtually unlimited access to the recording studio. Dickinson listened to what Alex had come up with and immediately agreed to help.

Alex and Lesa had begun dating around the time of *Radio City*'s ill-starred release, and several of Alex's acoustic demos were recorded with her engineering the sessions or joining Alex on background vocals. Like Alex, Aldridge was the off-spring of a well-off, well-educated, extremely liberal Memphis family, and although only eighteen years old when she and Alex met (he was twenty-four), Aldridge was his intellectual and spiritual equal. She was also beautiful—think pre-Raphaelite, dirty blond, with an attitude—and Alex was besotted. The new couple liked to drink and do drugs and stay up all night, which, combined with their youth, often led to nasty fights (verbal and physical), but what they liked to do best was listen to music, talk about music, and make music. Aldridge wasn't Alex's muse—she was his co-conspirator.

"Alex set the tone of the recording on the night of the first session, when he turned to me and shot Demerol down his throat with a syringe," Dickinson said. But even if the sessions were a chaotic mix of alcohol-and-drug abuse, highly combustible romantic fissures, and Alex's increasingly commercial contrariness (Dickinson: "Fry made the mistake of saying he liked [a certain song]... Well, the next thing Alex said was, 'I think we could do the snare drum with a basketball'"), listening to the demos gathered together on the three-disc *Third/ Sister Lovers* box set, released in 2016, reveals an artist who came to work prepared. (Because the original album didn't receive an official release for several years after the fact, its title tended to be in flux, sometimes going by *Third*—because it was Big Star's third album—and sometimes *Sister Lovers*, because Stephens was dating Lesa's sister Holliday at the time of its recording.) As unusual as the product sounded, by the time Alex and Dickinson were done with it, underneath it all were some very, very good songs—many among the best Alex would ever write—with, in many cases, relatively conventional, if exceptional, melodies and structures. And if there was any sonic weirdness added after the fact, it was good weirdness, the kind that helps the song better become what it's supposed to be.

Around twenty tunes were recorded during the sessions with Dickinson—several of them covers, which reveal Alex's endearingly eclectic taste. Who else, in 1974, would think to cover the Velvet Underground, the Kinks, the Beatles, Gram Parsons, Jerry Lee Lewis, and Nat King Cole? Of the originals, "Kizza Me," driven by Alex's effectively deranged vocal (name-checking Aldridge in the chorus) and Stephens' tasteful bashing, is rock and roll, all right, but it also benefits from some near-feral cello that essentially takes the place of the electric guitar as lead instrument. The defiant "You Can't Have Me," as clear a statement of Alex's mounting antagonism toward the music industry as he ever made, is another angry, all-out rocker, the squealing saxophone a nice, troubling touch. The upbeat "Thank You Friends" includes big backing vocals, and the tone is almost cheerful, but Alex's ode to all the ladies and gentlemen who have made his life not good, not happy, but...*probable* is evidence of Alex's new peekaboo sensibility: now you see who I am, now you don't. "O, Dana," a catchy celebration of a female friend who counsels some interesting self-pleasuring concepts, is sleekly sleazy. "Jesus Christ" is a catchy, unironic Christmas song (as unironic as a rock-and-roll Christmas song can be), inexplicably prefaced by a brief tack piano freak out. "Stroke It Noel" is pure joy, the violin break a cool, refreshing rain after so much emotional humidity and darkened skies. "Downs," an ode to Alex's drug of choice and cowritten with Aldridge, is the song Fry thought might be radio friendly—and it might have been, at least until Alex and Dickinson added the prominent use of steel drums, the aforementioned basketball, and someone hollering along in the background, somewhat in tune. Recalled Stephens: "We would record a song and it would be sweet and pretty, and then Alex would go back and throw the bass out of tune and do something wild and wacky to screw it up.... [Alex] thought it was a true reflection—this is what he was feeling."

Considering its eventual reputation as some kind of protopunk album, it is ironic that *Third/Sister Lovers'* best songs are the quieter ones. Which isn't to say soft or gentle or easily digestible. "Blue Moon" (an original—not the Bill Monroe tune Elvis covered for Sun Records) and "Take Care" are so tender they almost fall off the bone. "Big Black Car," particularly in its solo, acoustic demo form, would be impossibly despairing if it wasn't so beautiful. When Alex's boast that nothing can hurt him is followed in the next line with him asking himself why he should bother caring, it's a rare moment of sublime pop. The aural overhaul Dickinson performed on album highlight "Kanga Roo"—adding squalling feedback, waves of Mellotron, and a clanking cowbell, among other things—should have resulted in a cowriting credit, as essential as it is to the song's magnificence. Then there's "Holocaust," where Alex and Dickinson's deployment of Bartókian piano, sorrowful bassoon, and weeping slide guitar flawlessly complements the dim-and-dire lyrics.

In a perfect world, "Holocaust" would be the B-side to the hit "Stroke It Noel," and Alex would have been on the cover of *Rolling Stone*. That's not the world we live in, though. In this one, in early 1975, Fry and Dickinson pressed up promotional copies and began to shop them around to record labels only to receive not a single offer. Dickinson: "Karen Berg [a friend of Alex's then working at Elektra] accused me of destroying Alex's career.... Lenny Waronker [Warner Brothers] said, 'I don't have to listen to that again, do I?' Jerry Wexler [Atlantic] told me, 'This record makes me feel very uncomfortable'."

Third/Sister Lovers is *supposed* to make you feel uncomfortable. According to Dickinson, "The record was about deteriorating relationships. The band had fallen apart, Alex and Lesa were going through this soap opera that was their relationship, John [Fry] and Alex were not getting along," because the former found the drinking and drugging in the studio and the conspicuously uncommercial music unsettling. Alex wasn't merely hurling paint at a canvas and calling it art. He was exploring chaos—his own—not revelling in it. Not yet.

In the four years that separated the completion of the unsold *Third/Sister Lovers* sessions and the recording of his first full-length solo album to actually be released (*Like Flies on Sherbert*, in 1979), Alex continued to write and demo songs, among the first of which were "Take Me Home and Make Me Like It" and "The Walking Dead." Alex sent the tapes to friend and fan Jon Tiven, who was working for Chess Records at the time. "It was just chaos—a drum machine with some garbagey-sounding instruments and him intoning over the top. I said, 'Alex, I don't know if you can find an audience for that.' Alex was heading in a direction further and further from what people liked about him."

Tiven came to Memphis and produced several of Alex's new songs, helping to give them a vintage garage-rock sound, crude but undeniably catchy. Not that the sessions were without their challenges. "Alex was using a different vocal personality than I'd ever experienced, not much singing. He was like a clown entertainer. I thought, 'This is going to be very strange,' and it devolved very quickly when he started to sing 'Jesus Christ' [a *Third/Sister Lovers* song] with a German accent." At what point does not wanting to be defined by your past hinder more than help your future music? Probably when you sing a Christmas song with a fake German accent.

Perhaps Alex thought so as well, because in early 1976 he attempted to kill himself by cutting his wrists in the bathtub (although his drug and alcohol consumption and combustible relationship with Lesa also likely contributed to his desperation). He recovered quickly, and in the process stopped taking downers, although he continued to drink heavily. Then Terry Ork, owner of the tiny, independent Ork Records (who had released punk pioneers Television's first single, "Johnny Jewel," and Richard Hell and the Voidoids' EP *Blank Generation*), acquired from Tiven the rights to the songs he and Alex had recorded in Memphis and released five of them as an EP, *Singer Not the Song*. The best of these are a screaming version of "Take Me Home and Make Me Like It" (with barking background vocals) and a whacked-out, wah-wah–suffused cover of Eddie Cochran's "Summertime Blues." Once again, without trying, Alex was at the forefront of what was next—not power-pop this time, but punk. To the emerging punk crowd, loud, abrasive, and peculiar were virtues, not shortcomings.

Ork asked Alex to come to New York and promote the release of the EP with a local backup band anchored by bassist Chris Stamey, an enormous Big Star fan (there weren't many in the mid-'70s, but those that existed tended to be fanatical), whose band, the Sneakers, was clearly Big Star inspired. The show, at a small venue called the Lower Manhattan Ocean Club, was well received, even garnering a write-up in the *New York Times* that praised Alex's "blend of mid-'60s British pop buoyancy and New York punk energy." Alex and Stamey, with Lloyd Fonoroff on drums (other members would come and go), proceeded to play around town for the next year or so at punk-friendly places like CBGB, sometimes employing the moniker Alex and the Cossacks. The set lists were varied—songs from the recently released EP, some of the rockier Big Star tunes, a few covers, and a handful of new songs—but the sound was consistently loose, loud, and rock-and-roll rudimentary.

Alex continued to demo new songs, and he recorded a single for Ork, the rockafilthy "Bangkok" (backed with the Seeds' "Can't Seem to Make You Mine"). He also agreed to produce a record for his favourite among the new punk bands, the Cramps, whose intelligent primitivism in many ways mirrored his own refried-retro aesthetic. Eventually, however, when gigs became harder to come by, a potential record deal with Elektra didn't materialize, and Alex was evicted from his apartment and began drinking more than ever and popping pills again, it was time to go home. It was also time to make his last interesting record. Well, sixty percent of an interesting record. Which is still more interesting than most people's entire LPs.

Like Flies on Sherbert—Alex wanted to call it *Like Flies on Shit* (of course he did)—was commissioned by Memphis musician turned record-company owner Sid Selvidge for his microlabel Peabody Records (only five hundred copies were manufactured). It was coproduced by Alex and Jim Dickinson and imbued with even more of the quirky chaos of their previous collaboration, the unrealized *Third/Sister Lovers* (including false starts, flubbed vocals, and out-of-tune instruments), but contains only five original songs. They're five good ones, though, if not in the same superlative class as the *Third/Sister Lovers* material. The singing is frequently after-hours slurry and the playing often defiantly sloppy, which suits Alex's quintet of twisted tunes perfectly. "My Rival" is a nice-and-nasty love song, the only kind Alex seemed to write now. "Hook or Crook" is playfully menacing. The stomping "Hey! Little Child" is *cha-cha-cha* creepy. And the title track, with its primitive synthesizer screeches and Ronettes-meet–Wild Man Fischer vocals, is as uncompromising as anything released by any punk band, anywhere. Then there are the covers, all six of them.

"Girl After Girl," "Waltz Across Texas," "Alligator Man," and "No More the Moon Shines on Lorena" are Alex's first recorded forays into the classic rock-and-roll, country, and folk songbooks, but the off-key warbling and skronky arrangements, while entertaining the first time around, ultimately come across as not much more than lazy, tuneless piss-takes. If this is cow punk, give me Dolly Parton. The Bell Notes' "I've Had It", on the other hand, is *so* unhinged it's irresistible, the prominent pop-bottle percussion and Jim Dickinson's maniacal lead vocal (Alex content to pitch in on the shrieking chorus) making it a rowdy, charging charmer. And Alex's take on K. C. and the Sunshine Band's recent hit "Boogie Shoes" is a gleefully deconstructed, purposefully plodding hoot. Boogie to *this,* Alex seems to be saying.

For the next several years Alex drank a lot; performed occasional gigs with pick-up bands of varying worth, when someone asked him to; sat in with Memphis friends at their shows; played lead guitar for a while in art-blues band Panther Burns; broke up with Lesa (for good this time); and began driving a cab, because his record royalties were virtually nil, and club gigs paid in the hundreds (sometimes), not the thousands. In 1982, the year he turned thirty-two, he quit drinking (pot remaining his only indulgence) and moved to New Orleans, where he worked at various times as a dishwasher, a janitor, and an amateur arborist. Survival, not music, became what mattered most.

~

Ironically, it was around this time, Alex's personal and professional nadir, that Big Star began to shine just a little bit brighter. A few years earlier, in 1978, the British label EMI rereleased the first two Big Star albums as a double-LP set, the first time in several years either had been available outside of the second-hand market. That same year, a small British label, Aura Records, gave the much-bootlegged *Third/Sister Lovers* its first official release. After years of commercial indifference and outright rejection, this interest in all things Big Star was difficult for even some of band's inner circle to believe. In the liner notes to the 2003 Castle reissue of *Like Flies on Sherbert,* Aura label head Aaron Sixx remembered how "I loved the album [*Third/Sister Lovers*] so I contacted John Fry at Ardent and asked him if I could licence the LP. His response was, 'Why would you want to do that?'" In 1980 Sixx and Aura had also brought out a UK version of *Like Flies on Sherbert.*

People were discovering the group in their homeland as well. Listening to Big Star for the first time in the early 1980's, "I knew immediately that I had just heard one of my favourite bands," R.E.M. bassist Mike Mills recalled in the liner notes to the 2014 CD reissue of the first two Big Star albums, adding that "On *Radio City,* Chilton confirms his place as one of the best songwriters in rock and roll." In the liner notes for the 2009 box set, *Keep an Eye on the Sky,* Mills' bandmate Peter Buck articulated Big Star's outsider appeal:

> Big Star was probably the first band that brought home the whole idea of the "beautiful loser." Prior to that, pretty much everything you bought had been a hit. Even the Velvet Underground, they made four records and toured all over America. Iggy and Stooges LPs—you actually saw them in record stores; they weren't popular, but they were available. But with Big Star, I'd never seen a new record of theirs in a rack at a store. I don't know if that ever happened. They were like this weird myth of America: These guys who did this brilliant work, were ignored, and then disappeared.

Maybe not disappeared so much as had been temporarily eclipsed.

In 1986, the Bangles included a cover of "September Gurls" on their *Different Light* LP (generating for Alex his first real royalty money). The Replacements' main man and Alex Chilton admirer Paul Westerberg composed "Alex Chilton," which appeared on the Mats' 1987 release, *Pleased to Meet Me*. The next year, R.E.M., soon to become one of rock's biggest bands, paid their own tribute to Big Star by recording their album *Green* at Ardent Studios. Just when he could have rested on his godfather-of-outsider-rock status (it became compulsory by this time for all the happening bands to name-check Big Star) and made all of the cacophonous noise he wanted and have it heard by an audience finally ready to listen, Alex thought it would be more interesting and enjoyable to record and perform vintage vocal jazz and pop, blues, and R&B tunes (and the occasional trad-based original) and become a twenty-first-century Chet Baker, his very first vocal inspiration. Instead of embracing his growing reputation as the pop poster boy for the eternal tug of war between art and commerce, Alex became a wry musical archaeologist of traditional American music, content to record pleasant but inessential albums for a variety of small labels and ignore audience requests at shows for Big Star songs.

Before he died of a heart attack, age fifty-nine, in March 2010—long sober, happily married, and renovating a nineteenth-century cottage he'd purchased in New Orleans' Tremé neighbourhood—he even worked the nostalgia circuit with a partially reunited Big Star (Alex with Stephens on drums, plus a couple members of power-poppers the Posies) as well as with the band he fronted as a teenager, the Box Tops. The reunion gigs paid very well, it was his ass to sell, and he'd sell it to whoever he felt like.

How disappointing. How cool. How Alex Chilton.

JAMES BOOKER

While pensive poets painful vigils keep,
Sleepless themselves, to give their readers sleep
–Pope

Alphabetizing your records and CDs should be easy. Even if Big Bill Broonzy is technically blues, power-popping Chris Bell sits comfortably on one side and country-rocking Byrds on the other, the blues and rock and roll and country and folk close enough in origin and essence to allow all three to companionably share shelf space. But Bach beside the Beach Boys? It just doesn't work. So, you create a separate section for the classical stuff, and while you're at it, relocate the jazz albums to their own section, John Coltrane and Gene Clark each uniquely magnificent, but entirely different in sound and scope. Only one problem: where do you put James Booker?

A prodigy on classical piano who moonlighted playing organ on Sunday-morning gospel radio; a rhythm-and-blues session pianist as soon as he graduated from high school and owner of his own R&B instrumental hit in 1960; a coveted rock-and-roll sideman who played with everyone from Little Richard in the studio to Jerry Garcia on stage; a Chopin aficionado who thought nothing of slipping a version of the Polish composer's "Minute Waltz" into one of his wild solo live shows, right between a rousing Ray Charles medley and a slightly menacing cover of the Beatles' "Eleanor Rigby"; a delicate jazzy tinkler and a back-pew shouter: it's just the sort of tantalizing musical gumbo you'd expect to be cooked up by a New Orleans–born homosexual, African American, one-eyed, skeletally thin, false teeth–wearing, mentally ill heroin addict.

Actually, it shouldn't be that surprising. "Perhaps it's good for one to suffer," says one of the characters in Aldous Huxley's novel *Antic Hay*. "Can an artist do anything if he's happy? Would he ever want to do anything? What is art, after all, but a protest against the horrible inclemency of life?" James Booker's protest was his defiantly personal, delightfully unclassifiable music. He wasn't the first person whose joyful art was born of struggle and sorrow.

James Booker was born in 1939 in New Orleans' Charity Hospital, and although his father was a Baptist minister—and a piano player—and young James played the organ in his father's New Orleans church, he spent much of his adolescence in Bay St. Louis, Mississippi, where he and his sister were raised by a maternal aunt. Booker and his sister moved back to New Orleans to live with their mother when he was eight years old, and he enrolled in Xavier Preparatory, a distinguished Catholic high school where he received his initial classical music training.

Although he learned to love Bach and Chopin, this didn't stop him from regularly appearing on radio station WMRY's Sunday church services and soaking up the sounds of his birthplace, that amorphous mixture of jazz, blues, gospel, boogie-woogie, funk, pop, Latin (Cuban) rhythms, and whatever else flooded into the bayou and contributed to the indefinable but instantly recognizable sound of New Orleans. The protean Miles Davis—who helped to create, before leaving behind, several new musical forms, including cool jazz, ambient, and jazz rock—liked to say that there was no such thing as "jazz" as a musical genre; jazz was a *way* of playing music. To James Booker, jazz was definitely a verb and not a noun.

Booker (anyone who knew him well called him by his last name) was as creative with the truth as he was with his instrument, claiming, for example, that when the great New Orleans pianist Jelly Roll Morton died in 1941, his soul had immediately passed into Booker. He also maintained that, when he was hit by an ambulance at the age of nine, dragged thirty feet, and had his leg broken in eight places—which *was* true: he walked with a slight limp for the rest of his life—it was the morphine he received in the hospital that was responsible for his lifelong heroin and alcohol addictions. Booker had many nicknames (Gonzo, the Black Liberace, the Piano Pope, the Bayou Maharajah, Little Chopin, the Piano Prince, the Ivory Emperor), some of them self-styled, suggesting his lifelong compulsion to refashion reality. It is naive to expect a football player conditioned to be violent to be a peaceful citizen just because it's not Sunday and he's not wearing a helmet and shoulder pads; one should not be surprised when an artist as endlessly inventive and impulsive as Booker manifested the same iconoclasm and unpredictability in his life.

Not only were Booker's musical influences remarkably diverse, like the best jazz musicians he rarely played a song the same way twice. Unfortunately, sometimes he didn't even play a song the same way *once*. From the late '70s until his death in 1983, Booker played a regular hometown gig at Orleans' Maple Leaf Bar (which was low-down and low-key enough that it had a laundromat in the back). In the liner notes to *Spiders on the Keys*, a live album recorded at the Maple Leaf and released posthumously, journalist Michael Goodwin recalled:

> It was one of *those* Maple Leaf Monday nights. Booker had spent nearly half an hour adjusting the microphone, fooling with the piano bench, and talking to himself—and his little band had retired to the bar to wait it out. Finally he signalled that he was ready, and his sidemen made their way to the stage and picked up their instruments.... Booker took a deep breath, leaned backwards, and fell right off the piano bench. Laughing. So Tyler [Alvin "Red" Tyler, Booker's saxophonist] knew he wasn't hurt—but Tyler also knew there wasn't going to be any music tonight.

The first recorded music anyone heard from Booker was "Doing the Hambone," a funky slice of pre–rock-and-roll rhythm and blues, written and produced by Dave Bartholomew, which Booker cut for Imperial Records when he was only fifteen years old. Soon he was working as a session musician (such was his precocity, even occasionally subbing for Little Richard on his own records) and, after graduating from high school, touring with Shirley & Lee, Joe Tex, and even travelling with Huey "Piano" Smith's band when their namesake didn't feel like hitting the road and they needed a piano-playing impersonator. When he was home, he'd pick up a few bucks performing at the Dew Drop Inn, a predominantly African American nightspot. Racial segregation wasn't the only taboo he had to worry about. Like Little Richard, who also played the Dew Drop when in New Orleans, even if you were "out," Booker knew better than to be *too* out. In his unpublished autobiography—and why is it still unpublished?—he wrote that it never occurred to him that he wasn't a girl until he was about five. Other musicians and nightclub patrons might not care that you were homosexual, but society, circa the late 1950s, sure did. Even the Big Easy wasn't *that* easy.

Knowing first-hand how hard it was to make a living playing piano, and hoping to avoid the temptation of booze and drugs that went along with the gigging musician's life, Booker enrolled in Southern University's music department in 1960. His stay in academia was short, however, due to his fickle, fidgety personality and his uncommon musical proficiency. Fellow New Orleans musician Earl King: "His music teacher used to tell me, 'Earl, you a good friend of Booker?' I say, 'Yeah, I know Booker, what's it about?' He said, 'Tell him to cut my classes and I'm gonna grade him anyway, 'cause he come in and disrupt the class with all kinds of craziness and stuff.' He said, 'I can't teach Booker nothing.'" Those who can't, teach; those who can, scuffle the club scene and hustle for gigs and try not to get too loaded too often and hope to get a shot at making a record of their own one day.

Which is what happened in 1960, with the release of Booker's instrumental "Gonzo" on Peacock, a pleasantly hummable piece of Hammond B-3–driven fluff marred only by an entirely incongruous flute solo (he named it after the main dope fiend in *The Pusher*, a B movie that came out the same year). The tune ended up on the Billboard pop charts, getting as high as #43, and even if it didn't make him much money or lead to another hit in spite of several follow-up attempts, it did increase his profile and helped him obtain more session and touring jobs throughout the 1960s (working with, among others, Wilson Pickett, Freddie King, King Curtis, Bobby "Blue" Bland, and Roy Hamilton). Although he was paying his bills playing other people's music, he usually found a way to play it his way, like a jazz musician, producing an invigorating fusion of ragtime-rooted, greasy R&B, complemented by a seemingly ceaseless cascade of classical- and jazz-tinged filigrees, flourishes, and aural adornments. Booker at his best didn't need a band: his left hand kept it funky; his right hand kept it interesting.

Even at his happiest, Booker was never particularly emotionally grounded. The successive deaths in 1966 and 1967 of his sister and his mother were both distressing and debilitating. Friend, musician, and fellow New Orleans resident Aaron Neville, speaking in Lily Keber's documentary about Booker, *Bayou Maharajah*: "His sister died, and not too long after, his mother died, and he began to talk about how there was some kind of plot that somehow was responsible for the deaths, and that now he was being watched, and there were threats against him, and he began to get more paranoid and more . . . just angry." It is fair to say that, by this time, Booker wasn't simply eccentric—he was mentally ill. By the late

'70s, his paranoia was such that it was not unusual at his shows for audience members to beg him to quit ranting about the CIA and just play some fucking music.

Not surprisingly, perhaps, not long after his sister's and mother's deaths, he became addicted to heroin, the great eraser of sad memories and bad thoughts. Also not surprisingly, he was busted for possession outside the Dew Drop Inn one night in 1967 and served a year in Angola, the Louisiana State Penitentiary. There, he played in the prison band, learned how to type, helped teach inmates how to read, and managed to stay out of trouble. When Booker was released from prison he lived in New York briefly, before joining the exodus of Southern musicians to California, many of whom, like Texan native Doug Sahm, were evading their home states' draconian drug enforcement policies. Booker landed in Los Angeles, where to the surprise of many, he not only continued to find plenty of session and live work (Ringo Starr, the Doobie Brothers, John Mayall, Dr John) but also stayed on the methadone program—more or less—that he had begun in New York. He even took up yoga for a while.

He was still Booker, though. Dr John, from *Under a Hoodoo Moon: The Life of the Night Tripper*:

> Booker did the driving when we went out on the road, and before long he was driving us crazy. We might be leaving New York for Richmond, Virginia; I'd go to sleep and then wake up half an hour later to find we're coming back through the Holland Tunnel. I'd say, "Booker, what the hell's going on?" He'd say, "Oh I just got to make a little stop, then we'll cut out." Well, he would stop off someplace in Harlem to cop, and then we'd bust ass down to Virginia.

In 1973 former Dr John bassist Dave Johnson, whom Booker was living with when he first came out to California, helped put together a performing trio of New Orleans refugees living in LA, featuring Booker, himself, and drummer John Boudreaux. Johnson even managed to attract some label attention, and Paramount came up with a small recording budget and some studio time. Although Booker's distinctive keyboard work was occasionally sacrificed to full-band arrangements (which, in addition to the core of Booker, Johnson, and Boudreaux, included two percussionists, a guitar player, and a saxophonist), it was a most pleasing clamour, the sessions yielding excellent versions of old favourites like "Goodnight Irene," "Feel So Bad," and a mind-melting medley of "Stormy Monday" and "Hound Dog" (like the bebop-era Miles Davis, Booker would take a favourite standard, usually something slower—as Davis would do with time-tested ballads—and transform it into something distinctly different), plus excellent Booker originals like "So Swell When You're Well."

The latter is James Booker–band-style 101: rollicking stride piano (in this case, tack piano), an R&B beat, bluesy vocals, and enough jazzy twists and turns, courtesy of Booker's restless right hand, to make it all add up to much more than that. I don't know much about piano technique, but I know I'm never bored when James Booker plays piano. Unfortunately, the only evidence listeners have of any of this is eleven preliminary mixes that were done on the last night of the sessions, the songs that comprise the posthumously released *The Lost Paramount Tapes*; this, because Booker apparently checked the master tapes out of the Paramount library and lost them. It's just another wacky James Booker story now, but at the time, it was one more reason not to get into business with him, genre-obliterating keyboard prodigy or not.

Record labels and other musicians were not the only ones exasperated with Booker. It was during this period that someone forcibly removed his right eye. As to whom the amateur surgeon was, there are as many theories as Booker had friends and acquaintances. In one amusing sequence in *Bayou Maharajah,* several people give the confidential lowdown on what *really* happened to the missing organ: Booker pissed off some New York drug dealers to whom he owed money, who yanked it out with a pair of pliers; Ringo Starr—Ringo Starr!—did it in an argument over royalties; and—my personal favourite—a bouncer did it on the third consecutive night Booker showed up at the same bar, demanding to be paid for a gig he'd already been paid for. Adding to the modified visual effect, by now Booker was also regularly donning a large Afro wig (reputedly where he kept his weed) and a cape.

He also ended up back in New Orleans, where, at age thirty-six, he received an invitation (finally) to perform at the popular and well-regarded New Orleans Jazz and Heritage Festival. It went well enough that a European jazz fan and promoter who liked what he saw invited him to play at the Berlin Rhythm and Blues Festival, where he was even more enthusiastically received. And why wouldn't he be? There's a certain kind of European culture vulture who, no matter what he or she thinks of the United States' foreign policy, or of Americans in general, worships all of the indigenous American musical forms—blues, jazz, R&B, country, rock and roll—and Booker's style was a compelling combination of most of them, with the added European-friendly bonus of some good ol' Rachmaninoff or Chopin tossed into the mix.

The next year, playing on a session in New York, he was introduced to the producer Joe Boyd, who had a knack for bringing out the best in idiosyncratic musical talents (Nick Drake and the early, Syd Barrett–led Pink Floyd, to give just two examples). The result was 1976's *Junco Partner*, Booker's first album in his own right. There's refurbished Chopin ("Black Minute Waltz") right next to Leadbelly's "Good Night Irene"; there's one of Booker's typically untypical medleys (his own "Blues Minuet" into the traditional "Until the Real Thing Comes Along" into the early twentieth-century chestnut "Bill Bailey"); there's the joyful "Sunny Side of the Street" and the infectious, aforementioned title track; and wrapping things up, a soulful, stride-riding take on Liberace's "break" song, "I'll Be Seeing You." And whether featuring the inimitable plunking of his piano or his stirring voice (not as honey smooth as his hero Ray Charles', but maybe even more moving because of the occasional cracked note and plaintive phrasing and the periodic, involuntary, signature *wah wah* or *woo woo* used to punctuate a line), it all sounds like no one else but James Booker. *That's* jazz.

Junco Partner, while an aesthetic success, was only released in England, where it was respectfully received but soon remaindered. Having his own LP must have been a confidence booster, though, and more offers to appear at European festivals came in. One of these was recorded in Zurich and released in 1978 as *Live!* It is Booker at the peak of his dexterous piano powers and in an ideal setting—playing in front of a large, appreciative audience. Of special note are the yearning "Black Night" and the playful instrumental version of "Something Stupid." Sad, funny, angry, playful, lusty, desperate, witty, forsaken, elegant: the music Booker performed on these late-'70s European dates is where any James Booker neophyte should begin listening. If they do, they won't stop there. Friends recounted how, when he returned home, he would obsessively listen to the tapes of these concerts—but only to the applause, fast-forwarding through the music. This is endearing, this is sad, this is who human beings are: we get the acceptance, appreciation, and love we all need wherever we can get it.

Back in New Orleans, there were no packed concert halls or expensive grand pianos; instead, there were places like the Maple Leaf Bar, performing for maybe thirty people for forty bucks a night and all the booze he could drink. Hometown heroes seem a lot more heroic if you don't live in the same city as them. Booker's gigs began to occasionally resemble twisted TED Talks on the spectre of the CIA, sundry conspiracy theories, and the dangers of religious dogma as delivered by a manic, if amusing, one-eyed lecturer. To appreciate Booker's local live sides—as on the already noted *Spiders on the Keys* or on *Resurrection of the Bayou Maharajah*, also taped at the Maple Leaf—you didn't *have* to be there, but it would have helped. At best, it could be funny—Booker off his head is lot more entertaining and thought-provoking than most sane people *blah blah blah*–ing away—but sometimes it was simply irritating, and sometimes it was scary. Bassist James Singleton: "I did see Booker at Tipitina's on the stage, playing by himself, pull out a chrome-plated handgun and hold it to his head and [say] that he wouldn't play any more until someone brought him some cocaine right now. And there was kind of an awkward silence, and someone appeared at the side of the stage and he disappeared and came back and played."

Jerry Garcia's biographer Blair Jackson asked Garcia Band bassist John Kahn about Booker's short (two gigs), tumultuous tenure with the Grateful Dead lead guitarist's solo outfit in early 1976, and Kahn recalled the same mental instability:

> [Booker] wouldn't learn any of our songs. We tried to teach him songs and he refused.... He did half a set of solo piano and it was great; you could hear a pin drop. And he played things like the "Minute Waltz"; it was incredible. He could still play great. He could switch between piano and organ really easily and it would sound amazing. But he was out of his mind. He was watching cars go by and was checking out license plates and talking about the CIA. He saw a Louisiana license plate and then John Kennedy's name somewhere and that freaked him out. He saw bad omens everywhere and he was getting really weird.

In the liner notes to Booker's last LP, *Classified,* coproducer Scott Billington recounted how Booker would take a twenty-dollar cab ride to his manager (and Maple Leaf Bar co-owner) John Parsons' house, just so he could borrow twenty dollars. He would also dutifully take Antabuse to combat his alcoholism and then drink anyway, aggravating his ulcer. Harry Connick Sr, the district attorney of New Orleans and a big Booker fan, would offer Booker free legal advice and occasional representation, and Booker returned the favour by giving Connick's son, Harry Jr, the New Orleans–born musician- and actor-to-be, piano lessons. Harry Jr remembered a panicky

Booker calling the Connick home late at night looking for his father: "James would call my house. My parents [would be] asleep. And he used to say, 'Can you come get me, can you come help me?' And I'm like, 'James, I can't, I'm twelve.'"

These darker moments vied with the frequently brilliant music for the remainder of Booker's life, leading him to periodically check into Charity Hospital's psychiatric ward. Which was, of course, unfortunate for James Booker the person. James Booker the musician, however, might have benefitted. "One must still have chaos in oneself to be able to give birth to a dancing star," Nietzsche claimed in *Thus Spoke Zarathustra*. The oyster always requires the irritation to make the pearl.

In the early 1980s, Booker's manager received several lucrative offers from some of New York's hipper clubs, all of whom believed that Booker's musical reputation was worth the risk posed by his personal reputation. Regrettably, every offer was turned down, because Booker, who was living in relative poverty, refused to leave New Orleans. How horribly sad: the man who was reduced to listening to tape-recorded applause to boost his self-worth was unwilling or unable to get on a plane and go where real applause was waiting and people were yearning to give him lots of money and the recognition and adoration he both lacked and craved. Sometimes the irritation is just a goddamn irritation.

He was eager to record again, though, just as long as the sessions took place at home. Rounder Records employee Scott Billington had been a long-time Booker aficionado, and in 1982, the year before Booker's death, he convinced upper management to let him record Booker in New Orleans for the small, Boston-based roots label. His experience was equal parts maddening and gratifying. Much like Booker's life itself. From the *Classified* liner notes:

> As the session progressed, he [Booker] became distracted and would not play any of the songs he had planned. For the remainder of the day, he engaged in a cat-and-mouse game with the other musicians, randomly starting songs until they caught up, only to switch abruptly to something else. Then, Booker stopped communicating entirely and we called it a day.... [The next day,] after Booker left the piano and crouched in a corner, Red [Tyler, saxophonist] and I walked over and picked him up. I said, "Look, you're either going to play the piano, or I'm going to cancel the session and you're not going to get paid." He looked at me sheepishly and returned to the piano bench.

The album that Billington managed to extract, *Classified* (particularly the remixed, outtake-laden, 2013 edition), is a full-band affair that, while showing a slight slackening of Booker's nimble-fingered proficiency and his less-than-100-percent commitment, still came with plenty of highlights touching on the many facets of his genius: droll, good-time blues (the title track, an original); classical, Booker-style ("Warsaw Concerto"); oddly matched medleys (the Brazilian instrumental "Tico Tico" teamed up with two of his own compositions, "Papa Was a Rascal" and "So Swell When You're Well"); classic R&B (Lloyd Price's "Lawdy Miss Clawdy); songs that had become standards, particularly the sad, slower ones that Booker adored so much ("If You're Lonely" and "Lonely Avenue"); and just for the hell of it, even a dollop of dumb fun (Booker-fied renditions of "Theme from the

Godfather" and "King of the Road"). Booker at less than his best is still required listening.

Most of the people who knew Booker remember an intelligent man (he was a reader—a rarity for a musician) with a sardonic sense of humour, who, no matter how exasperating, was usually kind and never boring and, like a lot of sad people, always on the lookout for fun. And despite the drugs, the liquor, the mental illness, the loneliness (no one seems to recall any significant partner at any point in his life), and the career disappointments, Booker's friends tended to stick by him, even at his Booker-wounding worst. Like when Booker got clean around 1980 and decided he wanted an office job. Through the efforts of his friend Lee Madere, New Orleans' chief economist, Booker ended up securing a clerical job in the Department of Economic Analysis. Bet his buddies around the Quarter or his legions of European fans didn't see that one coming. Friends say he was proud of his sobriety and the regular paycheque and the three-piece suits he wore to work every day. It makes sense: if you're weird enough, normal can be a very interesting experience. It didn't last, though—did anyone really think it would?—and a year or so into his new life, after showing up at work one day smelling of booze (Booker claimed he had only gargled with whiskey), he was fired. Soon he was back to his regular routine: trying to stay (sort of) clean, playing small New Orleans clubs like the Maple Leaf Bar, and occasionally checking back into the psych ward.

No one seems to know how he got there, but on November 8, 1983, Booker ended up at Charity Hospital—the same hospital where he was born and where he had returned numerous times over the years, when his body or his brain needed healing—and was seeking treatment for some unknown malady, when he died before he could be helped. The official cause of death was renal failure, the quintessential alcoholic or drug abuser's disease. Someone play a sad song. The kind that's so beautiful, it can't help but make you feel good.

NICO

With these celestial Wisdom calms the mind
And makes the happiness she does not find
–Johnson

Nico was beautiful, but she wanted to be Bob Dylan. What the world wanted was for her to be satisfied with being beautiful. So she dyed her hair and got fat and became a junkie. Along the way, she ruined her talent and poisoned her soul and destroyed her body, but she didn't want to be Bob Dylan anymore. She didn't have to. She was Nico.

Before she could be Nico, though, she was Christa Päffgen, who was born in Cologne in 1938. Her father was a conscripted German soldier who suffered a serious brain injury during the Second World War and was likely executed by the Nazis, and her mother and she moved to Berlin after Germany's surrender in 1945. Christa was strikingly good-looking—no less an authority on feminine allure than Leonard Cohen describing her in a 1974 *Zig Zag* interview as "the most beautiful woman I'd ever seen." Tall, luminously pale, and with the high cheekbones and chiselled facial features that someone carving a German countess might come up with, Christa moved to Paris while still in her teens and found steady work modeling for the major fashion magazines and appearing in television commercials. It was around this time that she began calling herself "Nico" (a fashion photographer friend suggested the change because models didn't have names like Christa Päffgen).

Nico continued to model, appearing in TV ads and even scoring bit parts in several European films. Acting was more interesting than being a lingerie model or being instructed to stand there and be quiet and look alluring in the whiskey commercial, but Nico wanted more. Although she had left school when she started modeling, she was extremely intelligent—since the advent of her modeling and acting careers, she had added French, Spanish, and English to her native German. Focusing on her acting, she moved to New York and studied with Lee Strasberg, where Marilyn Monroe was one of her classmates, and in 1959 gained a role in Fellini's *La Dolce Vita*—as herself. She had been invited to visit the set by some actor friends, but when the director spotted her, he insisted she appear in the film. Lots of people, especially the sort of people who hang around movie sets, are good-looking; Nico was more than that. This is what is called *charisma*. More minor film roles, more modeling when financially necessary, and a baby, a son, the result of a short-lived relationship with the French actor Alain Delon. The child was raised, and later adopted, by Delon's relatives.

It was not until 1963 or 1964 that Nico began to sing professionally, doing the nightclub-diva thing at the Blue Angel in New York. She probably looked the part—Marlene Dietrich with long blond hair and a pair of cast-iron balls—

but the thought of Nico warbling "Falling in Love Again" to a roomful of martini-swilling drunks is too dismal to contemplate. She soon met Brian Jones of the Rolling Stones and, through him, the band's manager and producer, Andrew Loog Oldham, who was now running his own record label, Immediate Records. The A-side of the single Nico recorded for Immediate—a cover of Gordon Lightfoot's "I'm Not Sayin'"—is passable MOR folk-rock, the most interesting thing about the track being Nico's deep, heavily German-accented voice. Her impatient, resonant delivery nicely underscores Lightfoot's lively slice of amorous devilry.

Nico met the increasingly famous Andy Warhol and his studio assistant Gerard Malanga in Paris, and one or both invited her to drop by the Factory, Warhol's multimedia studio space and bohemian clubhouse, whenever she was next in New York. She brought along her chiseled cheekbones, a copy of her Immediate single, and her towering Teutonic mystique, and everyone was immediately overwhelmed. In Legs McNeil and Gillian McCain's compulsively readable *Please Kill Me: The Uncensored Oral History of Punk*, Warhol associate Paul Morrissey remembered that "Nico was spectacular. She had definite charisma"—that word won't go away—"She was interesting. She was distinctive. She had a magnificent deep voice. She was extraordinary looking. She was tall. She was somebody." It is undeniable that it was mainly Nico's looks that secured her a job as part of Warhol's latest discovery/art project, the Velvet Underground, a New York–based rock-and-roll band. Factory scenester Gerard Malanga, speaking to Clinton Heylin for his *From the Velvets to the Voidoids: The Birth of American Punk Rock*: "Andy decided to throw Nico into the act because the Velvets themselves were not very charismatic onstage, and Andy wanted a spotlight on someone." (Actually, it was Morrissey who convinced Warhol of the need for a stronger stage presence.) "So Andy threw her in on the act against the wishes of the Velvets."

Ah, the Velvets . . . How does one sum up in less than two hundred words one of the most important groups in the history of rock and roll? Easy. The Velvet Underground was one of the most important groups in the history of rock and roll. But *why* were they so great? For the best reason of all: because. Because the Velvet Underground sounded like no one else but the Velvet Underground, and because no one who came after them succeeded in sounding anything like them either. All genius is tautological. Shakespeare and William Blake and Emily Dickinson can be imitated, but only disastrously. They simply *are*. The Velvet Underground was the magnificently mongrelized result of four singular individuals who loved old R&B, but whose collective sound was almost entirely bereft of any blues. A band whose principal songwriter (Lou Reed) adored doo-wop and had worked for a songwriting sweatshop, cranking out made-to-order pop songs for a budget record label, but who went on to revolutionize rock and roll by composing tunes about scoring dope, paying someone to beat you up, and the agony and the ecstasy of heroin addiction. A rock-and-roll group whose original sound was seasoned with the chilling wail of a classically trained Welsh music expatriate (John Cale) sawing away on an electrified viola. A band whose drummer was a diminutive young woman (Maureen "Moe" Tucker)—virtually unheard of in rock-and-roll circles in 1966—who stood up to play her instrument, frequently using nothing more than mallets to bang away on a couple of kettle drums—Bo Diddley meets John Cage.

Nico might have gotten the nod to join the group because of how Warhol envisioned her looking on stage, but that only got her in the door. Once inside, it wasn't only her unusual, and unusually affecting, voice that legitimized her as a contributing part of the Velvet Underground, but also her mysterious, muted presence. Billy Name told the makers of the *Nico Icon* documentary that the "specialty of the Factory was a synthetic aura.... Most people at the Factory were very loquacious and verbose.... [But] Nico rarely spoke, and only when someone spoke to her." It soon became apparent that her long silences and general indifference to the hipster hubbub were not the result of shyness or a lack of confidence or a pouty pose, but a fundamental lack of interest. In *anything*. Alan Wise, who managed her career in the 1980s: "Life was a bore to her."

Because Warhol knew that no record label was likely to gamble on a group as odd as the Velvets, a backer was found to pay for the sessions that yielded most of *The Velvet Underground and Nico* (when Verve Records, a division of MGM, eventually bought the tapes, the band went back into the studio to re-record a few songs). Reed, at Warhol's instigation, came up with three songs for Nico to sing, and they are all VU classics. "Femme Fatale," although not written about Nico (it was about another Factory habitué, the doomed Edie Sedgwick), was an ideal vehicle for Nico's deep, ominous voice. Listen to anyone else's version—Alex Chilton and Lesa Aldridge's, R.E.M.'s—and the song tends to take on a gentle, almost tender timbre; Nico sings it like Reed intended it to sound: soothingly menacing. "I'll Be Your Mirror" is jaunty in comparison, the playful lyrics and music-box melody accented by Nico's playful, naughty-naughty vocals. "All

Tomorrow's Parties" is the only song on the album that hints at what's to come in Nico's solo career. The song is a nice mix of classic VU clatter and crash, and Nico's dark, droning delivery of Reed's strange tale of the poor girl and what happens when Sunday comes around is just right. Everything about the Velvet Underground—the sound, the lyrics, the philosophy (John Cale: "I had no intention of letting the music be anything other than troublesome to people.... We really wanted to go out there and annoy people.")—was indisputably the product of Reed's, Cale's, Tucker's, and guitarist Sterling Morrison's combined instincts and aptitudes, but without Nico's presence, their inaugural album wouldn't be nearly so satisfyingly strange.

Genuinely strange music necessitates genuinely strange people to make it and play it, and strange people are rarely the easiest to get along with. Even though Reed insisted that the Velvet Underground be given separate billing on the album cover (they might have had to acquiesce to Warhol's demand that Nico be included in the group, but that didn't mean they had to treat her like an equal member), Nico either didn't take the hint or didn't care what the others thought. Not only did she make it clear she wasn't happy with the mere trio of songs she had been allocated ("I'm Waiting for the Man" and "Heroin," in particular, were two tunes she was eager to claim for her own), but the band had difficulty getting what they considered satisfactory vocal takes from her in the studio. Warhol said, "The whole time the album was being made, nobody seemed happy with it, especially Nico. 'I want to sound like Bawwhhhb Deeelahhhn,' she wailed." Thankfully, she didn't. She might not have sounded entirely like herself yet—that wouldn't happen until she recorded her second solo album—but it wouldn't be long before people began wanting to sound like *her*.

~

Every time the Ramones brought out a new single or album, Joey Ramone would think, *Maybe this is it, maybe this is the one that helps us break through.* Even experimental poets and midlist novelists secretly suffer from the same delusion. Which lasts just about as long as it took for the latest Ramones album to come and go and get discounted and dumped in the remainder bin. There are, of course, exceptions, but *The Velvet Underground and Nico* was not one of them; it wasn't even the minor success that the group, and Reed in particular, had hoped it would be. It was not surprising, then, that Nico took a job singing at a New York bar, Stanley's, when she wasn't performing with the Velvets (still singing only a few songs per gig and looking increasingly uncomfortable on stage while the others cooked away on their instruments). Friends helped out with instrumental accompaniment (Morrison, Cale, and even an initially reluctant Reed, who had first dismissively suggested that Nico sing along to a backing tape), and new friends, like a sixteen-year-old Jackson Browne, lent a hand when the others couldn't make it. He also gave her an excellent song to add to her slender repertoire, "These Days."

Soon she was back in the studio, this time recording a solo album for Verve. Some have claimed that the label had only signed the Velvets because of Nico's involvement, so the decision to roll the dice with the still-glamorous ex-model and ex-actor is easy to understand. Good looks sell. Reed made up for his reticence about giving Nico a hand with her gigs at Stanley's not only by playing guitar on her album, but also by writing or cowriting four of its ten songs. Cale and Morrison volunteered their instrumental services, too (the former being especially busy, contributing not only electric viola, but organ, piano, and bass), but the result was not *The Velvet Underground and Nico: Part 2*, with Nico singing all the songs. *Chelsea Girls*, as the LP would be called, is mostly Baroque 'n' Roll, the then-fashionable hybrid of folk guitar and overdubbed classical instrumentation. But whereas, say, Leonard Cohen's first album benefited from producer John Simon's relatively restrained orchestral touch, *Chelsea Girls'* producer, Tom Wilson, tended to subscribe to the when-in-doubt-overdub-something-else recording philosophy. Arranger Larry Fallon's brilliant contribution to Van Morrison's *Astral Weeks* demonstrates that the hokey flute and general over-orchestration that mar Nico's album probably weren't his ideas alone.

Jackson Browne's "These Days" is such a wonderful song, it's indestructible, and if Nico's version doesn't convey its powerful pathos as well as Gregg Allman's interpretation of the song would do, on his own first solo album a few years later, it is still *Chelsea Girls'* standout cut. The remaining nine tunes include two more contributions of Browne's, forgettable folk-rock so willowy you barely notice they're there ("The Fairest of the Seasons" and "Somewhere There's a Feather"); an unrecorded Tim Hardin tune, most noteworthy for being an unrecorded Tim Hardin tune ("Eulogy to Lenny Bruce"); the song that Dylan supposedly gave Nico to record ("I'll Keep It with Mine"), that is too fast and too tarted up to allow room for her sensitive delivery to breathe and grow; and a rare Cale composition ("Winter Song") that suffers not only from flutitis, but from the bane of Cale's admirably adventurous solo career, a weak melody and pseudopoetic lyrics. That leaves the four Reed songs.

It is easy to hear why they didn't make it on to *The Velvet Underground and Nico*. "Little Sister" (cowritten with Morrison) is just minor-key mopey enough to be an ideal Nico vehicle, and Reed's lyrics are appropriately obliquely bleak, but the omnipresent cello and flute finish it off. The title track, another Reed–Morrison collaboration, is almost catchy, despite Nico's foghorn delivery, but suffers from the same production woes that plague much of the rest of the album. Reed's "Wrap Your Troubles in Dreams" and the Reed–Cale–Nico cowrite "It Was a Pleasure Then" aren't anything exceptional, but they are the only orchestration-free cuts on the album and suggest what a second VU-and-Nico album might have sounded like: spooky, twisted, highly idiosyncratic rock and roll.

Released in October 1967, half a year after *The Velvet Underground and Nico*, *Chelsea Girls* managed even to commercially underperform its predecessor. Nico continued with her intimate solo shows and played with the VU on the road (as much as they allowed). But when in March 1968 she was forced to choose between honouring a New York solo gig and going to Boston to play with the band at the Boston Tea Party, one of the Velvets' few strongholds, she decided to stay home. Then, she decided to go after all but arrived late, and Reed wouldn't allow her on stage. Soon after, she was either "fired" (her explanation), or the band and she decided to part ways due to creative differences (the semiofficial story). Nico was the first but not the last casualty of Reed's rock-and-roll coup: Warhol was dismissed as the Velvets' manager/overseer (against the rest of the band's wishes), then Cale, the group's cofounder and the source of so much of their confrontational fire, was canned (also against Tucker's and Morrison's wishes). Reed wanted to be a rock-and-roll star, and a German chanteuse, an art-world celebrity, and a barmy Welshman with a screaming viola and a hunger to antagonize audiences weren't part of the plan.

An ex-model, ex-actor, ex-member of the Velvet Underground, and now a failed solo artist, Nico was still somebody, even if it was just a semifamous ex-somebody. Luckily for her, she met and became friends with Danny Fields, an A & R man and publicist for Elektra Records. Fields had discovered and signed the MC5 and the Stooges and had also worked with the Doors, Elektra's flagship band. While Fields had little respect for Jim Morrison as either a person or an artist, he still worked for the Doors' record company, and he thought it would be a good idea for Morrison's image to be introduced to Nico, because he approved of the women Morrison tended to sleep with about as much as he did the singer's personality and poetry. Although Fields brought Morrison to "the Castle" (a notorious hipster house rented out to visiting rock-and-roll people staying in the LA area), where he, Nico, Edie Sedgwick, and several other chic couch-crashers were temporarily living, he later dismissed the relationship he initiated that night: "That was the affair—he pulled her hair, he walked naked, she screamed, and I kept his car keys hidden for a day or two until he straightened up."

That's how things might have started, but the two formed an instant connection, at least from Nico's point of view. She described Morrison as the first man she ever loved and referred to him after his death as her "soul mate." When they weren't beating each other up while drunk (Nico claimed they both "enjoyed the sensation"), or screwing, or driving out to the desert to take hallucinogens, they discussed Nico's musical ambitions. She had despised the orchestral glop dumped all over her first album as much as anyone, and more than ever, she craved another chance to assert her status as a legitimate artist. Nico claimed it was Morrison who encouraged her to quit covering other people's material and to write her own songs. She respected him, she was in love with him, and probably not insignificantly, his band had the number-one song in America ("Light My Fire"). By the end of summer 1967, their relationship was over, and Nico went back to New York. Not long afterward, with the help of Fields (and Jim Morrison's tacit support), she got a contract to make a new album with Elektra. She even had its title—*The Marble Index*—which she had cribbed from a Wordsworth poem (her muse, Morrison, was a master at literary larceny). The album would contain eight songs. And this time they would all be Nico's.

The self-penned tunes weren't the only thing new about Nico's music. Aside from the neoclassical touches, which frugally compliment her frosty, minimalist compositions, the dominant aural colour is the harmonium, played by Nico herself. Reports vary as to how she became enraptured with the instrument's droning enchantments—Fields thought that Leonard Cohen might have played a role; others suggest she got the idea from Allen Ginsberg—but however it happened, Nico had found the ideal objective correlative to her new music. Nico's melodies are not really melodies—they are rarely much more than a long line of drone, with a couple of chord changes thrown in to remind you that you're not listening to the sound of the ocean crying itself to sleep or the desert slowly dying of thirst. She liked to call her songs "Medieval," but they were more like Nico-centric soundscapes. Even the lyrics—bordering on the pretentiously opaque but saved from such charges because of their atmospheric aptness—are more ambient than representational or confessional, just another mournful voice added to the chorus of lost souls wailing in the night.

Aside from the platform and exposure that being in the Velvet Underground had given her, the biggest advantage Nico gained from being in the band was having worked with John Cale, who believed in her developing vision and was eager to help her realize it on vinyl. (Although Frazier Mohawk was assigned by Elektra to produce the album, Cale's mark is all over it.) One of the first challenges Cale was presented with, in the mere four days Elektra had budgeted for the album's recording, was Nico's new instrument. Cale recalled the difficulty in his autobiography, *What's Welsh for Zen?*: "The harmonium was out of tune with everything. It wasn't even in tune with itself. She [Nico] insisted on playing it on everything so we had to figure out ways to separate her voice from it as much as possible and then find instrumental voices that would be compatible with the harmonium tracks." Cale's approach was similar to that of David Gilmour a couple of years later, when he coproduced Syd Barrett's two solo albums, with Barrett's erratic guitar playing and timing as the wobbly foundation for Gilmour's tasteful sonic embellishments

A song-by-song breakdown of *The Marble Index*'s half hour of music isn't really necessary—it is best appreciated as one extended piece. As with the books of a writer like, say, Jack Kerouac, whose novels are not novels in the traditional sense—little structure, plot, or character development—it is his inimitable prose that provides the reader with his or her aesthetic reward. The best way to "get" Kerouac is to simply pick up any of his books and open it to any page and start reading—aloud. Nico's genius wasn't in her songwriting (or singing or harmonium playing) but in sounding like Nico—in sounding like no one else, the toughest task any artist can undertake, and at which few succeed. It is easier to appreciate the tunes she sang on the first Velvet Underground LP because, in spite of their louche subject matter, Lou Reed wrote well-structured, verse-verse-chorus songs with extremely catchy melodies. Which are wonderful and why we're still listening to them. But that's not what Nico was aspiring toward on her own records and why, to me, she's such an inspiring role model. Nico wanted her records to sound like what she heard inside *her* head and *her* body and *her* soul. And amidst the swirling sighs and moans of her voice, the mournful wheeze of her harmonium, the sometimes consoling, sometimes jarring instrumental ornamentation, what emerges on *The Marble Index* is something far greater than the sum of its austere parts: a half hour in hell with Nico as your somnolent tour guide.

A handful of individual tunes are slightly more memorable than others. "Ari's Song," written for her young son, could have been called "Postpartum Depression Blues," with its weary entreaty to her six-year-old child to disappear into the ether (one cannot help but recall rumours of how, years later, she turned him on to heroin). On "Julius Caesar (Memento Hodie)" Cale picks up his viola to accompany Nico's harmonium, and the result is suitably chilling, if mostly lyrically incomprehensible. Not that that matters much: it's the sound of Nico's fractured, yet oddly fastidious English that carries the song's melancholic "meaning." "Frozen Warnings" is equally unnerving, its nuclear-winter minimalism seamlessly melding with Nico's forlorn voice. After "Evening of Light," less than thirty-one minutes from the needle dropping on side 1 opener "Prelude," it's over, and even the biggest Nico fan wouldn't wish it otherwise. There was a reason that the Ramones' first album was only 29:04—that is just about as long as one can take the rush of that much pure rock-and-roll psychosis; any more, and you might have a heart attack (although you would die with a depraved smile on your face). If *The Marble Index* went on any longer, it would have had to come with a suicide-prevention-hotline number printed on the back of the LP.

It wasn't just the music that signified Nico's transformation: staring out at the listener from the cover is a red-headed Nico dressed in black (the hair-colour change wasn't difficult—it turned out she had been dyeing her naturally brown hair blond for years). Nico was still bewitchingly lovely, but it was an autumnal, not an April loveliness, which was precisely what she wanted. Cale, from *What's Welsh for Zen?*: "She hated the idea of being blonde and beautiful and in some ways she hated being a woman, because she figured all her beauty had brought her was grief." *The Marble Index* is suffused with sorrow, but Nico is its supplier, not the recipient.

~

Exactly when Nico began messing around with heroin is unclear—some say it was during the recording of *The Marble Index*; others, like Iggy Pop, with whom she had a brief affair in 1969, claim "she didn't do any drugs then. Neither of us did. I would smoke my grass, she would drink her wine"—but her attraction to the drug was understandable, if regrettable. It might be true that, as William Burroughs declares in *Naked Lunch*, "If God made anything better, he kept it for himself," but it is a misnomer to say someone is "high" on heroin. The sensation is undeniably paradisiacal, but it is a feeling of being deliciously indifferent to everything but simply *being*. *You* are no longer *you*—all *you* are is blissfully tranquil flotsam on life's oh-so-silly, busybody jetsam. It may have been the perfect drug for Nico, who preferred silence and shadows to fashionable babble and bright lights anyway, but it is also a heinous concoction that eventually seizes and obliterate the user's soul, robbing them of all but the minimum amount of vitality and humanity. Heroin helped Nico become more Nico; it also eventually all but destroyed her. Being yourself does not necessarily bring happiness. Which is one of the reasons why many people are content to impersonate someone else and call it a personality.

Nico probably didn't become a full-blown junkie until the mid-'70s, though, and none of the indolence, petty criminality, and endlessly whiny solipsism that accompany heroin addiction had yet manifested while she completed her third album, *Desertshore*. And as Iggy Pop's testimony makes clear, when she hooked up with him in New York (Danny Fields once again playing rock-and-roll matchmaker—he'd brought the Stooges, who were in town recording their first album for Elektra, to the Factory), she was narcosis-free enough to blow open the young mind of the Stooges' front man. As Pop told Nick Kent for his essay "The Four Ages of a Man Named Pop: Pictures of Iggy" (included in his superlative essay collection *The Dark Stuff*), "She was the one who took me in when I was a skinny little naïve brat and taught me how to eat pussy and all about the best German wines and French champagnes." Yes, life might often be boring, but if your brain and your body aren't corroded with poison, good head and good wine can certainly make the time go by a little more pleasantly.

For *Desertshore*, Cale was an officially designated overseer, sharing the duties with Joe Boyd, an American-born, British-based producer. Nico was recording for Reprise this time. Elektra did not expect *The Marble Index* to fly off record-store shelves, but it was among the worst-selling albums in the company's history; in addition, Nico wasn't exactly a team player—not interested, for example, in spending a good portion of her life in the back of a cramped van attempting to persuade popular-music fans that the drone of a harmonium was the equal of an electric-guitar solo, and that sex, drugs, and Thanatos were a winning rock-and-roll combination. The album, which came out in 1970, two years after *The Marble Index*, was an extension of the latter: more elegantly inchoate lyrics mournfully wedded to bewitchingly monotonous music, all of it decorated with light neoclassical instrumentation and the odd mad slam of a piano. In other words, another triumph of unwavering individualism. Put on *Desertshore* and forget about which song is which and simply let the sonic fog roll in and over you. Of note is "Janitor of Lunacy," her ode to the recently deceased Brian Jones; she'd later pay the same honour to Jim Morrison. Jerry Garcia said that Grateful Dead music is like licorice: some people don't like it, but the people who do, really, really like it. Ditto Nico's music. To her fans—as few as there were—more of the same was a good thing because there was nothing else anywhere quite like Nico's sameness.

In the 1980s, if an interviewer noted the paucity of material she had produced in the previous decade and asked what she had been busying herself with during this time, Nico would take a long pull on her ever-present Marlboro and answer, "Making avant-garde films." One such film was Philippe Garrel's *La cicatrice intérieure* (1972), which starred Garrel, Nico, and her son (still living in Paris with his father's family). If your idea of "avant-garde" is watching long stretches of Nico plunked down upon a horse, surrounded by a ring of fire in a desert, then Garrel is your go-to moviemaker. For the full effect, turn down the sound and listen to Kevin Ayers' chilling Nico tribute, "Decadence," instead. The cover shot of Nico's *Desertshore* album is a still from the film of an inscrutable-looking Nico sitting on the same desert-marooned horse, so it wasn't entirely a waste of time. Another still—this time from Garrel's film *Les hautes solitudes* (1974)—would later serve the same purpose for her album *The End*...

Nico was involved with Garrel during this period and lived with him in Paris. Lutz Graf-Ulbrich, Nico's German sometimes lover/guitar accompanist described chez Garrel in his grammatically challenged but occasionally revealing memoir, *Nico—In the Shadow of the Moon Goddess*: "The winter was cold. Philippe's apartment was without electricity and the heating was cut off. Philippe used to hang around in his fur coat and smoked one cigarette after another always to the end. Even when you had been away for a couple of hours and you came back he was in the same position as before. You did not miss anything." Red wine and heroin and cigarettes: breakfast of the doomed.

Nico didn't have a permanent band—have harmonium, will travel—and when she did play live, it was rarely a typical one-nighter, but more often something a little more special, like a European music festival. One such gig took place in 1972 at the Bataclan, a Paris theatre, involving herself, Lou Reed, and John Cale—a mini–Velvet Underground reunion. Reed, still attempting to complete his first solo album and not yet transformed with David Bowie and Mick Ronson's assistance into a glam-rock superstar (with a Top 40 hit), appeared in full Afro and looking slightly chubby. He not only looked lost, but he sounded that way as well, his bluesy improvisations during such songs as "I'm Waiting for the Man" simply embarrassing. (He would attempt the same nonsense during the VU's reunion shows in the mid-'90s—perhaps to illustrate how he wasn't imprisoned by his most influential work—with about as much success.) Cale brought along a few of his own songs and his viola and provided his usual sensitive accompaniment, but it was Nico who excelled. Of course, she hauled out a couple of VU golden oldies ("Femme Fatale" and "I'll Be Your Mirror"), plus "No One Is There" and "Frozen Morning" from *Marble Index* and "Janitor of Lunacy" from *Desertshore,* all of which illustrated that hers was clearly the most unique and uncompromising solo material. It must have been revitalizing—perhaps even revelatory—for Reed to share a stage with two real artists, as opposed to the session men he'd been working with. According to Victor Bockris' *Transformer: The Lou Reed Story,* the Velvets' one-time leader was so overwhelmed by the experience that he immediately suggested that he, Cale, and Nico continue working together. Nico and Cale declined. Revenge is a dish best served solo.

Nico and Cale did work together again, though, on 1974's *The End...,* her fourth album. Recorded for Virgin (her fourth company in as many tries and her last with a major label), it was another helping of Nico's dependable brand of doom and harmonium-laden gloom, occasionally spiced up with some muted Arabic touches, and with instrumental assistance this time not only from Cale, but Brian Eno (keyboards) and Phil Manzanera (guitar). The album did get more attention than usual, likely because of the title track, her cover of the Doors' own magnum opus of melancholy, which manages to out-gloom the original; and because of "You Forgot To Answer," a song of her own, about the last time she saw Jim Morrison before his death in 1971, getting into a Paris taxi. No longer insistent on recording exclusively her own material—partly because she had established herself by now as an independent artistic entity, partly because drugs and apathy had diminished her creative zeal—"The End" is worthy of its album-title status. It didn't hurt that, while not "Love Me Two Times" or "Light My Fire" catchy, it at least contained a few more chord changes than Nico's usual dirges, providing a nice tonal change of pace. And it was no stretch for her to sing a song about patricide and incest, the decline of Western civilization, and endless Roman wildernesses of pain (whatever those are). It is a reminder, too, of how much of Nico's lyrical style was inspired by Morrison's own opaque brand of ominous pop poetry.

A little controversy never hindered anyone venturing into the marketplace, and *The End*... concludes with an unexpurgated rendition of "Das Lied der Deutschen" (Germany above all others), the version of the German national anthem adopted by the Nazis, the public performance of which had been banned in that country since the Führer and his dreams of world domination went up in flames in the bunker. Satiric?

Sensationalism for sensationalism's sake? Cryptic neo-Nazi confessional? You'd have to ask Nico. What is for sure is that, to paraphrase her old pal Jimbo, when the music's over, the music's over, turn out the lights.

It would be seven more years before another Nico studio album was released (*Drama of Exile*), and unfortunately it can't be said that it was worth the wait. Which might help explain why it (and its successor, 1985's *Camera Obscura*) sounds so crappy—no one was waiting. The music industry had changed significantly since Nico last recorded, and by the 1980s most record labels were more concerned with following popular trends than allowing maverick artists like Nico to dictate them. From this point on, Nico would record with a series of watered-down New Wave ensembles, hoping, one supposes, to capitalize on her rising credibility with the post-punk and goth crowds (who was more goth than Nico?). When *Drama of Exile* was released, Nico told the media she was tired of playing only slow, sad songs, but the answer, if there was one, wasn't saxophone solos or chirping synthesizers or electronic drums. There were still some good original songs buried underneath the busy goo (e.g., "Henry Hudson" from *Drama of Exile*), but the cold, processed, mainstream sound of both records utterly undermines what had made Nico's music so inimitable. *No one* sounded like the Nico of *The Marble Index*, *Desertshore*, or *The End*...; a *lot* of albums made in the 1980s sound like the Nico of *Drama of Exile* and *Camera Obscura*.

A fully committed heroin addict now, and with no more major-label record advances forthcoming, Nico spent much of the rest of her life on the road, touring with one low-budget band after another (it helped that she didn't have a permanent residence or own many material possessions). With his book *Nico: Songs They Never Play on the Radio*, James Young, the keyboardist in her last band, wrote not only a disturbingly intimate memoir of Nico's final, drug-addled years, but also one of the best books ever written about what it's like to travel hundreds of tedious miles every day in an unreliable, filthy van with a bunch of other underpaid, undernourished, unstable musicians, hoping there will be more people in the audience at that night's show than there will be performers on stage.

It wasn't all doom and dopey gloom; in Jennifer Otter Bickerdike's *You Are Beautiful and You Are Alone: The Biography of Nico*, sound engineer Phil Rainford recalled how, when on the road, he and Nico "used to sing together quite a lot. Both of us were big fans of the American songbook: Frank Sinatra and Ella Fitzgerald. When we were travelling, quite often she'd sit in the front with me, driving everybody else mad in the bus, and we didn't care! 'Fly Me to the Moon' and 'My Funny Valentine' and stuff." A smacked-out Nico singing Frank and Ella tunes to make the miles disappear. But of course.

Even though Nico was over forty now (ancient in rock-and-roll years, particularly at the chilly dawn of MTV), and nearly always broke, nearly always almost out of heroin, nearly always complaining and fighting with her manager and the members of her band (and sometimes ripping them off), she was still defiantly Nico. Young, from *Nico: Songs They Never Play on the Radio*: "She was almost proud of the fact that her teeth were rotten and her hair was grey and, you know, her skin was bad and she had needle tracks all over…

she liked that. That was her aesthetic." Nico might have rejected the image foisted upon her by fashion photographers and filmmakers and the well-meaning Andy Warhols of the world, and the image she adopted and developed and perfected instead—the tortured, drug-addicted, misunderstood artist—might have been just as much of a cliché and a creative cul-de-sac, but it was an image *she* adopted, *she* developed, *she* perfected. "I must create a system," William Blake wrote in *Jerusalem*, "or be enslaved by another man's."

When she died in Ibiza in 1988 of a brain hemorrhage, she had traded in heroin for methadone, had begun to ride a bicycle for exercise, and was determined not to tour anymore. And if she did return to limited performing, it would be entirely solo, just her and her harmonium. She even talked about writing an autobiography. It's best not to sentimentalize and speculate how good it would be. One thing is fairly certain, though: it would sound like Nico.

THE STAPLE SINGERS

And weep the more because I weep in vain.
–Gray

If the twentieth century taught us anything, it is that, as Auden wrote in "In Memory of W. B. Yeats," "poetry makes nothing happen." The last time public opinion in the Western world was affected en masse by anything an artist said or did was someone like Kipling confirming Edwardian England's conviction that invading and occupying other countries and looting their natural resources is a magnanimous act. Or Hemingway in full-blown, late-career *Life* magazine mode, reaffirming every cliché that ever existed about what it means to be a successful artist (loud, drunken, loutish, ostentatious). Mostly, though, it's mass-media sensations like the Beatles, who persuaded a large segment of the male population to grow their hair a little longer, or Kurt Cobain, who singlehandedly made flannel shirts hipster haute couture among the mopey masses. Poets are no longer the unacknowledged legislators of the world (if, pace Shelley, they ever were). Social-media influencers now call the cultural-seismic shots. Want to change the world? Get on television or become a TikTok sensation. Ten million Twitter followers can't be wrong.

And that's okay. Art tends to save souls one soul at a time. I remember reading an interview with John Updike when I was a young writer—when one of the spurs that keeps you scribbling and enduring the repeated punishment of rejection and indifference is the prospect of literary acclaim—where he defined success as something akin to a lonely young woman in Iowa pulling down one of his dusty books from a library shelf, long after he was dead, and reading it and feeling different about language and the world and her place in it. At its best, a gospel song is the essence of this. Existential exploration doesn't get much deeper than a soul-searching song like Blind Willie Johnson's "It's Nobody's Fault but Mine," the salvation we all seek always slipping out of our ungrateful, grasping hands. You don't need to believe in Jesus to participate in Johnson's anguished examination of human frailty. It is not only Christians who wonder what it's all about and where God does or does not fit into the cosmic jigsaw puzzle we call life. As with all good art, you don't have much choice in the matter: you're *compelled* to partake in the spiritual struggle Johnson sings about. And at *their* best, gospel music rarely got better than the Staple Singers.

The Staple Singers' rock of ages was Roebuck "Pops" Staples, the father of Mavis and her other singing siblings, and the source of the uncanny instrumental sound underpinning the group's finest music. Pops was born, raised, and married in

Mississippi, but like many African Americans around this time seeking a better life (he did his time in the cotton fields, and was adamant about never doing any more), Pops moved with his wife, Oceola, and their first daughter, Cleotha, from Drew, Mississippi, to Chicago in 1936. There, Oceola gave birth to three of the couple's four children and Pops found work as a manual labourer, spending long hours, according to Greg Kot's *I'll Take You There: Mavis Staples, The Staple Singers, and the March up Freedom's Highway*, variously in an abattoir, an airplane parts factory, a soft-drink factory, a steel mill, and a construction company (while Oceola toiled as a maid). The money was much better in the North, but shovelling figurative shit for a living, whether he was well compensated or not, was not how Pops envisioned his life—or that of his children. Characteristically, although he never attended high school in Mississippi—where learning was easily trumped by earning—Pops took night classes in Chicago and worked hard and gained his high school diploma. His children were healthy, his marriage was happy, and unlike back in Mississippi, he even had a few dollars in the bank. But something was missing: music.

In Mississippi, living and working on the plantation, Pops had not only sung in the Baptist church, but also had the opportunity to see and hear many wandering, guitar-playing performers, including the seminal bluesman Charlie Patton (who influenced and inspired another restless young field-worker who would end up in Chicago, Howlin' Wolf). Pops learned to love the sound of a guitar and the feel of the blues, as well as the idea of making a living doing something that made oneself and others happy, as opposed to merely filthy and exhausted; this, even though some people in the religiously conservative community scorned the playing of or listening to the blues, including Pops' parents—the slow, pulsating rhythms of the blues a clear invitation to all sorts of worldly trouble. Mavis recalled how, as an eight-year-old, after her grandmother discovered that she had sung a bluesy tune at a school variety show that she'd heard somewhere,

> Grandma says, 'Oh, you singin' the blues, huh? You go out there and get me some switches.' I didn't understand. Nobody told me what I could and could not sing. I came back with a handful of these switches, and she whipped me pretty good. Tore my legs up. Each time she whipped me she said, 'You...don't...sing...no...blues! In this family you sing church songs.'

In the Chicago neighbourhood the Staples called home in the early 1940s, however, music of all kinds flourished—not just the blues and gospel, but also pop, jazz, and early R&B—and, when not working or studying or helping to raise four young children, Pops eventually joined a gospel sextet called the Trumpet Jubilees. And he might have remained a member of just one more amateur Baptist singing group if he hadn't been quite so...Pops. Although he was only one voice among six, he was the group's self-appointed overseer and taskmaster and found himself increasingly exasperated with the rest of the quartet's lax attitude toward rehearsing and their general unprofessionalism. So he started a new group composed of members he knew he could rely on: himself and his adolescent children (Mavis, Cleotha, and their brother Pervis). Yvonne, the self-described "quiet one," was allowed to opt in and out of the group—mostly out.

From their first tentative rehearsals in the family living room, the Staples' sound was pretty much set: Pops playing guitar and singing tenor; the diminutive Mavis covering the low notes; Pervis taking care of the higher ones; and Cleotha laying her voice, even higher still, on top of his. Later, Mavis would take over most lead vocals when Pervis' voice changed—they were children, after all. It was basic, if dependably stirring, Baptist-style vocalizing, but something new to secular ears. Levon Helm, one of the Band's three distinct, outstanding lead vocalists, recalled in his autobiography *This Wheel's On Fire: Levon Helm and the Story of the Band* that "one of the things we'd always loved about soul music was the way groups like the Staple Singers and the Impressions would stack those individual voices on top of one another, each voice coming in at a different time until you got this blend that was just magic." Helm goes on to claim that "those multiple voices" were a key part of how the former rockabilly band "discovered our sound" (listen to "The Weight" or "We Can Talk" and hear how it was so). To non-churchgoers, the sound was—and still is—revelatory. Talking to Robert Love, editor of *AARP* magazine, Bob Dylan recalled discovering the sound of the Staple Singers: "One night I remember listening to the Staple Singers, 'Uncloudy Day.' And it was the most mysterious thing I'd ever heard. It was like the fog rolling in. What was that? How do you make that? It just went through me." In time, Mavis' voice became *the* voice associated with the Staple Singers, but it is the asymmetrical intermingling of all the family members' individual voices that remains most moving. It is a Greek chorus with tempo and texture—an anguished exorcism of metaphysical angst; hillbilly high lonesome from the other side of town; cubist blues with a steady beat.

But the power of the Staples' sound wasn't solely vocal; Pops' guitar is an integral part of what gives their most enduring music what Neil Young and his producer David Briggs used to call "the Spook." Some records have it, most records don't (in Young's case, there's *Tonight's the Night* and *On the Beach* and then there's all the rest), but however it's defined—the sublime, the transcendental, the uncanny—if a song doesn't have it, it's just, at best, entertainment. Not that there's anything wrong with entertainment—the world would be an even more sombre, less interesting place without silly love sings or the poppy froth of something like the Monkees—but Pops was aiming for something more substantial. Pops wanted to *save souls*. And a mission such as this requires the employment of every spirit-unlocking, mind-expanding, goose bump–inducing tool available. It requires "the Spook." And Pops' tremolo-laden electric-guitar playing is spooky. It's not just the eerily reverberating tone he coaxes out of his instrument (although that's a big part of it)—it's also the measured, almost wary way his fingers stroke the strings, as if he believed that if he played any more notes than were absolutely essential, he would be showboating, showing off, detracting from the crucial task at hand. One can't help but hear Pops' less-is-more aesthetic as an influence on the Band's Robbie Robertson's uniquely—for late-'60s rock and roll—economical lead-guitar style, although it's just as possible that he took his cue from the Impressions' Curtis Mayfield, who definitely did know the Staples' music inside and out.

The group began playing local churches in 1948, then a few out-of-town churches, then a few churches in nearby states, gaining attention and acclaim along the way, not only because of the unusual visual configuration of a father performing with his young children (in his pioneering *The Gospel Sound: Good News and Bad Times,* Anthony Heilbut dubbed them "an appealing novelty"), but because of their sound. In addition to the stacked vocals and reverberating guitar, there were two other noteworthy aspects to the Staple Singers' music. First, there was Mavis' unusually deep, girly-growly lead vocal, which seemed like it could not only, as in the Reverend Gary Davis song "Samson and Delilah" (which the Staples cut in 1964) "tear this whole building down," but could also seduce you into walking in the light of the Lord. There's nothing cutesy or flirtatious about Mavis' voice—its appeal is rooted strictly in the irresistible strength and passion of her guttural wails and moans and cries. Niagara Falls isn't sexy—its attraction and fascination come from proximity to something natural that, because of its awe-inspiring power and size, seems to border on the supernatural.

Second, the Staple Singers sounded *country*—as in, came from the country and sounded like where they came from. Pops was the only one who'd been born and raised rural and had actually done time working the fields, but because he was the band's sole instrumentalist and arranger (and its only adult), the songs the group sang and how they sang them tended to reflect his background and musical predilections. Pops' delicately rumbling electric guitar was bluesy, the group's harmonies were Baptist country churchy, the rhythm was understated, Sunday-service clappy, but the overall effect is blues-tinged gospel with strong hillbilly undertones. "Will the Circle Be Unbroken" is a turn-of-the-twentieth-century Christian hymn written by two white songwriters, Ada R. Habershon and Charles H. Gabriel, and made famous by the all-white Carter Family, a folk-based country group, but the Staples Singers' version sounds as authentic as anyone else's, or as any song they ever recorded. More, in fact, than their much better-known, borderline MOR, gospel-folk and gospel-pop hits of the late '60s and '70s.

To end up in Pops' ecumenical songbook, a tune had to pass two tests: (1) it had to reflect God's glory; and (2) it had to be a good song. Pops heard "Will the Circle Be Unbroken" sung by whites and Blacks alike back on the plantation and the skin colour of the person singing it didn't matter. As a teenager, Jimmie Rodgers, also Mississippi born and raised and sometimes called the "father of country music," worked as a water boy on the railroad and picked up plenty of musical influences from the African American railroaders, including his trademark yodelling. Chuck Berry, sometimes called the "father of rock and roll," grew up playing the blues and ballads but, coming of age in the American Midwest, also listened to country music on the radio, and its backwoods bounce eventually found its way into what everyone now identifies as the "Chuck Berry" sound. "In order for one's book to sweat truth," Flaubert wrote to a friend, "one has to be stuffed to the ears with its subject." Pops' ears were stuffed with the sounds of God's glorification, regardless of what the person who wrote the song or sang it looked like.

The Staple Singers became popular enough that they recorded some sides for United Records in 1953, and while the results are excellent—just Pops' ringing guitar, a little piano, and a whole lot of Staples lung power—the label wanted something more commercial (this wasn't just gospel, this was... country gospel) and never released them, although after the group's subsequent success they ultimately found their way onto vinyl. When Pops signed a deal with Chicago's Vee-Jay label in 1955, he joined a company (owned by two African American evangelicals and gospel buffs) willing to let the group make their music *their* way, the hit parade be damned. The Staple Singers would go on to make Vee-Jay a lot of money, but only because the label initially encouraged them to do their own thing. That that "thing" became a popular "thing" was a very nice dividend; the principal prize, however, was putting the Staple Singers' unique sound before the public, where Vee-Jay believed it needed to be.

"Each Day," "God's Wonderful Home," and "If I Could Hear My Mother Pray Again" were the initial results, the only real departure from their United Records session being Mavis, who was now a teenager, taking a larger role vocally. These records also did nothing commercially, but their next single, 1956's aforementioned "Uncloudy Day," was a hit. It was the same old Staple Singers—Pops and his trembling, mesmerizing tremolo, Pervis' and Cleotha's voices swooping and soaring and helping keep the beat, Mavis laying down the divine law with her impossibly (she was sixteen) sonorous wisdom—but the tune, a nineteenth-century hymn, was catchy enough that it attracted the attention of gospel-record buyers along with those intrigued by the group's uncommonly uncluttered, unhurried sound. Significantly, Mavis doesn't sing of a home beyond the skies, a home where no storm clouds rise, but of how she's been *told* of all of these wonderful things. I'm sure that when she sang it Mavis had no doubt that such a celestial paradise existed, but to agnostic ears the impact is equally profound. "Uncloudy Day" is a Kierkegaardian country-gospel blues, two minutes and fifty-seven seconds of funky fear and trembling. Even songs imbued with assurances of everlasting serenity and joy like "I Got Religion" and "Come On Up in Glory" are, via Mavis' polygonal vocal gifts (alternately joyful, despairing, assured, bewildered), permeated with a wobbly wisdom. Like any great poet, it's not what Mavis says—it's how she says it.

With a bona fide chart hit, gigs got bigger, and the money got better, enough so that it made more economic sense for Pops to quit his job at the steel mill and focus on captaining the group's burgeoning career. Staple Singers shows were a lot like their songs: unadorned and unfussy and all about the music, although many concert-goers must have been surprised to see sweet-sixteen Mavis, instead of a wizened gospel veteran, belting out all those odes to the Lord. When Mavis graduated from high school and her brother and sister quit their jobs, the Staple Singers were officially full-time professionals, touring all over America on gospel package tours as well as on their own. The Staples' bread and butter was the American South, and in spite of having to endure segregation and pernicious concert promoters (Pops carried a gun on tour because the Lord helps those who help make sure their family gets paid) the group was a very popular concert attraction. DJ Al Bell remembered how a typical Staple Singers show reflected Pops' undeviating values:

> They would take a break just as things were peaking, and not a moment later. There would be an intermission, then they would play their latest album over the PA, and the girls and Pervis would take the albums out to the audience and he [Pops] would be onstage asking people to buy them, or take a picture with the family. He did it in such a way that you didn't feel offended. It was very casual and good-natured.

"You see my son, Pervis, over there? He's a good-looking fella. Why don't you take a picture with him?" Then they'd get back onstage, and they were back into it. He was just masterful at keeping that vibe, pushing out this powerful, moving music, but selling it, too.

God might have been on his side, but Pops knew how to put his shoulder to the wheel, as well.

One expertly arranged, passionately performed, gorgeously austere gem followed another (the jaunty interpretation of "Swing Low Sweet Chariot," Pops' own, equally sprightly "Help Me, Jesus," the near-pop appeal of his "This May Be the Last Time"—parts of which the Rolling Stones "borrowed" for their own song of the same name), but it would be difficult to top the self-penned "I'm Coming Home," released in 1957. (Its omission in full-length studio form from the otherwise excellent box set *Faith and Grace: A Family Journey 1953–1976* is dumbfounding.) In "I'm Coming Home," Pops' near-hypnotic guitar undulations (the sound of the earth slowly cracking and crumbling underneath your feet) cosset his and Mavis' high-wire, call-and-response, nearly seven-minute cosmological conversation. The words Mavis sings might say that she's coming home someday, home to that place where the streets are paved with gold and one's burdens are abolished forever, but her—sorry, there's no other word for it—*tortured* tone makes it a far-less sanguine situation and song than the words alone might indicate. Keats wrote about what he called "negative capability," when an artist "is capable of being in uncertainties, Mysteries, doubts, without any irritable reaching after fact & reason," and this extraordinary (and extraordinarily rare) perspective is made incarnate in

Pops' sometimes uplifting, sometimes sinister-sounding guitar, and the unfathomable depths of Mavis' many-sided vocals.

The Staple Singers left Vee-Jay in 1961 for Riverside, and if the rhythm section is beefed up a bit and there's the occasional inclusion of organ and syncopated hand-clapping, tunes like Pops' "Hear My Call, Here" and "Let That Liar Alone" and Stapleized renditions of gospel mainstays such as "Great Day" and "I Can't Help From Cryin' Sometimes" are, on the whole, comparable with the group's Vee-Jay material, and continued the group's run of aesthetic, if not commercial, success. Maybe this was one of the reasons why the Staples' sound began to change. Pervis Staples:

> I was always like, 'Hey, gospel is not selling.' Yeah, we could play this on the five-thousand-watt gospel station or we could play on this fifty-thousand-watt commercial station. I was having beers and stuff with cats who made a step above where we were. We started singing the folk songs. We ran into Dylan, Baez, and Johnny Cash, people we respected. We saw this was a whole different market we could be part of.

Artists are inclined to like it when people read their books or look at their paintings or listen to their music, and the Staple Singers' desire to reach a wider audience is not only understandable, but consistent with their acknowledged proselytizing aim: more listeners mean more saveable souls.

But there was another reason for their eventual desertion of the haunting, near-naked truths of their early sound: the civil rights movement, of which Pops and his entire family were, naturally, enthusiastic champions. By the early '60s, folk—and, later in the decade, soul and funk—would be the most popular musical means of getting out the word about racial inequality and the predicament of all of America's long-suffering underclasses, and Pops exhibited his usual good taste in selecting Bob Dylan's "A Hard Rain's Gonna Fall" and "Masters of War" (and later, when they moved to Epic, the Buffalo Springfield's "For What It's Worth") for the Staples treatment, as well as composing several civil rights anthems himself, like "Freedom Highway" and "Why (Am I Treated So Bad)." And although Pops' human rights ardour was no less sincere than his religious zeal, and the group still sound like the Staple Singers underneath the increasingly busy arrangements—Pops' guitar and Mavis' voice guarantee that—the frugal singularity of their musical vision became slowly sacrificed to their admirable, if aesthetically compromising, agenda.

Meaning: the majority of the folk-gospel protest songs that the Staple Singers recorded for Epic (and the personally empowering, horn-heavy, funk-lite fare they laid down for Stax in the '70s, including million sellers such as "Respect Yourself," "Heavy Makes You Happy (Sha-Na-Boom-Boom)," and "I'll Take You There") are worthy slices of righteous good sense, but lacking in that special musical something that allows a song to rise above the topical and approach the universal. They lack "the Spook." The four-CD *Faith and Grace* box wraps up in 1976, and although the group, and Mavis and Pops as solo artists, continued to record long after this, it's the right critical call. Anything Mavis Staples sings is worth hearing, but it's the spooky stuff that we come back to. Despite some celebrity-assisted albums (like the Jeff

Tweedy–produced *You Are Not Alone* from 2010 and 2013's *One True Vine*), Mavis' best solo LP is probably her second, 1970's *Only the Lonely*, which contains a brief but punchy version of "Son of a Preacher Man," with which Dusty Springfield had a hit the year before. Pops made only four solo LPs before his death, at age eighty-five, in 2000, and they're all good, honest music. But it is the Vee-Jay material that remains essential.

After it was revealed that a very young Bob Dylan proposed to Mavis during those early, exciting folk music/civil rights days, she stated in interviews that, although they loved each other, it simply never occurred to her at that time that marrying a white person was a viable option. Too bad. A mixed-race celebrity couple like Bob Dylan and Mavis Staples could have immediately furthered American race relations fifty years. That's something no song is likely to do. No matter how righteous. Or even spooky.

CAPTAIN BEEFHEART

Hated by fools, and fools to hate
Be that my motto, and my fate
–Swift

The blues is the best, everybody knows that, but the blues gets boring, admit it. So, Captain Beefheart (aka Don Van Vliet) came to the rescue and weirded things up and saved the blues. Besides, listeners want weird. *Need* it. Living prosaically, we desire to cozy up to crazy, to experience vicariously, through the music of others, the poetry and passion so often lacking in our own lives. But the madness can't be manufactured—a shaman isn't a salesman, enlightenment isn't a savvy career move—and sometimes bringing the magic means being a conniving, dictatorial, abusive, and exploitive magician. Sometimes, if that white whale called keeping-the-blues-alive is going to get caught, Captain Beefheart has to be Captain Ahab.

Born in 1941, Don liked to emphasize to credulous interviewers just how extraordinarily precocious he was growing up (whistling when he was two; at three insisting upon addressing his parents by their given names; at the same age attempting his first sculpture; as a teenager, becoming so fixated on one or another of his art projects that he stayed in his bedroom for nearly three weeks). Frank Zappa, a close friend of Don's since they met in high school (they were born less than a month apart), provides an illustrative anecdote about Don's youth in the 1997 BBC documentary *The Artist Formerly Known as Captain Beefheart*:

> He spent most of his time at home. His girlfriend lived in the house.... His father had had a heart attack [and] drove a Helms bread truck; part of the time Don was helping out by taking over the bread truck route.... The rest of time he would just sit at home and listen to rhythm and blues records, and scream at his mother to get him a Pepsi.

Self-absorbed; autodidactic; obsessive; ceaselessly curious; indulged and entitled: Don was neither the first nor the last aspiring somebody to depend upon the kindness of his or her parents. One of his heroes, Thelonious Monk, enjoyed his own mother's free room and board in Harlem well into his twenties, while he went about the busy business of helping to revolutionize modern jazz, much as thirty-something Gustave Flaubert, while living with his mother in the French countryside, directed his energies toward transfiguring the contemporary novel.

As indulgent as they might have been, Don's mother and father forced him to decline a scholarship he had been offered as a teenager to study sculpture in Europe because they were afraid, according to Don, that such a move might turn him into a homosexual. Soon afterward his parents moved from the LA suburb of Glendale to Lancaster, California, a small town close to the Mojave Desert. This was a different kind of sprawl: there was still nothing to do, but desert nothingness was better, at least, than subdivision sterility. And it was here, while attending Antelope Valley High School (sounds like a Beefheart song title), that he met Frank Zappa.

Zappa shared his new friend's love of blues (especially Howlin' Wolf and his band's stutter-step rhythms, an obvious influence on the mature Beefheart sound), R&B, and jazz (particularly the free jazz of people like Ornette Coleman). Their mutual musical education continued when he and Don enrolled at Antelope Valley Junior College. Zappa, studying music, was the more academically committed of the two; he was also the first person to convince Don to sing on tape—a parodic, scatological blues captured on a school tape recorder. Don, enrolled as an art student, soon dropped out. While Don continued to enjoy his mother's home cooking and worked as little as possible, Zappa was busier, joining a local rock-and-roll band and spending a lot of time at a Cucamonga recording studio, becoming increasingly interested in the technical aspects of record production (he would eventually purchase the tiny studio and rename it Studio Z). Soon after, he formed his own band so he could play something other than hits of the day for bar patrons, and it wasn't long before he roped in his old pal Don to handle vocals on some studio sessions.

The recorded results are lo-fi, shaky R&B, distinguished, if that's the right word, by the singer's impenetrable, seemingly associative lyrics and half-growled vocals. Another one of Zappa's ideas was a rock opera (in 1963) called *I Was a Teenage Maltshop* that thankfully never got beyond the songwriting stage. The problem with Zappa as a satirist is that too often what he targeted was so obvious as to not really warrant the effort. Zappa is an intellectual to the same sort of people who believe Jim Morrison is a poet. One thing that did come out of the aborted project was the name of one of the characters that Don was pegged to play: Captain Beefheart. Zappa's next brainstorm was the making of a sci-fi movie called *Captain Beefheart vs. The Grunt People* (another, uhm, satire of the straight world). This, too, didn't get much beyond the pre-production stage, but there was that name again. It would come in handy later.

While Zappa went off to LA, in 1965, to form the first Mothers of Invention, Don stayed home and eventually got together with some of the local guys he had jammed with at Zappa's studio. Equipped with a love of the blues that only middle-class white kids growing up on Cornflakes and *Ozzie and Harriet* can have, the band also had its name: Captain Beefheart & His Magic Band. In his memoir of his time with Beefheart, *Lunar Notes: Zoot Horn Rollo's Captain Beefheart Experience,* guitarist Bill Harkleroad remembered this early incarnation as "a pretty straightforward blues band doing Howlin' Wolf, Muddy Waters, Jimmy Reed, John Lee Hooker" plus the obligatory Rolling Stones covers (by 1965, even the residents of Lancaster, California, had succumbed to the British Invasion). As traditional as they might have sounded live, behind the scenes things were already getting a little odd. Although he played the harmonica, the non-music-reading captain was entirely self-taught and frequently had to resort to metaphors to get the rest of the band to understand what he was trying to say. One is reminded of another musical visionary, Syd Barrett, and his attempt to get the musicians assembled to record one of his solo albums to play a certain passage "a little more middle-of-the-afternoonish."

The captain and his band were a reasonably successful local attraction, but it was an appearance at something called the Teenage Fair at the Hollywood Palladium that led to the formation of the first "real" Magic Band. Gary Marker, bass player for the Rising Sons, another group performing that day, told biographer Mike Barnes (*Captain Beefheart: The Biography*),

> I looked up at the crowd and right up front was this really weird-looking guy.... It gets pretty toasty in Hollywood in April, even outdoors at night-time, but this dude with an unruly shock of hair was wearing a leather coat that hit him about mid-thigh. He had an absolutely stunned and perplexed look on his face.... The song wound down, and this weird dude turned to one of the guys with him and grabbed him by the arm—and I mean grabbed him really hard. He pointed at Cooder [Ry Cooder, the Rising Sons' bottleneck-playing guitarist], then snarled at his prisoner through clenched teeth, "There, that's the shit I mean. That's what I've been fucking talking about. Get it? Now do you know what the fuck I'm talking about?"

Cooder wouldn't join the Magic Band until they recorded their first album, but the captain had found his man.

The group scored a deal to record a single with A&M Records and had a modest local hit with a version of Bo Diddley's "Diddy Wah Diddy." The choice of cover had been their producer's idea, but it was a good fit for the still-developing band. It is basic, bluesy garage rock, if a little catchier than most specimens of the genre, but it is Beefheart's voice that demands one's attention more than either the song or its performance. Although he possessed a four-and-a-half-octave range, he doesn't sound like Howlin' Wolf on LSD quite yet, but it is still like nothing else that was being cut in the rock-and-roll world in 1966. According to friend Jim Sherwood, Beefheart didn't come by his raspy vocal style naturally, which only makes its eventual gravelly voiced, hiccup-syncopating grandeur all the more impressive. "He would wash his hair and keep it wet and do things to get a cold," Sherwood recalled. "He used to stay sick with a cold so that he'd get that voice and sing like Howlin' Wolf. Then when I saw Don a few years later, his voice was really torn. I don't know what he did, whether he tore his vocal cords, but he had a real gruff voice and it pretty much stayed that way. That's what he wanted and he got it." If you want to sing the blues, you've got to pay your wet-hair dues. Just add to it to the captain's tab.

"Diddy Wah Diddy" did well enough for A&M to issue a flop follow-up (the patchouli-dusted, "Smokestack Lightnin'" rip-off "Moonchild" b/w "Frying Pan," a forgettable, almost poppy blues song), but the best cut recorded for A&M was the unreleased (until the appearance of 1984's *The Legendary A&M Sessions*) "Here I Am, I Always Am," a stomping, slightly dissonant dose of proto-Beefheartian peculiarity, made slightly more accessible by the unrequited-love lyrics. The band continued to gig around California, and although the captain's voice certainly made them unique on the teen concert circuit, bootlegged tapes reveal a group not that far removed from any above-average garage band, circa 1966, such as the Standells or the Chocolate Watch Band.

Then five things happened: (1) A&M officially dropped Captain Beefheart & His Magic Band from their label; (2) a new group sound was being developed by Beefheart, and a new drummer, John French, joined up; (3) the band moved to a communal house in Laurel Canyon because the captain thought it was time to get out of the desert and closer to LA and the music industry; (4) the small Kama Sutra label offered Beefheart a deal on their subsidiary label Buddah to make a full-length LP; and (5) Ry Cooder, the Rising Sons having broken up, was convinced to join the Magic Band. It was time to make *Safe as Milk*.

~

Initially reluctant to join the Magic Band as a full-time member, Cooder could not have felt very sure of his career choice when, at one of the first practices he attended, Beefheart brusquely informed guitarist Doug Moon that he was now no longer part of the band (Alex Snouffer, the other guitarist, was judged worthy of keeping). Beefheart also told Cooder, who had been brought in as unofficial arranger as well as lead guitar player, that Jerry Handley, the bass player, couldn't play the goddamn parts he'd been taught, goddamnit—this, in front of said bass player and the rest of the group. The major difference between Don's fine art projects (both before and after his career as Captain Beefheart) and his vocation as a musician was not in the raw materials employed—the contrast between paint and musical notes—but in the contrast between working in isolation and working with other people. Some individuals—novelists, for example—tend not to play well with others. A musical group is just that, however—a group. From this point on, the captain was a painter of musical landscapes, and what he viewed as his instruments, the musicians in the band, were not always keen on being treated as mere tools of his trade.

The mission the captain set for himself and his crew on their maiden-LP voyage was nothing less than the resuscitation of the blues. On the one hand, the blues, the real, elemental blues—Son House, Howlin' Wolf, Muddy Waters, John Lee Hooker—was Beefheart's first and deepest musical love, for many of the same reasons that other people adore it: its intense, emotional honesty, its trance-like rhythms, and the slow, deep grooves it rides. Even if a blues song's subject is sorrow, it usually still *feels* good because of the sturdy, reassuring rhythmic pulse. Beefheart, who also loved contemporary jazz (John Coltrane, Ornette Coleman, Roland Kirk) wanted to retain the emotional and rhythmic appeal of the blues without being controlled and constrained by musical formulas or potentially numbing repetition (something Coltrane et al. were up to in the jazz field). Beefheart derisively referred to the rhythmic inflexibility of most blues music as the "mamma heartbeat," and he made it his task to avoid its seductive, simple-minded allure by any musical means possible.

Future Beefheart guitarist Bill Harkleroad recalled how Beefheart "would say, 'Play a high note like a low note. Play a low note like a high note. Play something staccato but play it like you're imagining it lasting longer.' Any way to change something to make it less predictable in the musical sense." Beefheart also formulated what he called his "exploding note theory," whereby one note doesn't follow from the one that preceded it or followed it, neatly summed up by Harkleroad in his memoir, *Lunar Notes*: "The best description I can come up with is to call it sound sculptures. It was both polyphonic and polyrhythmic—with some repeated shapes. We would play in various time signatures, often at the same time. For instance, one part might be in 3/4 time while another was in 4/4 time." The blues is great; playing it your own way is even better.

Safe as Milk was released in 1967 and consists of twelve songs, eleven of them originals (of these, Beefheart is credited with all the music and collaborated with a friend, Herb Bermann, on the lyrics). Cooder's creaking electric bottleneck-guitar figure that announces opening track "Sure 'Nuff 'n Yes I Do," which is really an amped-up, lyrically revised version of Muddy Waters' "Rollin' and Tumblin'," is an ideal introduction to the band's version of postmodern blues. It sounds like horror-movie, Mississippi Delta music, reassuringly familiar but still slightly unsettling. The same effect is achieved when the captain sings the song's opening stanza, his cracked, growly voice and odd, punctuating vocal hiccups, unusual enough—and that's before he sings the last line, the one about the moon getting stuck in his eye. And when the drums kick in—now you know this isn't the blues, at least not any you've ever heard before. Like the best jazz drummers, new skinsman John "Drumbo" French (Beefheart liked to give his band members nicknames, perhaps as a way to dictate their identities as much as he did the instrumental parts they played) always keeps the beat, but without falling into a predictable, repetitive pattern, his style a nonstop, stop-and-start, polyrhythmic blizzard of tom-tom attack, sizzling hi-hat, and galloping aggression. The essence of the Beefheart rhythm sound is feeling just grounded enough that you're able to soar through the universe without feeling in danger of evaporating.

Which leads to a question that has to be raised at some point when discussing Beefheart's music: how much did the captain contribute to his band's unique sound and how much were the individual musicians responsible for it? Here is French discussing the drums on the *Safe as Milk* track "Electricity" in his memoir, *Beefheart: Through the Eyes of Magic*:

> The drum parts to "Electricity" were taught to me in the studio, ten minutes before we did the song. Don came over and started talking to me about these new parts he had.... They were simple enough, because Don only had a rudimentary knowledge of drums, so he basically sang the ideas to me. However, it really made the song come together. When I say rudimentary knowledge, again, I am referring to being specific about what to play on what drum. He could vocalize drum sounds, like saying "ka-chomp boom" and I would interpret what he sang into the beat.

French freely admits that Beefheart attempted to show him what he wanted to hear played, but no matter how much instruction he received, it was French who ending up playing it. Ambition is limited by ability, and a less-talented musician than John French might not have been capable of developing and eventually mastering the signature frantic-but-funky Captain Beefheart drum sound. The captain supplied the vision, but his soldiers made it a reality.

As for the other eleven tunes, "Zig Zag Wanderer" boasts an acrobatic Beefheart vocal and distinctive, shifting time signatures (a jazz hallmark). "Call On Me" is eccentric folk-rock with a tough, R&B-tinged vocal. "Dropout Boogie" features a deranged vocal to go along with the fiercely chugging rhythm and with a delightfully disconcerting, slowed-down middle section as well. "Glad" is the kind of glorious doo-wop that Don and Zappa were obsessed with as kids, but whereas Zappa would have been incapable of playing it straight, Beefheart croons it for all of its simple street-corner beauty. The aforementioned "Electricity" could be considered corny—the squealing theremin is definitely period specific—but Drumbo's rampaging drums and Beefheart's ghoulish vocal delivery more than compensate. "Yellow Brick Road," despite its nastily sung chorus, is little more than not-entirely unenjoyable flower-power nonsense. "Abba Zabba" is a tongue-teasing treat, a bubbling obscurity riding a complicated but cleanly executed rhythm. "Plastic Factory," highlighted by the captain's crude-but-effective harmonica, is a wailing, almost-straight blues. The remaining three tracks are a mixed bag (the souped-up soul ballad "Where There's a Woman"; the sole cover, a rhythmically rearranged version of Robert Pete Williams' funky "Grown So Ugly"; and the pretentious, overly out-of-sight "Autumn's Child"). Despite its flaws, *Safe as Milk* is one of my favourite Captain Beefheart albums, partly because it was the first Beefheart LP I owned, partly because, even in this unrealized form, it's the first formulation of a vision of the blues that I hadn't even known existed. That really no one knew existed until *Safe as Milk* was released in October 1967. (The Grateful Dead were up to something similar in the folk-rock vein with such time-signature-twisting compositions as "The Eleven," "New Potato Caboose," and a few others, but not until a year or so later.)

There was trouble in Magicland, however. In his memoir, French acknowledged not only how well the band liked and valued Cooder, but also how much the twenty-year-old guitar player and arranger contributed to *Safe as Milk*'s one-of-a-kind sound. Yet French ultimately had to side with the captain when it came to Cooder's increasing unwillingness or inability to comprehend the value of Beefheart's pioneering vision:

> I could see that Ry was upset [one day]. He was talking to Don…in the hallway and in the conversation I heard there was the overriding theme of this music not being blues. I was disappointed, because I felt what we were doing was blues-based, and certainly as valid, but also original and contemporary.…Instead of wanting to do something fresh and new, which was certainly a definition of what we were creating here, he [Ry] seemed more inclined to copy, to imitate.

Virtually all of the Magic Band's members lamented Beefheart's unprofessionalism, parsimoniousness, and overbearing egotism, but not one of them, except for Cooder, ever questioned the importance of the inimitable music they were creating together. Sometimes it's difficult to see the forest for the weirdness.

It wasn't musical differences or a lack of money that led to Cooder's departure from the group (according to French, Beefheart lied to the band about the advance they had received from the record label and kept most of it for himself). Just before they were scheduled to perform at the Monterey Pop Festival, Captain Beefheart & His Magic Band booked a gig at another outdoor festival, the Magic Mountain Fantasy Fair. Monterey Pop is famous for hosting the breakout performances of Jimi Hendrix, the Who, Janis Joplin, and Otis Redding (in terms of white American youth, anyway); the Magic Mountain Fantasy Fair is infamous for being the show where Captain Beefheart either got high on acid or experienced an acid flashback, thought he was having a heart attack (he was a lifelong hypochondriac), and fell off the stage. When French tracked down a disgusted Cooder, who was walking to his car, and tried to convince him to give the band another chance, the guitarist told him, "Nope, can't do it, got better things to do, can't work with that man."

Considering the absolute penury that the Magic Band would endure over the group's career, a high-profile gig like Monterey might have made a significant difference in their lives. Another neoblues band, Canned Heat, while not as popular a success as some of the other performers on the bill, nonetheless used the opportunity to publicize itself and its own first album. Many excellent musicians who "got" the captain's musical message were forced to leave the band over the years for primarily financial reasons. And yet others—like French—did stay on, and not because things got monetarily better. *Beefheart: Through the Eyes of Magic* is full of French's anti-Beefheart vitriol, much of which is hard to argue with. And yet... After the Magic Mountain Fantasy Fair debacle and Cooder's exit, French admits, "I am not sure why I stayed. My dreams of being a famous drummer were gone if I stayed with this man, yet there was a curious bond forming between he and I that I couldn't seem to shake." Recognition is nice, money is nicer, art is the best. Give French et al. credit for feeling this, if not, even now, quite understanding it.

To no one's surprise, the record was a commercial nonstarter, but Buddah allowed the band (fortified by Cooder's replacement, Jeff Cotton) back into the studio to commence work on its next intended album, provisionally entitled *It*

Comes to You in a Plain Brown Wrapper. Even more than on *Safe as Milk*, the musical language was still the blues, but it was now being spoken in a very distinct dialect that takes some getting used to. The material they recorded in the late fall of 1967 (released four years later as *The Mirror Man Sessions*) eliminated the majority of what traditional blues and rock elements had been evident on their first record by extending the length of the songs, emphasizing the two guitarists' interweaving, slashing bottleneck playing, and cultivating even rubberier rhythms. The overall sound is very appealing, alternatively propulsive and supple, driving yet cagey, the captain's periodic drive-by harmonica attacks and shrieking, shouted lyrics adding to the twisted deconstruction.

Too often, however—especially on longer songs like "Tarotplane," "25th Century Quaker," and "Mirror Man"—the frantic riffing and cunningly shifting time signatures and overall bubbling trouble eventually grow slightly tedious, the listener waiting for a punchline that never arrives. Unlike, say, Thelonious Monk's beautiful disassembling of traditional jazz piano technique—what his biographer Robin D. G. Kelley (*Thelonious Monk: The Life and Times of an American Original*) identifies as Monk's "cling-clang sound of surprise, rich with deafening silences, dissonances, and harmonic ambiguities"—Captain Beefheart & His Magic Band during *The Mirror Man Sessions* do a much better job of gutting the house of the blues than renovating it.

After a few gigs and a smattering of promotional work in Britain and France (where the BBC's John Peel, who had fallen in love with *Safe as Milk* when he had briefly DJed in the US, featured the band on his highly influential radio show), Captain Beefheart & His Magic Band returned to

California to discover that Buddah had not only released the group from their contract, but insisted that the material that had been recorded on their corporate dime was their property. Fortunately, Bob Krasnow, who had produced *The Mirror Man* sessions, was in the process of leaving Buddah and starting his own label, Blue Thumb. He signed up Beefheart as his first act and secured them the studio time that resulted in their second album, 1968's *Strictly Personal*. Many musicians, after they have been dropped by their label because of a lack of commercial success, might want to make a good impression on the new company paying the bills by giving the sense that they are willing at least to consider compromising, commercially speaking, but Beefheart wasn't one of them. French, from his memoir: "Although still very difficult to understand at times because of his lack of musical knowledge, he would sing, whistle, play harmonica, or attempt to play guitar—often breaking strings—to get his vision across.... He kept pressing us into stranger and stranger music and more and more tempo changes and less song form." In for a penny of sonic oddness, in for a pound.

Although the songs on *Strictly Personal* (some new, some rerecorded from the *Plain Brown Wrapper* sessions) were, as French said, growing "stranger and stranger," they were also much more satisfactory than the material that was eventually released on *The Mirror Man Sessions*. For one thing, they *are* songs—the meandering blues jams having been replaced by eight tunes with discernible beginnings, middles, and ends. These are very peculiar beginnings, middles, and ends, however, the captain's biting harmonica, the duelling bottleneck guitars, busy drums, and dodgy bass working together to create some almost-catchy melodies while simultaneously fighting for their respective right to be listened to individually. It's all weird, but not, one feels, simply for the sake of weirdness.

Opening track "Ah Feel Like Ahcid" sets the tone for the album, Beefheart's rhythm-keeping foot stomping, ragged harmonica, and unhinged, Son Housesque vocal sounding almost like something dug up on an old 78. *Almost.* With its spiky bottleneck guitar and herky-jerky tempo and references to things like his woman's great big chicken legs, there's something off about the whole thing—delightfully so. "Safe as Milk" (the song didn't appear on the album of the same name) is a woozy, twangy joy, the locomotive groove sliced apart by the razored, wobbly bottleneck guitar, the nervous time changes never allowing the tune to bog down in 4/4 boredom. And the captain's lyrics are a surrealistic hoot, American Dada at its finest. Musically and lyrically, "Trust Us" is a magnificent mess, alternately tuneful and disruptive, peace loving and cynical. "Son of Mirror Man—Mere Man" and "On Tomorrow" are more of the strange same—the blues broken down so as to be built back up again as Captain Beefheart & His Magic Band see fit. If there was any doubt about how the captain felt about his rock-and-roll peers, "Beatle Bones 'n' Smokin' Stones" answers that question clearly. Another gutbucket blues turned inside out by tempo shifts and a deranged vocal performance, it took a different kind of guts to openly mock rock's reigning royalty, and in particular the Beatles' laughably naive "All You Need Is Love" philosophy. Unlike Zappa's *We're Only in It for the Money* album, his pedantic satire of *Sgt. Pepper's Lonely Hearts Club Band* and hippie values, "Beatle Bones 'n' Smokin' Stones" needs less than five minutes to excoriate the collective delusion of an entire good-hearted, empty-headed generation. Plus, Beefheart's na-na-na-na-na sneering send-up of all things "strawberry," including "Strawberry Fields," is a gas. "Gimme Dat Harp Boy" is the captain gone gonzo on the harmonica, Ornette Coleman on the Mississippi saxophone. He doesn't just play his instrument—he talks to it, sings into it, and hoots and howls and blows some more whenever the spirit moves him. "Kandy Korn" wraps things up, and although it's nothing extraordinary, either musically or lyrically, that's okay because it is still reconstructed raunchy fun.

But we haven't talked about the excessive use of phasing, backwards recording, treated vocals, an embarrassing coda (meant, one presumes, to give the album a thematically "heavier" significance), and various other production inanities that sometimes obscure the music beneath the pseudopsychedelic sheen. And why would we? Beefheart said he hated it all and that producer Krasnow added it without his consent. Others claim that Beefheart signed off on it and only acted aghast once it was clear that the album was another commercial dud. As with most arguments, it was probably a little bit of both. It's still prime, raving, naked Beefheart underneath the Day-Glo dress, however, and that's good enough.

After another brief British and French promo jaunt, the group lost guitarist Alex Snouffer, who chafed under the captain's increasingly eccentric musical vision and was probably simply tired of being broke. New member Bill Harkleroad (soon to be baptized by the captain as "Zoot Horn Rollo") moved into the band house and was witness to the next Magic Band defection, recalling that "the first indication of the direction the music was taken [*sic*] was when [bassist] Jerry Handley left the band. I'll never forget him turning round and saying, 'Where's the blues tunes?'" Handley would soon be replaced by Mark Boston (dubbed "Rockette Morton" by Beefheart). Meanwhile, Zappa, always a very smart self-propagandist and businessman, was doing well leading the Mothers of Invention and had secured major-label support for the formation of two new Zappa-overseen record companies, Bizarre and Straight. The idea was that Zappa and his band would see their work released on Bizarre, while any interesting acts Zappa spotted and signed would appear on the subsidiary Straight imprint. Zappa knew that Beefheart was upset about how Krasnow had supposedly corrupted *Strictly Personal* with his intrusive production touches, so he offered the captain an opportunity to make a record with absolute artistic autonomy.

~

As you get older, it seems like every year another cliché comes true. "Be careful what you wish for," for instance. James Joyce scuffled and hustled to make his art, just as much as any couch-surfing musician, and one of the principal ways he provided for himself and his wife and two children was through the patronage of the editor (*The Egoist*) and philanthropist Harriet Shaw Weaver. Which was wonderful—Joyce was able to concentrate on composing his increasingly allusive, labyrinthine works without having, for example, to teach English as a second language, something he had done throughout his long exile from Ireland—and which was for many readers disastrous, just as it had been for one of Joyce's oldest and most fervent supporters, Ezra Pound, who wrote to the former after having been sent early sections of what became *Finnegans Wake*:

Dear Jim:

Ms. arrived this A.M. All I can do is wish you every possible success.

I will have another go at it, but up to present I make nothing of it whatever. Nothing so far as I can make out, nothing short of divine vision or a new cure for the clap can possibly be worth all the circumambient peripherization.

One of the primary reasons that Joyce was able to so entirely indulge his ardour for things like trilingual puns (*Finnegans Wake* took thirteen years of hard, steady work to complete) was because, made indifferent to the "common reader" and his or her fondness for such mundane matters as plot, demotic speech, and clearly discernible characters, the subsidized Joyce need only think about what interested Joyce (and as he continued to lose his eyesight, puns were much more compelling than people). Regardless of how bafflingly Byzantine his creation, he knew it would get written and published. About *Ulysses,* Joyce famously boasted, "I've put in so many enigmas and puzzles that it will keep the professors busy for centuries arguing over what I meant, and that's the only way of insuring one's immortality." To each writer his or her own idea of posthumous acclaim. But Joyce was right: most literate people have at least heard of *Finnegans Wake,* long after many initially better-known works have been lost to time. Aside from graduate students and those still-busy professors, however, there are not that many people who actually read it.

It is tempting to think of *Trout Mask Replica* as the *Finnegans Wake* of rock—no one's read it, but everybody's got a copy—but the album that Captain Beefheart & His Magic

Band recorded for Straight Records (with Zappa producing) certainly has its listeners. Indeed, it has become a sort of hipster litmus test: if you don't "get" *Trout Mask Replica*, you may be viewed as musically conventional, conservative, and uncool. Tellingly, the most common epithet applied to it is "avant-garde," almost as empty and worthless an aesthetic term as "experimental."

The facts are these: (1) Beefheart composed most of the *Trout Mask Replica* tunes banging on the piano (an instrument on which he was barely competent) or by simply whistling them; (2) John French would then heroically attempt to transcribe them for the rest of the band; and (3) the album is impressively assembled and expertly performed, it's pretty funny in places, the lyrics and the "poetry" that the captain periodically recites are good goofy fun that occasionally hit the mark, it's like nothing else you've ever heard, it's the kind of music that's more enjoyable to talk about than listen to.

Maybe this last point isn't a fact—no doubt there are people who genuinely take pleasure in listening to nearly eighty continuous minutes of savagely jagged inversions of harmony, melody, and traditional song structure. The furthest I can get is to find it undoubtedly interesting and invigorating, but ultimately—cover your fish eyes, *Trout Mask* aficionados—sort of boring, at least by the time you're on to the second LP of the original two-record set. Everything that made *Safe as Milk* and *Strictly Personal* so appealing—raw, instinctual blues, radically offset and augmented by vigorous, discordant deconstruction—has been replaced by prolonged, hyperplayful cacophony, all tension and little release. It is still tasty, but it's like losing the entrée and ending up stuck with only the spices. It's flavourful, all right

(Harkleroad's and Cotton's guitars are a swarming, elastic treat, and French manages to hold the entire thing together without abdicating his own percolating, polyrhythmic contribution), but something is missing. There are twenty-eight songs on the album (wisely, most are very short, somewhat attenuating the zany sameness), but the one that stays with me is "China Pig," certainly *Trout Mask Replica*'s most anomalous track. Doug Moon, the guitarist who had been booted out of the Magic Band when Cooder joined, was hanging around the group's communal house at some point during the *Trout Mask* sessions and happened to play a Delta-blues riff that caught Beefheart's attention. He recorded Moon and his own lyrical improvising on a portable tape recorder and decided to include it, lo-fi and undoctored, on the finished LP. It's got soul, it's got its own mind (try to imagine John Lee Hooker singing a song called "China Pig"), it's what Captain Beefheart & His Magic Band did best: combining the best of the blues and free-form jazz and knocked-off beatnik doggerel to create something fresh, fascinating, and—like the blues itself—enduring.

Much has been made of the captain's Synanon-like treatment of the Magic Band members during the writing and recording of *Trout Mask Replica*. That the group was pitifully poor during these eight or so months was one thing (French recalls subsisting on soy beans at one point). That "life in the Magic Band seemed to consist of these gruelling marathon practice sessions—sometimes for up to 16 or 17 hours a day," as Harkleroad writes in *Lunar Notes*—was another. "Then I'd curl up in a corner on the floor and sleep, just to get up and practise some more." But the way that the band members were discouraged from leaving their cramped, communal house—ever—and the psychological pressure that Beefheart foisted upon his musical subordinates was another level of callousness altogether. Harkleroad: "When we weren't rehearsing, Don would subject us to long sessions of being 'brainwashed.'... We might be in a room talking for up to twenty hours—that is no exaggeration.... He would hone in [*sic*] on whatever it was that we were doing that he didn't approve of. Many of these were personal assaults on our weaknesses as human beings—from eating habits, to how we dressed, how we were sitting, our relationships with people."

The masochistic manipulation that Beefheart inflicted upon his bandmates may be reprehensible, but as unpleasant as he made things, he also manufactured the working conditions he deemed necessary to create his music. The Magic Band members' recollections of their lives during this time conjure up nothing so much as an army boot camp—the maniacal discipline, the discouragement of individual thought, et cetera—but, whatever one feels about war, most people would agree that they tend not to be won by undisciplined freethinkers. Beefheart made sure that everyone knew that *Trout Mask Replica* was a collection of *his* songs that *he* taught to the band. Which meant that Beefheart had the satisfaction of hearing on vinyl what he had heard—more or less exactly—in his head. Which is one way to lead a group and make a record.

But consider Miles Davis as another kind of band leader, someone who admitted in his autobiography, *Miles,* that when he was searching for a different kind of sound, it was the younger members of his mid- to late-sixties bands that influenced *him*. Davis—never someone who lacked confidence in his abilities or belief in his titanic reputation—acknowledged that Tony Williams and Herbie Hancock and all "the other young dudes" in his band helped him develop the funkier, electrified version of the sound he was groping toward. It was still Davis' name on the covers of *In a Silent Way* and *Bitches Brew*, and his horn that was the centrepiece, but both LPs were composed and recorded by a band of individual musicians who listened to, and learned from, each other. In John Szwed's *So What: The Life of Miles Davis*, Hancock reflected that "I think Miles doesn't like to overexplain things, or to explain things to the point where it becomes crystallized in your head and you'll do only that. He wants to give impressions so that you have a wider range of discerning what he wants. You know, if he tells you specifically something, you'll do that and only that, see.... He wants to point you in a direction, and your talent and creativity will let you do maybe five things."

Trout Mask Replica did far better commercially in Britain than in America, climbing as high as #21 on the UK charts (partly because of John Peel's ceaseless championing on the BBC, partly because the Brits have always been an easy target for purveyors of what they perceive as American primitivism), while not even making the *Billboard* Hot 100 at home. What buzz that did exist around the album and Beefheart himself was mostly the result of the media's typical fascination with the more titillating tidbits that the captain would let drop in interviews, such as how he wrote the entirety of his beguiling new album in eight straight hours and spent the next several months patiently teaching it to the band, or that he was telepathic, or that he could break glass with his voice. Most of it was self-aggrandizing bullshit, but most people would rather read about an artist's peculiar personal life (even if they are fabrications) than a discussion of his or her art. In the aftermath of *Trout Mask Replica*'s release, a few gigs were followed by two more Magic Band departures: Cotton, who quit after having his ribs broken (although not by Beefheart himself) during another one of the captain's infamous marathon band meetings; and the beleaguered French, who according to his memoir, was literally thrown out of the group ("[Beefheart] grabbed me by the shirt collar and belt from behind, like a barroom bouncer, and propelled me to my right toward the staircase. I lost balance and fell about halfway down to the second landing, in a heap").

As an added insult, Beefheart also excluded French's name from the list of musicians credited on the album jacket. And in a move reminiscent of his bad-mouthing of Krasnow when *Strictly Personal* failed to connect with the record-buying public, Beefheart began to castigate Zappa at every opportunity, complaining to reporters about everything from the label's distribution woes to how Zappa treated him as just another one of the "freaks" that he had produced for his customized label (Wild Man Fischer, the GTO's, et cetera). As cantankerous and staggeringly ungrateful as Beefheart was (who else but Zappa would have not only encouraged him to indulge his wildly eccentric musical vision, but okayed its release as a *double* album?), his bile was still infused with his characteristic Captain Beefheart wit. Once, he grew so angry during an interview with Nick Kent that he called Zappa a "cataract." The style is the man, and whatever else you might think about him personally, Captain Beefheart definitely had style.

In the interim between *Trout Mask Replica*'s release and the recording of the next Beefheart album, 1970's *Lick My Decals Off, Baby*, the band members decided (meaning Beefheart decided) that communal living wasn't for them, and the captain met the love of his life, a seventeen-year-old college student by the name of Jan Jenkins. Although he was nearly thirty and was, well, Beefheart, the two immediately got married and, even more surprisingly, stayed married until Beefheart's death in 2010. Friends claim that she was the most stabilizing influence in his life. It only takes two people to construct a world, and it's an even colder, more indifferent cosmos when they don't.

Professionally, things were looking up, as well—the Magic Band family got back one of its own when French, a year after being physically ejected from the group, was deemed irreplaceable by Beefheart because his intended replacement, ex-Zappa drummer Art Tripp, was found incapable of replicating that "Beefheart drum sound" (i.e., French's drum sound), although Tripp was retained on percussion and marimba. The captain assured French that the . . . unconventional interpersonal relationship techniques that had previously dominated the group had changed for the better, that *Trout Mask Replica* was an underground hit with college students (which it was), that the group was set to become rich with its next record (which it was not), and that French was the missing percussive piece. French agreed to return, a decision he called "probably the most incredibly stupid thing I've done in my life. . . . I had completely lost my sense of how shrewd and devious this man could be. I had lost my defenses and been sucked right back in." Elsewhere in *Beefheart: Through the Eyes of Magic*, however, he lets slip a far more prosaic, but probably more accurate reason for why he returned: "I missed the music horribly."

Captain Beefheart fans missed the music as well, which was why *Lick My Decals Off, Baby* was so welcome. Released on Warner Brothers' Reprise label, which wasn't afraid at that time to take chances on outsider artists (ex–Magic Band member Ry Cooder was a recent signee as well), the album is an appealing blend of the pre– and post–*Trout Mask Replica* sounds: concurrently pliable and taut, ballsy and subtle. With French back, banging away in his signature crashing, polyrhythmic fashion, Art Tripp supplemented the sound with plenty of tasty fills, rolls, and crazy clatter (and occasional marimba). Perhaps because of Cotton's departure and Harkleroad being the sole guitarist, there is more unison playing along with Boston's dependably supple bass. As a result, there's additional space between the notes, and the songs are allowed more room to breathe. It is still an intricate, tension-teasing, slightly insidious sound, but also radiantly clean and focused. The highlights are many: the raunchy title track, Beefheart's raspy, rascally voice an instrument all on its own; the superbly shambolic "Doctor Dark" which is as scary as it sounds; "I Love You, You Big Dummy," a semiconventional blues-rock tune (the instruments tend to play in unison and in the same key throughout, the drums jungle-jumpy but steady) offset by the captain's unhinged vocal, laughter, yips and yells, and furious chromatic harmonica playing; the uncharacteristically minimalist guitar and bass beauty of the delicate, plunking instrumental "Peon" (there are two other short instrumentals on the album); the frolicsome, marimba-dominated "The Clouds Are Full of Wine (Not Whiskey or Rye)"—notable if for no other reason than its title—which is only partly compromised by the captain's Ornette Coleman–inspired horn work, his free-form excursions on sax and clarinet adding little but abrasion to the musical mix. Overall, the album's typically Beefheartian discordances are supplemented by an almost breezy—dare one say?—joyfulness. Maybe it was because Beefheart was in love.

Another album briefly in the UK charts (one spot higher than *Trout Mask Replica*) and commercially underwhelming at home, more touring to sometimes adoring, sometimes dumbfounded concert-goers, more complaints from the band members about unpaid tour wages, and at some point, the captain decided the entire group should move to Santa Cruz so they could concentrate on making their next album, *The Spotlight Kid*. This time, however, there were in-group musical concerns, the captain's cultivation of a somewhat more basic rock and blues sound not sitting well with some of the band members. Whether the captain was feeling corporate pressure from Warner Brothers (unlikely) or was just tired of being broke and relatively unknown (compared to, say, his sometimes friend, sometimes nemesis, full-time rival, Zappa) or was simply desirous of a different sound, theoretically, anyway, the move wasn't a bad one. There is nothing ignoble about getting back to the blues.

Beefheart "getting back to the blues," however, is not the same as someone like Eric Clapton doing something similar; whatever it is, *The Spotlight Kid* is not reverentially imitative—it still sounds like Beefheart—and is still plenty strange in the best possible way. Apart from the aching absence of the once-again departed French's highly idiosyncratic drum technique, the biggest problem with the album is not any commercial compromise, but the mix, which places the captain's vocals and his harmonica (which is the dominant instrument throughout) too far upfront. Propelled by a transfixing opening guitar riff, courtesy of recently added second guitarist Elliot "Winged Eel Fingerling" Ingber, "I'm Gonna Booglarize You Baby" may lack French's polyrhythmic pulse (he would endure the indignity of being replaced at one point during the recording sessions by a more conventional session drummer), but in what world would a song with "Booglarize" in its title and so prominently features the captain's slithering, steaming vocal be considered a potential hit? It sounds like a hip, horny Barry White on downers. And it is doubtful that Art Tripp's playful marimba was what rock-record buyers in 1972 were dying to fork over their hard-earned dollars to hear.

One might characterize the album as sluggish, but voodoo-slow songs like "When It Blows Its Stacks," "Glider," and "Grow Fins" create a pulsing, ominous atmosphere. The lyrics are still the usual engaging shower of cracked images and wonky Beefheartian wordplay (except for the preachy ecological lament "Blabber 'n Smoke"), and aside from the more-predictable drum sound, the only conspicuous mainstream element on the entire LP is Ingber's impressive but conventional blues-rock guitar solo on the instrumental "Alice in Blunderland" (one has no difficulty imagining Clapton playing it—something you cannot say about almost any other Captain Beefheart tune). "Click Clack" is the album's highlight and a good example of how "traditional" doesn't have to be a bad word: it chugs and churns along just like the train in the song, but at a slightly irregular, invigorating tempo, the harmonica and slide guitar (too-little employed throughout the record) giving it the necessary grit that a tune about a train, a girl, and the blues requires.

The Spotlight Kid might not have made anyone wealthy, but rapturously received performances at London's Albert Hall and the 1972 Bickershaw Festival and several well-attended, if much smaller, gigs in the US had to have been rewarding after so many years of banging one's head against the wall of rock-and-roll orthodoxy. Playing before appreciative audiences must also have whetted Beefheart's populist ambitions and likely contributed to the appointment of Ted Templeman as producer of *Clear Spot*, the band's second release of 1972. Templeman may have been the man in charge of such radio favourites as the Doobie Brothers and Van Morrison, but he was also at the helm of Little Feat's quirky *Sailin' Shoes*, and head-Featster Lowell George, like the captain, didn't allow anyone in his kitchen who he didn't believe could contribute to his band's atypical stew of sound.

Not surprisingly, given Templeman's mainstream credentials, *Clear Spot* is Beefheart's best-sounding album. It is big and warm and roomy, without ever compromising the captain's vision (which, lyrically, now included a pronounced feminist bent, which Beefheart was happy to extrapolate on in interviews, along with his recent, antidrug stance—with a brain like Beefheart's, mind-altering drugs must have seemed superfluous by this point). The album sounds great, Beefheart is still blowing his harp and hiccupping and howling and huffing and puffing away, and the end result is never less than enjoyable. It sounds like Captain Beefheart trying to get along and doing a pretty damn good job of it.

Leadoff track "Low Yo Yo Stuff" is funky-lite, a pleasing groove that stays where it is and doesn't bother anyone. "Nowadays a Woman's Gotta Hit a Man" is the same, Women's Lib Beefheart in standard time. With horns, background singers, and an unabashedly emotional vocal, "Too Much Time" was the closest the captain had come to straight R&B

since some of the material on *Safe as Milk* five years before. You can imagine him singing it over a prerecorded backing track on *Soul Train*. "Circumstances" is a welcome return to old-school Beefheart (nasty harmonica honking, tempo changes, stinging slide guitar, a fierce, acrobatic vocal); slight, perhaps, but skewed and solid. ("Sun Zoom Spark," the title track, "Crazy Little Thing," and "Long Neck Bottles" employ much of the same archetypal Beefheart sound, but as applied to better tunes.) "My Head Is My Only House Unless It Rains" and "Her Eyes Are a Blue Million Miles" are downright tender; one-groove snoozes musically, but impossible to dislike for their lilting vulnerability and emotive conviction. There's even the prominent employment of acoustic guitar on the latter. The jumpy, jostling "Big Eyed Beans from Venus" is what *Trout Mask Replica* might have sounded like if Templeman had been in the producer's chair—it is angular and opaque, but accessible, even hummable. And Harkleroad is a motherfucker on slide, monstrous and momentous. Play it for a Captain Beefheart neophyte and they'll be hooked. And if they're not, why are you wasting your time with someone like that? The album unfortunately ends with "Golden Birdies," a brief, mostly spoken-word piece that, if nothing else, demonstrates that Beefheart's lyrics—as beguilingly bizarre and cerebrally visceral and crammed full of cosmic cartoon consciousness as they usually are—simply don't stand up as musically unadorned poetry.

Clear Spot was not the breakthrough that either Beefheart or Warner Brothers was hoping for (and thank goodness—a breakthrough to what? A package tour with the Doobie

Brothers? A featured appearance on *The Midnight Special*?). But better-paying, better-attended live gigs were getting easier to secure, and Beefheart was able to snag a new record deal with Mercury without much difficulty. He also changed management, signing on with the di Martino brothers, who sound more like small-time mobsters than music managers. Later, after the twin artistic failures that would be his next two albums, *Unconditionally Guaranteed* and *Bluejeans & Moonbeams* (both released in 1974), Beefheart wouldn't be shy about doing a little damage control—or a lot. He blamed the di Martinos for interfering with his work (they claimed writing credits on several songs, as did Beefheart's wife, Jan); he maintained that he only made the two records because he wanted the band to finally make some cash; and he even told interviewers that fans should return their copies of the LPs to the record stores and demand their money back. Whatever. It's his name on the front of the albums. You're the captain: take responsibility and at least go down with the ship with some dignity.

In *Lunar Notes*, Harkleroad sums up the sad situation that was Beefheartville circa 1973–74 and isolates the main cause for the artistic decline: "We were thinking, 'God, let's just do something and maybe we can pay the rent!' Some people might have said, 'Oh man, they sold [out],' but that was easy for them to say, they weren't still living off of mom's tit." Not that the predictable rhythms and unadventurous playing and unimaginative songs and the shiny production made any difference in the marketplace. Middle-of-the-road Beefheart sold even worse than the real thing.

When, finally, the entire Magic Band mutinied ahead of a proposed European tour, because of poor wages, and the captain was forced to assemble and tour with an ad hoc group of musicians wholly unsympathetic to the Magic Band sound, he essentially retired from the music business for a year or so, spending his time at home on the Northern California coast with Jan, painting and scribbling poetry and doing whatever it is that anyone does who's thirty-three years old and burned out and broke. He couldn't have recorded and released anything, anyway—apparently, he had signed a contract he should not have, or did not sign something he should have: the upshot was that he could not release any new music until the lawyers sorted it all out.

Enter old pal Zappa in 1975, who told his own biographer, Barry Miles (*Zappa: A Biography*), "He [Beefheart] apologized for all the garbagio [he said about Zappa] and asked for a job." Zappa invited him to go on tour with him and the Mothers, where Beefheart played a little harmonica, sang a few tunes, and made some cash, because the lawyers couldn't touch any money earned from performing. Selections from the tour appear on Zappa's album *Bongo Fury*. It was not long, however, before the old animosities resurfaced. In the documentary *The Artist Formerly Known as Captain Beefheart*, former Mothers drummer Jimmy Carl Black remembers encountering Beefheart backstage, "drawing pictures of Frank as the devil with horns and a tail." As initially appreciative as he might have been for the modest cash infusion and the chance to re-enter the music business, the captain needed to be charge of his own ship.

By 1976, he was. He had formed a new Magic Band with some old mates (John French was back for further musical adventures and more abuse) and some new ones (Jeff Moris Tepper and Denny Walley on guitars and, a Magic Band first, a keyboard player, John Thomas). Surprisingly, it was Zappa who facilitated (financially and otherwise) the sessions that led to what was to be called *Bat Chain Puller*. Just as the album was completed, however, Zappa became embroiled in his own legal troubles, resulting in the tapes being confiscated by the suits, who refused to allow them to be released until Zappa's business woes were resolved—or Beefheart bought them outright, which he couldn't afford to do. Beefheart and Zappa never worked together again.

Two years later, litigation free and ready to make another record, Beefheart was back on Warner Brothers and released a reworked version of the confiscated *Bat Chain Puller* material, entitled *Shiny Beast (Bat Chain Puller)*. French was out (though he would return in a reduced capacity), Tripp was back (though he would leave after the completion of the album), and aside from Tepper, it was a whole new Magic Band, composed of young musicians thrilled to be working with a legend (legendary status is what they give you instead of money and fame when you get old enough and still haven't sold many records). *Shiny Beast*, as well as its successors *Doc and the Radar Station* (1980) and *Ice Cream for Crow* (1982), both recorded for Virgin, is new wave Captain Beefheart. Each album is sprinkled with standout songs ("Ice Cream for Crow" has to be on any Beefheart best-of, and "A Carrot Is as Close as a Rabbit Gets to a Diamond" is downright sublime, even though it would have sounded even better performed on an old guitar instead of an expensive electronic keyboard), and all three LPs are full of an expert approximation of that signature Beefheart sound (jagged guitars, jumpy time-signatures, et cetera)—a relief after the mostly SoCal snore of the previous two records.

But the musical deviations have begun to sound routinized to the point of predictability and "modernized" for an audience who had finally caught up to what the captain had been doing for a decade and a half. It is an uncomfortably glossy, overly tidy sound—well played by a group of musicians who obviously deeply respected Beefheart and his legacy, but without any of the gamble and grease of the original Magic Band. In its own clanking, cacophonous way, the old Magic Band swung; the new Magic Band was merely tight. Contemporary touches like synthesizer, Mellotron, electric keyboards, and background vocals might have made the albums more palatable to an audience intrigued by the captain's avant-garde reputation but more accustomed to the sound of the Talking Heads than Howlin' Wolf, but at the cost of cooling down the boiling madness that made earlier Magic Bands such great groups. When Beefheart does occasionally blow his harp, for example, it's almost as if it's there because someone thought, "Hey, it's a Captain Beefheart album, we should probably get some harmonica on here." And too many songs aren't so much songs as backing tracks to a Beefheart spoken-word recitation, which is great if your idea of a poet is Henry Rollins; if not, not so much. Vocally, the captain sounds tired; when he barks and hollers and howls, he too often sounds like he's impersonating someone undergoing a particularly manic episode, as if he's trying to sound deranged. For weird to be weird, it has to be *weird*.

Maybe he was beginning to feel the effects of the multiple sclerosis that would take his life in 2010. Although the long-awaited, much-desired "breakthrough" seemed to be finally happening (the albums still didn't sell much, but the captain appeared on *Saturday Night Live* and on David Letterman's show, twice), Beefheart went home to the California desert, where it had all begun, and put away his harmonica and became Don Van Vliet again and devoted himself to his first love, painting. I don't possess the critical acumen to comment on the quality of his visual art (which made him much more money than music ever did, at least), but until the MS physically incapacitated him, he spent most of the remaining twenty-eight years of his life working industriously at his paintings and spending time with his wife and doing whatever he wanted to do, all by himself. Pretty much just like he always did.

HANDSOME NED

The childhood shows the man,
As morning shows the day.
–Milton

When my wife and I were in Serbia several years ago, the man who was hired to drive us around—an army veteran who still suffered from wartime nightmares and who worked very hard just to make enough money to live under conditions that many North Americans might be tempted to call "third world"—told us, "Smartest thing you ever did: be born in Canada." I'm not proud to be Canadian any more than I feel proud that I was born with ten fingers and ten toes. How could I? I didn't have a lot to do with it. I do feel fortunate, though. Lucky. Thankful.

In the same way, I don't feel proud that Handsome Ned—who grew up on West German NATO air bases and in Stoney Creek, Ontario, but spent the most significant part of his life in Toronto, my adopted hometown as well—helped keep country soul alive in the predominantly aurally ugly 1980s, and whose music and story continues to engage and inspire, but I do feel thankful. We don't choose our parents or our birth certificates, but we do get to pick our heroes and what to live and die for. And because Robin Masyk wanted to be Gram Parsons, he became Handsome Ned, and his shows at Toronto's tiny Cameron House, the handful of neo-hardcore country and rockabilly records he released, and the alt-country radio show he hosted once a week were like holy water and a crucifix in a vampire world of Phil Collins and Kenny Rogers and Bryan Adams. Ned and his music set an example—for honesty, good taste, and devotion. That he's from around these parts? Well, I guess that's good, too.

~

Robin David Masyk was born June 4, 1957, in Zweibrücken, West Germany. He and his brother were army brats (actually, Royal Canadian Air Force brats) who moved around a lot (the family would not come back to Canada permanently, to Stoney Creek, until 1970). His father was a big country-and-western fan, and his mother always had music of some sort playing around the house. In the fine documentary *You Left Me Blue: The Handsome Ned Story*, his mother tells the filmmakers that her son once said, when he was only a child, that no one had ever heard of a cowboy named Robin. This is dedication and purity of purpose before it even knows what it is.

In the same film, according to his brother and sometime musical partner, Jim Masyk, Ned's true country-music epiphany occurred when he heard Gram Parsons and the Byrds' *Sweetheart of the Rodeo* playing on a British pirate radio station when he was twelve or thirteen, definitely not your average teenybopper's usual musical pin-up. Parsons had—and still has—that kind of effect on listeners; he is one of those artists who may not be well known because of their uncompromising aesthetic, but those who do know them and their work know it extremely well and become lifelong enthusiasts. If someone was looking for an artistic role model, they don't come much better. Or, as a pharmaceutical role model, much worse.

Being that hip, that young, while growing up in the suburbs of Hamilton could not have been easy, so it's not surprising to learn that Ned dropped out of high school after grade ten and hitchhiked around a bit and read a bunch of writers, like Kerouac and Bukowski, who wouldn't have appeared on his high school English syllabus, even if he had bothered to show up, and listened and listened and listened to a lot of music. Judging by the set lists of his first band, the Velours, which he formed with his brother at the end of the '70s, Ned had a nose for the real thing, irrespective of its genre, rootsy renditions of Velvet Underground and New York Dolls songs served up back to back with rockabilly covers.

He also knew what was going on in the burgeoning "outlaw" country music scene, literate-but-earthy musicos like Billy Joe Shaver and Jerry Jeff Walker providing excellent songwriting examples. He made a yearly pilgrimage to Texas to attend Willie Nelson's Fourth of July Picnic and to buy a new cowboy hat, and in the late '70s moved to Austin for a year or so, at that time the epicentre of all things outsider-country cool. It was there that he and his brother cooked up the idea for the Velours, and when they moved back to Toronto in 1979, they were ready to country-rock and roll. And Robin Masyk became Handsome Ned, an appellation of his own making. At least he sounded like a cowboy now.

By 1981, the band, with a new drummer and bassist, changed their name to the Sidewinders and got their first break. Speaking to the authors of the invaluable history *Have Not Been the Same: The CanRock Renaissance, 1985–1995*, Ned's brother, Jim, remembered how "Steven Leckie [lead singer and founder of seminal Toronto punk rockers the Viletones] went nuts over us and blessed us, and then we started opening for the Viletones. We started taking their audience and pretty soon we started headlining. We were packing Larry's Hideaway, and it was the Demics' [another pioneering Toronto punk band] and the Viletones' audience that came to see us. We were the new punk in a way. We cranked it up, it was more rockabilly and fun, and less snarling and spitting." Musical fashions come and go, but energy and integrity never go out of style. Ned may have never been seen onstage (and rarely offstage, for that matter) without his trademark cowboy hat and chunky sideburns, but the Sidewinders were a fast and fun band to drink and dance and get up to no good to, so ditch the nose ring and the mohawk and grab your partner and let's have another beer and hear another hurtin' song.

Two things happened in 1982 that would enrich the remainder of Ned's short life and help define his legacy: (1) he began hosting his weekly radio program on Ryerson Polytechnical Institute's CKLN, the Handsome Ned Honky Tonk Hardwood Floor Show; and (2) he launched his weekly Saturday matinee at the Cameron House (which frequently extended into the evening). The gigs are legendary, and the radio show was important, and both happened because Ned made them happen.

Not long after he was a guest on another CKLN program, Ned talked his way into securing his very own show and began broadcasting his Cosmic American Music message to the world (or as far as CKLN's signal would reach) every Tuesday, the dusty voices of Hank Williams and Jimmie Rodgers and Ernest Tubb alive and well, thanks to Ned, on downtown Toronto's airwaves. He also played lots of records by newer, lesser-known artists who passed the Ned sniff test. To listeners like me, besotted with country-rock but finding little to no evidence in the record stores or on the radio that anybody else was, it was consoling to know that you weren't alone. That you weren't wrong to care about the Flying Burrito Brothers and Dillard & Clark and the New Riders of the Purple Sage. The first time I heard Steve Earle's music was on Ned's show.

The Cameron House was an old bar with new owners who were receptive to local musicians looking for a place to play (Toronto at that time had very few venues where bands could perform original music) and who might be able to draw more than the existing, primarily geriatric clientele whose idea of a good time was sipping seventy-five-cent glasses of draft beer all day. Not that flogging the idea of country music to the bar's owners—and other Queen Street West habitués—was an easy sell. Talking to *Post City* journalist Ron Johnson, Blue Rodeo bass player Bazil Donovan remembered that Ned said "he wanted to do country music matinees, and at first we scratched our heads and told him they play country music down the road in Parkdale. He was like, 'No, I'm doing cow punk.'"

Yes, he was: whenever he stepped on stage, whether at the Cameron or the Horseshoe or anywhere else around town, you could count on Ned providing punky energy and good-time irreverence combined with dependable country-music melodies and plenty of dynamic twang. Ned was a very physical performer—sweating underneath his ubiquitous cowboy hat, straining for the high notes and the low notes both—and, with his big smile and bigger charisma, he was hard to take your eyes off. Like Gram Parsons before him, another magnetic Pied Piper, Ned wanted everybody—the old and the young, the punks and the drunks, the already country converted and the merely country curious—to hear the music he loved so much, and that he knew everyone else would love, if they would just give it a try.

Eventually, Ned's brother recalled, "There was this whole scene built around Ned. You could depend on him being there [at the Cameron] every Saturday, and you knew the faces. I can't imagine how many people he knew. Once he met people he remembered them. He was very street level—'Hey, you coming out to see me?'—just a promotional machine."

Ned didn't know who I was, but that was okay, because I knew who he was. I was a four-eyed philosophy undergraduate from a small town living in the big city for the first time, and he was Handsome Ned, the only guy on Queen Street West who wore a cowboy hat and the first person I'd ever encountered outside of books who also believed that Gram Parsons meant more than whatever was in the Top 40. Once, though, drinking beer with a friend and listening to the Cameron's jukebox, which was as wonderfully eclectic as Ned's musical taste, he caught me staring at him leaning against the wall sipping his own bottle of beer. Before I could lower my eyes and look away, Ned touched the brim of his cowboy hat with his right hand and nodded. I think I blushed.

No one becomes famous—even virtually unknown-outside-of-your-hometown famous, like Ned was—without wanting to and working hard to get that way. In *Have Not*

Been the Same, Blue Rodeo's Greg Keelor claims, "Ned was the king; he was the scenester"—for example, organizing the Handsome Ned Picnic on Toronto Island, his own annual Willie-style musical bash (without an event permit or a liquor licence, of course). "Every Saturday, at his fantastic matinee," Keelor continues, "he just played on and on until the band [slated to follow Ned] that night had to say, 'Get off'!" In the *You Left Me Blue* documentary, Handsome Ned's bassist Rene Fratura remembered how "he was Handsome Ned from the moment he woke up, walking the streets, he did the gunfighter thing every day, marching up and down the street, greeting bands, greeting people, there on Queen Street, I'm Handsome Ned, howdy, howdy, howdy, this band's playing there, this band's playing there, we're playing here. See this guy at seven, see that guy at nine, then wind up at the Cameron House at eleven if you really want to hear something."

That Keelor and plenty of others have maintained that Ned's pioneering, proselytizing presence laid the infrastructure for the eventual alt-country boom downtown that included bands like Blue Rodeo, the Skydiggers, and the Cowboy Junkies is undeniable, but Ned did what he did because it was the right thing to do, because people *needed* to hear his music and the music where his music came from. All the best, most effectual magnanimity is born of near-fanatical egotism. Jesus saves because that's just what Jesus does.

None of which would have mattered if Ned had not possessed such an eerily echoey voice, a deeply powerful instrument that sounded like Carl Perkins or early Elvis after they'd popped a couple of Bennies. It was no gimmick, and neither was the band's sound, which was tight and muscular, but capable of smouldering subtlety if the song demanded it. Ned's voice contained none of the corn-porn self-parody or southern-accent fakery that many rockers intentionally or unintentionally adopt when slumming in the world of C&W. (It is to the rest of the Rolling Stones' considerable credit, for example, that the insufferably artificial Mick Jagger didn't always ruin their occasional forays into country music, as on "Factory Girl" or "Dead Flowers.") Anybody can get up on stage after a few drinks and warble a little country karaoke, but only a real artist can pull off something as vocally demanding as the old country song "Ghost Riders in the Sky." It takes a Johnny Cash or a Handsome Ned to supply the necessary spooky sonority and acrobatic vocal skills that a song with this many precipitous register changes demands. This is not someone trying to sound like somebody else—this is someone trying to sound like the voice they hear inside their head and heart. Handsome Ned's lead guitar player, Steve Koch: "He had an amazing voice, a really great set of pipes. Sometimes I wonder if it really comes through [on recordings], but he could sing louder than the average guy, had great sustain and really good control. It's an honest kind of sound. He talked the same way he sang. There's nothing fake about it, and people liked that."

As a songwriter, early tunes such as "Rockabilly Girls" show the promise that would be fulfilled with classics like "Put the Blame on Me" and "In Spite of the Danger." "Rockabilly Girls" is the sort of song that Marshall Crenshaw might have cut—clean and crisp and pleasantly hummable, if slightly nostalgic in both topic and musical texture. In 1983 Ned and the Sidewinders (who would disband not long afterward) released a single, "Put the Blame on Me" b/w "Cryin' Heartache Misery." The B-side is a clever amalgam of early

Elvis, early Conway Twitty, and a whole lot of Sun Studio–inspired production magic. It's a good little song that a hardcore honky-tonker from the '50s, someone like Webb Pierce, might have covered and turned into a minor hit, but "Put the Blame on Me," while still an echo-drenched slice of neo-rockabilly, has such smart lyrics and such a catchy chorus, it's simply irresistible. It is also admirable that the songs were not reverbed into irrelevance in the mixing stage, as were so many of the records released by '80s underground roots-rockers like Lone Justice or the Beat Farmers or the Del Lords. If Ned had lived past thirty, he might have done well financially by providing songs for mainstream country artists, like fellow alt-country outsider Fred Eaglesmith has done. Although the more-than-likely mushy, mainstream results would have certainly soured some of the obvious appeal of the cash infusion.

A lack of money was one of the reasons the Sidewinders left Ned temporarily without a band. It was the classic country-rock conundrum, going all the way back to Gram Parsons' unending troubles with the recording industry: record labels like their artists to slot into easily defined genres, and rockabilly- and honky-tonk–inspired, contemporary, acoustic punk didn't ring cash registers in any label executive's head. Undeterred, Ned formed a new band, the Handsome Neds, as well as piloting side projects like the Cajun-inspired Handsome Ned and the Hayseed Hellions.

In 1985, the Handsome Neds released "In Spite of the Danger" b/w "Ain't No Room for Cheatin' (in a Song About Love)." The flip is another honky-tonk weeper that you're too busy tapping your toes to and singing along with to get too sad about, but the A-side is something else entirely, certainly Ned's finest moment on record. "In Spite of the Danger" is recognizably classic-country influenced, but the moody, minor-key melody, electric guitarist Steve Koch's jangly lead, and the general forebodingness of both the song's overall sound and its thoughtful lyrics (reputably about an affair Ned was having) push it way beyond its influences. It sounds like Roy Orbison sitting in with Chris Isaak's band at a honky-tonk, but it also sounds—*still* sounds—absolutely contemporary. It also resembles Isaak's equally moody and echoey hit record "Wicked Game," which wouldn't appear until four years later. A lot of the posthumously released material that make up the studio portions of *The Ballad of Handsome Ned* and *The Name is Ned* compilations are energetic, honest, engaging neo-rockabilly and hardcore country, but would have been best enjoyed with a bottle of Black Label and the dance floor only a short stumble away. "In Spite of the Danger" is the kind of song that other people cover and keep singing long after you're gone.

~

On January 10, 1987, the night before what would have been the five-year anniversary of his Saturday matinees at the Cameron—and a week before he was scheduled to begin recording his first full-length record—Ned, who lived in one of the Cameron House's upstairs rooms, was gone, victim of a heroin overdose at age twenty-nine. Koch: "Nobody likes to say it, but there were dope problems, which leads to 'not getting paid' problems. We were losing a bit of focus as to what's important." Interviewed by Liz Worth for her *Treat Me Like Dirt: An Oral History of Punk in Toronto and Beyond, 1977–1981*, Chick Parker, guitarist for the Ugly, among other

Toronto punk bands, recalled how, unfortunately, "the last time I saw [Ned], he ripped me off on a junk deal. But that's what happens. Junkies steal, they lie, and that's it."

I read about Ned's death in *The Strand*, Victoria College's student newspaper. Making the experience even stranger, I was eating lunch between classes at Ned's Cafe, Vic's commuter cafeteria (even though it was named after the poet and Victoria College alumnus E. J. Pratt and not, of course, Handsome Ned). I was twenty years old and not used to people dying, particularly of drug overdoses. People in books, like Gram Parsons and Hank Williams, sure, but they weren't people, they were myths. But Ned was someone you'd see around town, someone who seemed as permanent a part of the local landscape as the Brunswick House or Honest Ed's department store. And now he was gone.

Ned. A dead junkie. It didn't sound right. It *wasn't* right.

Why would someone so full of vision and vigour do something as stupid as stick a needle in their arm? Was he pissed off that bands that used to open for him had scored major-label deals while he was still surviving month to month? Who wouldn't be? Was he experimenting, like a lot of young people did and still do? Why would he be any different? Was Ned following the Gram Parsons script a little too closely, messing around with dangerous pills and powders just like ol' GP did, because that's what outlaws do? If so, he wouldn't be the first person to get what he wanted because he wasn't careful enough about what he asked for. Just like *his* hero. We forget sometimes that our idols have idols, too, and Gram Parsons' was Hank Williams, who checked out at age twenty-nine, the same as Ned when he died, from a morphine-induced heart attack in the back of a

'52 Coupe de Ville. Williams put morphine in his veins because of a chronic, crippling back problem; Parsons did it, in part, because Hank did it, but with the same result, overdosing in a Joshua Tree hotel room at twenty-six years old.

Feel bad for Ned's family and friends—and for us, for the music we never got to hear and the shows we never saw—but don't feel too bad for him. The high-school dropout from Stoney Creek, Ontario, wanted to grow up to be like his heroes. He did. He was. He is.

Duane Allman

All human things are subject to decay,
And, when Fate summons, monarchs must obey.
–Dryden

The Allman Brothers always seemed like one of *those* bands. You know: hairy rednecks born to boogie, proud sons of the American South who never passed up an opportunity to demolish a hotel room, impregnate a groupie, or inflict an interminable guitar solo upon their slack-jawed followers. *Southern Rock*. Labels are one of the ways human beings attempt to make a little more sense out of the frequently bewildering morass that is our lives. Inevitably, though, labelling falsifies as it simplifies, leaving us feeling a little less lost but still stumbling and fumbling in the dark. Case in point: the Allman Brothers were, yes, hirsute Southerners who lived to jam; by 1971 they were also the world's best rock-and-roll band, until October 29, 1971, the day Duane Allman's motorcycle collided with a truck on a Macon, Georgia, street and he was killed. "Grey, my friend, is all your theory," Goethe wrote in *Faust*. And he never even had a chance to hear the forty-four-minute version of "Mountain Jam" captured on *Live at Ludlow Garage 1970*.

Willis Allman came home from World War II to a job as an army recruiter based in Nashville, where he and his wife, Geraldine, doubled the size of their family with the addition of two sons, Duane, born in 1946, and Gregg, who arrived a little more than a year later. A month or so after Gregg's birth the boys' father was shot and killed by a man that Allman and a friend had met at a bar and offered to drive home at the end of the night. The widow and her two young children moved to Daytona Beach, Florida, although they returned to Nashville in the summertime to visit relatives. It was on one such visit that the brothers attended an R&B revue at the Nashville Municipal Auditorium, where they saw Jackie Wilson, Otis Redding, B. B. King, Johnny Taylor, and a few others. As recounted in Gregg's memoir, *My Cross to Bear*, if he was thrilled with what he heard, Duane was near catatonic: "My brother was just mesmerized—he was frozen, and he looked stuffed, like a taxidermist had gotten through with him. Nothing on his body moved during the whole concert. I had to poke him a couple times to make sure he was still there with us."

No epiphany was built in a day, however, and it was Gregg, not his older brother, who saved up his paper-route money and bought a guitar. In their early teens now, "as soon as I got the guitar," Gregg recounted to Allman Brothers biographer Alan Paul (*One Way Out: The Inside History of the Allman Brothers Band*), "[Duane would] look at it and go, 'Now what you got there, baby brother?'...And I'd go, 'Now, all right,

Duane, that's mine.' He would slip into my room and play it. We had more fights over that guitar than you'd believe.... Finally, to stop all the fights, my mom got him his own guitar....Then there was not only peace in the family but we started playing together; we had a twosome. Within a few weeks, he could play it really good. It was pretty amazing."

Duane's interest in the guitar was preceded by the near-systematic destruction of his first motorcycle, his previous passion. "He drove the damn motorcycle into the ground and brought it home in a bag," Gregg recalled. *Passion* was Duane's passion. Musician and friend Dr John: "Duane knew he lived on the edge. I don't think he had a death wish, but he knew that he was pushing it—that his lifestyle wasn't necessarily compatible with life. I remember...he got an Opel because that was supposed to be the car that you couldn't turn over and he just wanted to prove he could flip it."

Eventually, the brothers started playing with other apprentice musicians, and although naturally the music was lousy and derivative, the interesting thing was what they were busy attempting to imitate: not surf, not folk, not even rock, but R&B. To add to the visual incongruity of a bunch of white kids attempting to sound like James Brown and Bobby "Blue" Bland, blond and blue-eyed Gregg resembled a cross between a male model and a slightly butch beauty queen, and pale, freckled, strawberry-blond Duane looked just plain strange. Not so incidentally, because Duane and Gregg were such R&B and blues obsessives (both were devoted listeners to WLAC, a clear-channel radio station, broadcasting from the South, that played everything African American from Little Milton to Little Richard), neither fell for the usual red-herring race nonsense that young whites their age, growing up when and where they did, often succumbed to. This was only accentuated when they began to mix with actual Black musicians. Regardless of skin colour, hat size, or horoscope sign, if a person could play, great; if not, goodbye. Art is a great leveller.

Although they might have struck some club goers (underage—they played youth dances, mostly) as a little on the pallid side to be playing what they played, the brothers' love of rhythm and blues was the real thing, and what Gregg refers to in his autobiography as "our first real band," the Escorts, was good enough for him to have to skip his high school graduation because the band had a gig (Duane had dropped out of school long before). They played not only the R&B hits of the day, but *all* the hits (Beatles covers, Motown, even the theme song to the latest James Bond movie), the same dues that every band working the clubs had to pay. But they were also getting paid, if poorly, to learn how to play, which beats having to do so for free in the garage or in somebody's basement.

By the time the Escorts became the Allman Joys (because Duane and Gregg thought the Escorts was a silly name!), they added some good, committed players to the band, began playing clubs outside of Florida (where they would usually perform five forty-five-minute sets a night, six nights a week), discovered marijuana and what it's like to live on three dollars a day and go hungry, and attempted to get something down on tape. And when things got bad, Duane, according to Gregg, "always believed. He kept that light going." While playing a residence in St Louis in the spring of 1967, the manager of the Nitty Gritty Dirt Band caught their impassioned, if not particularly original act and invited them to come out to LA where he swore he could help them become stars. Enticing them with gas money to get there, the band packed up and began the long drive to California.

~

The newly named Hour Glass (at least it was better than the Allman Joys) led a peculiarly schizophrenic existence in Los Angeles. The Dirt Band's manager followed through on his promise to score the band a recording contract, and it signed with Liberty. With its tough, no-nonsense R&B sound, it was a popular live draw and opened for many much-more-established bands such as the Doors, the Paul Butterfield Blues Band, and the Buffalo Springfield. Although by now Gregg had switched from guitar to the Vox organ, made fashionable by some of the British Invasion bands, they were still primarily a snarling rhythm-and-blues machine that, to those with ears to hear it and a soul to feel it, was a refreshing change of pace from the incense-and-peppermints deluge of the Summer of Love. The Springfield's Neil Young was a fan and even wrote the liner notes to the Hour Glass' second and final LP.

Their record label, Liberty, however, not only forbade its recording of any of their concert-tested, beloved R&B covers for its 1967 self-titled debut, but also anything that Gregg, who'd started to compose original material for the band, wrote. The record's producer, Dallas Smith, also severely downplayed the band's main musical strength—Duane's increasingly accomplished guitar playing—in favour of busy horns and groovy female background singers. The follow up, 1968's *Power of Love,* was better—Duane's guitar is featured much more prominently, and seven of Gregg's apprentice compositions are included, even if they are only so-so and slightly saccharine—but the overall sound is still closer to Herb Alpert than B. B. King. The single most noteworthy thing about *Power of Love* is Duane's slide-guitar playing, a new-found passion. Every maestro begins as a novice, and Duane's path to six-string virtuosity began with him falling off a horse.

Gregg had talked his reluctant older brother into an afternoon of horse riding, which ended in Duane spraining his arm badly enough that it had to be in a splint for six weeks. When Duane's birthday came around, Gregg attempted to make up for his blunder by dropping off a copy of the first Taj Mahal record and a bottle of Coricidin cold-medicine pills on his brother's doorstep (in addition to his bum arm, Duane also had the flu). That evening, Duane called Gregg and demanded he come over—*immediately*. When Gregg got there,

> he said, "Man that record you bought me is out of sight. There's this guy called Jesse Ed Davis on there, this Indian dude, and he plays guitar with a damn wine bottle. Dig this." And then I looked on the table and all these little red pills, the Coricidin pills, were on the table. He had washed the label off the pill bottle, poured all the pills out. He put on that Taj Mahal record, with Jesse Ed Davis playing slide on "Statesboro Blues," and started playing along with it. When I'd left those pills by his door, he hadn't known how to play slide.

By the time of his death four years later, Duane Allman would be a slide-guitar master with virtually no living peers, and all it took was a spooked horse, a bottle of cold medicine, and a record album. From tiny Coricidin bottles grow mighty musical oaks.

The only thing worse than selling out is selling out but nobody buying, which was the situation the Hour Glass found itself in by 1968: broke (at one point the entire band lived in a single hotel room), bullied by its label (who became convinced that blond, blue-eyed lead singer Gregg was the only Hour Glass member with a chance of "making it"), and burned out. On tour promoting the *Power of Love* album and realizing that they were within driving distance of FAME Studios, Alabama's renowned recording complex, the band members pooled their money and decided to lay down a few songs played the way they wanted to play them and produced the way they wanted them produced. They recorded another not-quite-there-yet song of Gregg's entitled "Been Gone Too Long" and another tune called "No Good to Cry," but the core of the session was a medley of B. B. King songs including "Sweet Little Angel," "It's My Own Fault," and "How Blue Can You Get?". Gregg sings the hell out of all three—you can almost hear the relief in his voice as he tears into some material he can finally get his entire soul behind—but he sounds a little too much like B. B. himself for his vocal to be a complete success. The band, however—the church-time organ, a tighter-than-tight rhythm section, and Duane's blistering electric guitar—is simply feral, what Cream might have sounded like if they had played as a band and not as three competing soloists. B. B. King never sounded like *this,* and neither did any other blues artist that the Allman Brothers Band covered down the line. Except that "covered" is the wrong verb. No matter how old or how iconic the tune (e.g., Blind Willie McTell's "Statesboro Blues" or T-Bone Walker's "Done Somebody Wrong"), the Allman Brothers made it their electrifying own, the blues for a tripped-out new generation of blues fans.

As might be expected, Dallas Smith, their producer, and the other suits at Liberty Records didn't like it. The band members were equal parts dumfounded and dispirited, but Duane was something else as well: pissed off. According to Gregg, he told Smith and every Liberty executive in the room to go fuck themselves and announced that the band was done with La-La Land and attempting to be pop stars and was heading back home, to the South. The only problem was, Liberty had signed the band to a recording contract that forbade any of them from recording with any other label, and eventually a deal had to be worked out whereby Gregg went back to LA and worked as a session singer, in exchange for the rest of the Hour Glass—whom Liberty couldn't have cared less about by this point, anyway—being released from their contract. Duane lambasted his brother for selling out; Gregg said he only did it to help everyone else; but the end result was that the Hour Glass was no more and Gregg went his way and Duane went his.

Gregg claimed that the year he and his brother spent apart—the longest they had ever been separated—felt like three. Sometimes not getting what you want, though, is precisely what you need. Gregg suffered through session after session of singing along to the most egregious pop pap (thankfully, none of it caught on with the public) and making enough cash to get by and getting laid a lot, but what mattered most was that he was beginning to blossom as a songwriter. Although, when the Allman Brothers later recorded several of the songs he composed during this time, it was the entire band that worked up the arrangements (and in some cases, probably deserved a cowriting credit), much of the Allman

Brothers' songwriting legacy was created during this twelve-month span.

Duane, meanwhile, had ended up at FAME Studios in Muscle Shoals, Alabama, as a session guitarist and was making good money playing music for the first time in his life, but he had not given up on the idea of leading his own band—it was just that, until then, he was busy blowing away everybody he came into contact with. People like Rick Hall, FAME Studios' owner and overseer, who, when Duane showed up looking for work as a session player, told him he didn't need any more guitar players. When Duane asked if he could pitch a tent on the grounds of FAME Studios and wait around just in case, Hall could not help but be impressed with Duane's determination to be heard. After a couple of weeks, Hall felt compelled to give the kid a chance. By now, Duane had begun to master the bottleneck technique (and was still using a Coricidin bottle on his finger, as he would for the rest of his life) and when "Duane played bottleneck guitar on a session," Hall remembered, "you had to have plugs in your ears because he would rattle the shingles... Of course, you can't capture that on a piece of plastic—the bigness and the funkiness and the whole thing of it."

If Duane had never recorded a song with the Allman Brothers, or they had never performed a single concert, his legacy as a session man would have been secure. Highlights are many (especially considering how short his life was): his ferocious electric guitar solo and vicious vamping on Wilson Pickett's rendering of "Hey Jude" (which was Duane's idea and which he worked hard to convince Hall and Pickett to attempt); his hijacking of Boz Scaggs' thirteen-minute take on "Loan Me a Dime," Duane's searing electric guitar saying all sorts of things that poor Boz could only wish he could conjure up with his voice; the extra-stinky electric bottleneck he supplies to Eric Quincy Tate's "Comin' Down"; his scintillating and often-underappreciated acoustic and dobro work on Delaney & Bonnie's Robert Johnson cover "Come On In My Kitchen"; Johnny Jenkins' rendition of Dr John's "I Walk on Guilded Splinters"; and the deeply moving Cowboy song "Please Be With Me" (his last-ever session gig). Because while he was alive the Allman Brothers never made enough money to live above a subsistence level, Duane would continue to work intermittently as a session player for the rest of his life. Among some of the other artists whose records he endowed with his electric and acoustic gifts were Aretha Franklin, Clarence Carter, Doris Duke, Ronnie Hawkins, John Hammond, King Curtis, Laura Nyro, Otis Rush, and Sam Samudio.

As rewarding as it was to be the hottest guitar player for hire in Muscle Shoals and to be working with so many excellent artists, Duane still desired to be the one with *his* name on the front of the album (on Pickett's *Hey Jude* LP, he is even credited as "David Allman"). In time, Hall grew so impressed with Allman's playing and personality that he signed him to a deal with FAME. He had been wanting to get into the business of producing his own artists anyway, and although he knew that Duane was not a songwriter or a great singer, he felt optimistic that something worthwhile might come out of it. The musicians Duane assembled for what was going to be his solo album included familiar faces (Hour Glass alumni Johnny Sandlin, Paul Hornsby, and Pete Carr) and some new ones, future Allman Brothers members Jai Johanny "Jaimoe" Johanson on drums and bassist Berry Oakley.

Duane had crossed paths with Oakley's band, the Second Coming, in Florida and liked what he heard and convinced him to make the trip to Alabama. Although Duane and Jaimoe had never met, the latter received a phone call from a friend who told him "They got this white boy down in Muscle Shoals—this hippie with long, reddish-blond hair. I'm not kidding, Jai—I never heard no white boy play like this. You gotta hear it—they call him 'Sky Man.'" Rick Hall claims in his autobiography, *The Man from Muscle Shoals: My Journey from Shame to Fame*, that he dubbed Duane "Dog" because "when you looked at him with all that hair and stringy moustache, he looked like a sad-eyed old hound dog." According to Wilson Pickett's biography, Tony Fletcher's *In the Midnight Hour: The Life and Soul of Wilson Pickett*, "Sky Man" was what Pickett dubbed Duane because he was always sneaking off to the bathroom for a reefer break; because people were already calling him "Dog," Duane eventually became known as "Skydog."

Jaimoe told biographer Scott Freeman (*Midnight Riders: The Story of the Allman Brothers Band*) that he, Duane, and Oakley would jam at FAME "and none of those guys [the other Muscle Shoals session players] would pick up an instrument. They'd just come in, sit around the wall and look at us. You'd try to get them to jam and they'd say, 'No, not with you.' Man, the three of us used to play and we scared the hell out of people. Some of that shit used to scare me."

The songs that Duane and his band cut for Hall were undeniably soulful and well played (his howling guitar solos on Champion Jack Dupree's "Goin' Down Slow" make it, along with the Hour Glass' "B. B. King Medley," required listening for any serious Duane or Allman Brothers fan), but there was a problem: Duane couldn't sing and didn't write songs (as his sole original composition, "Happily Married Man" made clear). Hall admitted that he also wasn't comfortable with all the pot smoking and amphetamine taking that the band indulged in, and he was equally frustrated that they were not putting in the sort of nine-to-five hours he expected of musicians in his studio. Duane must have sensed that the sessions weren't turning out the way he hoped either, because, after convincing Jaimoe to accompany him, and detouring to St Louis to visit a girlfriend (from whom he would soon split after she bore him a daughter), the pair headed for Florida, where Oakley had returned when the solo sessions were aborted.

One of the people Duane looked up in Jacksonville was Butch Trucks, the drummer in the 31st of February, a Florida band that Duane and Gregg had briefly played with after the collapse of the Hour Glass. Two drummers in the same band can be a recipe for rhythmic disaster, but because Trucks was a rock-and-roll drummer who prided himself on keeping a steady pulse, and Jaimoe was essentially a jazz musician who thrived on supplying compelling taps and splashes of cadenced colour, they were complementary players. Berry Oakley participated in informal jam sessions with the two drummers, and Duane's appreciation for Oakley's uniquely adventurous bass playing combined with his unshakeable sense of time only increased the more they played together. Like the Grateful Dead's Phil Lesh, another rock bassist who was capable of contributing his own twists and turns to the tune at hand, Oakley wasn't originally a bassist—he switched to bass from guitar, while Lesh had formerly been a classical music student and sometime horn player. Oakley would also eventually become Duane's closest friend in the band and number-one follower of the faith. "Duane had the vision and Berry got it done," harmonica player and band buddy Thom "Ace" Doucette recalled to Alan Paul in *Brothers and Sisters: The Allman Brothers Band and the Story of the Album that Defined the '70s*. "They were just so close."

Then there was Oakley's Second Coming bandmate Dickey Betts, who joined in on the jamming and not only shared Duane's love of the blues and good rock, but grew up on country, bluegrass, and western swing. Still, two drummers is one thing—the Dead, after all, featured Bill Kreutzmann and Mickey Hart on the skins—but two *lead* guitar players? Like the drummers, however, right from the start Duane and Betts listened to each other, were willing to learn from each other, and were different enough players that, again, symbiotically it worked. Listening to an Allman Brothers song, if Duane is not playing slide, you can tell Duane from Betts because the former's tone is (still) slippery smooth, while Betts' is sharp and hard. They had the sound, but what they did not have was a singer and their own songs. Duane knew just the person to complete the puzzle.

~

When Duane called Gregg in LA in March of 1969 and told him he was sick of session life and was ready to rock and roll again and had found the musicians to make it happen and that all it lacked was his baby brother, Gregg was initially wary. Not only because of the lingering bad feelings about the Hour Glass breakup, but because, in his mind, two drummers and two lead guitar players equalled a musical mess. But he was just as restless with the life he was leading in LA as Duane had been with his in Muscle Shoals, and he knew that if his brother was excited about something, it must be good. A couple of days later he was back in Florida and joined the as-yet-unnamed band.

After Gregg was officially part of the group, Duane had a surprise for his little brother: a Hammond B-3 organ that Duane had decided was going to be an integral part of the band's sound. That Gregg had only played the instrument a handful of times was irrelevant (although he was a fan of soul-jazz pioneer Jimmy Smith). Duane knew his band needed it and he knew his brother could learn to play it and that was that. And when Gregg—who, in spite of his assured, growling-and-howling singing voice, was actually quite shy and self-conscious—needed the occasional confidence boost, Duane was right there. A good leader knows who needs a pat on the ass and who needs it kicked. Trucks:

> One day we were jamming on a shuffle going nowhere so I started pulling back and Duane whipped around, looked me in the eyes, and played this lick way up the neck like a challenge. My first reaction was to back up, but he kept doing it.... The third time I got real angry and started pounding the drums like I was hitting him upside his head and the jam took off and...he smiled at me, as if to say, "Now that's more like it." It was like he reached inside me and flipped a switch and I've never been insecure about my drumming again.

Phil Walden, recovering from the death of his prize managerial client and close friend, Otis Redding, was in the process of setting up his own label, Capricorn, with backing from industry heavyweight Atlantic, and it was the latter's Jerry Wexler who bought out Duane's contract with Rick Hall for $15,000 (both had been stunned by Duane's work on "Hey Jude"). Walden had the prescience to see that, even though Duane couldn't sing, didn't write, and his new band didn't even have a name yet, Duane was someone worthy of building a record label around. Walden's only condition was that the group move to Macon, Georgia, where he was busy setting up not only Capricorn's offices but a recording studio as well.

The entire band, as well as their roadies, moved into a one-bedroom apartment, where the mattresses spread across the floor were their own only domestic luxury. They practiced constantly (they were so poor, there really wasn't much else to do), hung around the nearby bucolic Rose Hill Cemetery, played a lot of free concerts in Macon, took a lot of psychedelics, particularly mushrooms (each member got a mushroom tattooed on his leg), and generally made the local citizenry uncomfortable with their long hair, loud music, and racially mixed group personnel. They also played a few shows at the Boston Tea Party, their first non-Macon dates as the Allman Brothers Band (the moniker was the other members' idea, not Duane's or Gregg's). Things were so tight financially, when they were invited to come back three weeks later for a series of gigs opening for Dr John, the only way they could pull it off was to hang around Boston until it was time to play again, some of the members living in a squat with no electricity, a few others with the local promoter in his already cramped apartment.

Ironically, the Allman Brothers' eponymously titled first album was not recorded in Macon, but in New York, because

Capricorn and the band wanted to work with veteran Atlantic producer Tom Dowd (Ray Charles, John Coltrane, Otis Redding, et cetera). Ultimately, it didn't matter because Dowd proved unavailable at the last minute, and the band ended up with another Atlantic staff producer, Adrian Barber. Many, including members of the band, have criticized Barber's role in the recording (the vocals were not recorded properly, the band was rushed, the recording equipment was old), but it is difficult to imagine that, even with Dowd behind the console and with a bigger production budget, things would have come out sounding much different (although, admittedly, the mix is slightly muddy and the vocals are somewhat echoey). To the outside listener, the only real problem is that the album is simply too short. For a group that built its reputation as a live band given to long, improvisational flights, it's impossible for an LP that is only a little over thirty-three minutes long to do anything more than hint at what the Allman Brothers were all about. What's there, though, is good—very good.

Opening track "Don't Want You No More" is a charging instrumental borrowed from the Spencer Davis Group and shorn of its pedestrian lyrics and served up roaring and raw, an unorthodox but ideal opening salvo of bruising R&B- and soul-jazz–infused rock; when it segues into the slow, simmering Gregg original, "It's Not My Cross to Bear," the other, smouldering late-night-blues side of the band is highlighted. "Black Hearted Woman" and "Every Hungry Woman" are average songs performed spectacularly—the guitars play off and with each other, the Hammond B-3 bubbles underneath, the bass holds down the bottom but nips at the guitar players' rising notes, and the two percussionists swing like a good jazz band with a bad case of the rock and rolls. Any other band including a cover of Muddy Waters' "Trouble No More" on their debut LP would produce a ho-hum response, but not when the song features Duane Allman and his first use of slide guitar on an Allman Brothers record. It might be sacrilegious to say so, but no other studio version of the song—by anybody, including Muddy—ever sounded this dynamic, driving, and mean.

The final two tunes are the longest—together, they add up to almost a third of the LP's total playing time—and the best. Even in its embryonic state, "Dreams" is a measured, organ-heavy blues that manages to be both melancholic and maniacal. Live, as on the posthumously released *SUNY at Stonybrook 9/19/71*, "Dreams" often exceeded twenty minutes and is a marvel of Duane's improvisational genius. The closing track, "Whipping Post," wasn't the monster it would become live, but it was still a teeth-rattling explosion of betrayal and catharsis.

Because they weren't yet touring regularly and the album was not exactly radio friendly, no one was surprised when *The Allman Brothers Band* failed to rise higher than #188 in the charts. Besides, there was no time for feeling sorry for themselves—it was time to bring the music to the people, and the only way to do that was to cram into the Econoline and hit the road. Additionally, despite Walden's belief in Duane and the band, the group was poor. Not can't-afford-to-buy-a-Cadillac poor, but *begging* poor. Once, even literally. Trucks: "We went all the way to California, got as far as the Golden Gate Bridge, and didn't have the fare to pay the toll to get across. So Oakley's out going from booth to booth looking for young ladies to get the money to get across the bridge."

One thing that helped both the band's finances and their growing musical gestalt was the large house in Macon that several of the group members (including Duane) moved into, which everyone called the Big House. Those that didn't actually live there hung out there all the time, and it was here that Duane's jazz education progressed to the PhD level, principally courtesy of Jaimoe.

Duane and Betts had each been exposed to jazz before, of course—what guitar player doesn't adore Django Reinhardt?—but it was because of the Big House's communal record player and Jaimoe's LP collection that the entire band became saturated in the work of several contemporary jazz masters. While insisting that "Duane had listened to Miles and Coltrane before he met me," Jaimoe said, "we did spin those a lot. His two favorite songs were Coltrane's version of 'My Favorite Things' and Miles's 'All Blues.' Those two songs were the source of a lot of our modal jamming, without a lot of chord changes." Betts grew up with a deep love of all aspects of country music and claimed that the twin-fiddle lines often employed in Western swing music were also an influence on his and Duane's unique, interweaving dual–lead guitar style, but without Jaimoe's jazzy leanings it is difficult to imagine the pair's sparring, improvisational flights, as well as the entire band's increasingly fluid, yet still fiery sound.

The Allman Brothers Band's growing confidence with the jazz idiom is most apparent in the instrumental "In Memory of Elizabeth Reed" (the song was titled after a gravestone in Rose Hill Cemetery near where Betts liked to sit and think and play and write in peace), the longest and most striking cut on their next record, 1970's *Idlewild South*. From the gentle, opening volume swells produced by Betts, its composer, to his and Duane's ringing, singing dual harmony playing, to the funky soul-jazz organ break provided by Gregg, to Oakley's leaping bass lines, to the drummers' brief tandem solo spot, "In Memory of Elizabeth Reed" is jazz-rock for real.

Despite its puny playing time (30:48), the remainder of the album, produced by Tom Dowd this time, is first-rate as well. Opening track "Revival" is most noteworthy for being Betts' initial ABB original composition, its pronounced country-gospel feel, and for being the first Allman Brothers Band song to prominently feature the use of acoustic guitars (courtesy of Duane), which was a welcome change-up from the usual sonic assault. Gregg's "Don't Keep Me Wonderin'" is another funky, been-done-wrong-for-too-damn-long blues, pushed along by Duane's screaming slide and guest Thom Doucette's harmonica. "Midnight Rider" is something else completely: a song that is not only both soulful and superbly memorable, but also a sad reminder of how the band, if Duane had lived, could have gone to so many other musical places: the hook is played by Duane on an acoustic guitar, the electric solo sounds like it is coming from a hopped-up pedal steel, and Jaimoe's feathery conga playing supplies a menacing percussive touch. As tight and tough as it is, the Berry Oakley–sung cover of "Hoochie Coochie Man" is album filler, a nice vocal break for Gregg when performed live, but entirely superfluous on record. "Please Call Home" is not only a great, slow-burning R&B original (it's easy to imagine James Carr or Percy Sledge covering it), but sung with such wrenching feeling by its author, Gregg, that again, one wishes this side of the band's talent had been explored more when Duane was alive—the spare beauty of his playing between the lines of Gregg's repeated pleas in the chorus is simply gorgeous. "Leave My Blues at Home" wraps things up nicely, the by-now trademark twin lead guitars and lively rhythm section in place, but the band's sonic palette further extended by Gregg's employment of piano in the intro.

In contrast to their debut, *Idlewild South* took several months to record, mainly because the band seemed to be on the road all the time (over three hundred days during 1969). It was largely because of this near-constant touring (and their incendiary live act) that *Idlewild South* made it just inside the Top 40 album chart and their audiences started growing larger. The road giveth and the road taketh, however, and along the highway there was a murder (a club owner who refused to pay the band, stabbed to death by Twiggs Lyndon, one of their loyal roadies), a lot of physical and mental exhaustion, and a lot of drugs—too many and too often the wrong kind. The impetus changed from getting high to have a good time, to staying high to get the job done and survive the road and get to the next show on time. The band even endured a near-fatal overdose when Duane took too much opium after a Nashville gig and turned blue and could not be revived. Although he eventually recovered, band members recalled hospital personnel advising them to temper their expectations for Duane's recovery and Berry Oakley pleading with God to spare Duane for just one more year.

It wasn't only drugs that Duane could be reckless with. Alan Walden, brother of Capricorn head Phil Walden, recalled how "one night the Macon police caught Duane out riding [his motorcycle]. He had no tag, no driver's licence, no helmet, and he ran a red light. They pulled him over, found out who he was, and escorted him home. They told him, 'Now, Duane, you stay home tonight.' They caught his ass about 35 minutes later, running another red light."

It was during the protracted *Idlewild South* recording sessions, when they were working in Miami at Dowd's preferred recording studio, Criteria, that Dowd mentioned to Duane that he had been asked to produce Eric Clapton's next project, which would eventually become Derek and the Dominoes' *Layla and Other Assorted Love Songs*. Being a fan of Clapton's, Duane hoped to meet the British guitar hero and asked Dowd if he could drop by Criteria once Clapton and his new bandmates got settled in Miami. It turned out that Clapton was a fan of Duane's as well, particularly his brilliant soloing on Wilson Pickett's "Hey Jude." When the Allman Brothers Band was back in Miami a couple of weeks later for a gig, Clapton insisted that his entire group (Bobby Whitlock on keyboards and vocals, Carl Radle on bass, and Jim Gordon on drums) check out the show, and afterwards most of the Allman Brothers Band came back to Criteria with Clapton and company and embarked upon a marathon, coke-fuelled jam session. Thrilled with Duane's playing—particularly his scintillating slide work—Clapton invited Duane to join the album sessions, which Duane did after first honouring a few ABB concert dates.

Much—too much—has been made of the domestic drama behind *Layla and Other Assorted Love Songs*, specifically that Clapton was hopelessly in love with Pattie Boyd, his close friend George Harrison's wife, and that the entire album is a tortured paean to his unrequited love. All of which may be true, but it is equally true that once Clapton and Boyd became a couple, he was almost immediately serially unfaithful, and the couple divorced nine years later (during which time a girlfriend of his gave birth to one of Clapton's children). Most relationships—no matter how passionate their genesis or epic their scope—don't last; great art does. Pattie Boyd may have been the muse behind *Layla and Other Assorted Love Songs*, but Duane Allman was the reason that it is perhaps the only one of Eric Clapton's albums that can be recommended unreservedly.

It's not only what Duane's guitar playing brings to the party (the filthy bottleneck on "Tell the Truth," for example, or the celebrated introductory riff he contributed to the title song, "Layla"), but also what he brought out in Clapton, who never played electric guitar as intensely or as inventively. *Layla and Other Assorted Love Songs* is that rarest of things: a blues album that doesn't sound like a blues album because it *is* the blues. There's symbiosis at work in every successful musical collaboration, and Duane was certainly inspired by Clapton's playing as well, but it's impossible to imagine *Layla and Other Assorted Love Songs* becoming the masterpiece it was without Duane's involvement.

Clapton was so inspired by what they'd accomplished that he asked Duane to permanently join the band, which Duane briefly considered before gratefully declining. His equivocation wasn't as disloyal as it might sound. Circa 1970, Eric Clapton was certified rock-star royalty, traveling by jet, not van, and living in the large home he owned in the English countryside, not in a shared rental in Macon, Georgia. But the Allman Brothers Band had unfinished work to do. Duane and the rest of the group knew that they were at their best in front of an audience and that the depth and scope of their sound had yet to be captured on tape, so they talked their label into recording and releasing a live double LP. One of their favourite places to play was Bill Graham's Fillmore East, and so, with a recording truck in tow, the band headed to New York in March 1971 to make it happen.

~

At Fillmore East was not supposed to be Duane Allman's musical epitaph (and technically it wasn't, as the three tracks he cut with the band before he died, for their next studio album, chronologically succeeded it), but in light of his death, it is not hard to view it as a scorching summation of everything that the Allman Brothers Band were about to this point: Duane's explosive slide guitar, as on kick-off cut "Statesboro Blues," the very tune that had sparked his bottleneck infatuation only a few years before; Betts' stinging, complementary playing alongside Duane, particularly on the two lengthiest tracks, "You Don't Love Me" (19:06), a tune they probably learned from Junior Wells' *Hoodoo Man Blues*, and a titanic version (22:40) of Gregg's "Whipping Post"; the silkily propulsive rhythm section, no matter how blues-based the tune (only Trucks and Jaimoe could make a gutbucket Elmore James blues like "Done Somebody Wrong" *swing*); Oakley's rumbling, acrobatic bass (listen to him soar alongside the guitar players on the sparkling, definitive, thirteen-minute version of "In Memory of Elizabeth Reed"); Gregg's always apposite Hammond B-3 organ playing and pained, primeval voice, as when he slows things down to a funky crawl on "Stormy Monday."

There's also the near-telepathic level of musical communication among all six members, the more-improvisational songs suffused with tempo changes and shifting light-and-dark textures, no matter how loud or furious the playing (as on the short but fierce instrumental "Hot 'Lanta"). When the hurricane of electricity that is "Whipping Post," the double LP's final song, ebbs to a hushed moment near the twenty minute mark, Betts briefly quotes the melody from "Frère Jacques," after which Duane and Oakley almost bashfully join in, and it is as if the band and the listener both were suspended on floating purgatorial notes; until the entire band comes crashing back in and we are inescapably—and inevitably—once again slammed back down into the depths of Gregg's anguished hell, his every tortured wail answered by his brother on shrieking, sobbing guitar.

At Fillmore East was culled from two nights of gigs, two shows a night, October 12 and October 13. Tom Dowd produced the double LP, and it sounds as good as the playing is hot. Duane might have been the undisputed boss when it came to the band, but he also knew to listen to somebody else when it made the music better. The group actually began their Fillmore run on October 11, but unbeknownst to Dowd, who arrived at the Fillmore late on the first night and had not had a chance to confer with the band before settling into the recording truck parked outside the venue, the group had invited three horn players to sit in. "All of a sudden," Dowd recalled in the liner notes to the six-disc *1971 Fillmore East Recordings*, "I hear horns and I nearly wet my pants! I came tearing-ass down and when they came offstage I grabbed them and said, 'Get those horns out of my life. They are out of tune and they don't know the songs.' I was pissed and I gave them hell." Duane was adamant that the horns stay—until Dowd played back the evening's recording. The next night the horn section was gone.

Even *At Fillmore East*'s album art is superb: a full front-cover black-and-white shot of the entire band, assembled in an alley in front of their ubiquitous road cases, all of them inexplicably cracking up except for Duane, who sits in the front row with a smirk on his face and both hands linked in front of his crotch. The shot was taken after Duane, spotting a local dealer, popped up, scored some coke, and returned to the photo shoot with the bag of blow strategically hidden from the photographer's lens. Unfortunately, by the time the Fillmore concerts were recorded, and the album was being readied for release, cocaine was not the worst of Duane's chemical vices.

It's elementary rock-and-roll physics: what gets high must come down. Between the overpowering music the band was creating and the powerful stimulants they were using to help make sure it happened night after night, heroin was a convenient way of soothing threadbare nerves and getting body and soul rested up and ready for the next day's rock-and-roll onslaught. When the insomnia-suffering Macbeth cries out for sleep—what he calls "Nature's soft nurse"—he might have been talking about heroin. Every drug takes just as much or more than it gives, and since no drug gives more than heroin, no drug takes more, either. Duane's playing began to suffer. Trucks:

> One night in the summer of '71 in San Francisco, Duane followed me to my hotel room and jumped in my face. He said, 'I'm pissed off! When Dickey gets up to play, the rhythm section is pumping away and when I get there you're laying back and not pushing at all.' I looked him dead in the eye and said, 'Duane, you're so fucked up on that smack that you're not giving us anything.' He looked me in the eye and walked out the door.

The criticism must have stung, but it didn't take Duane long to decide to seek help. This wasn't about his health or even endangering his life, this was about something important. This was about the music.

After spending enough time to get clean at a primitive rehab clinic in Buffalo that October, and a few days in New York hanging out with friends (Duane conceded he had a smack problem—the only problems he had with alcohol and cocaine was getting enough of them), Duane flew back to Macon heroin-free, reenergized, and ready to get back to work on the band's next studio album, *Eat a Peach*, for which they had managed to record three tracks. These included Betts' bouncing, beatific "Blue Sky," an irresistible jazz/country hybrid that pointed towards a fresh, new direction for the band, as well as the delicate acoustic instrumental "Little Martha," Duane's first and only original composition for the group.

On October 29, a day after arriving home, the motorcycle he was riding slammed into the side of a truck. Duane rode his motorcycle like he did everything else: very fast and indifferent to such trivialities as fastening the chinstrap on his helmet. He never regained consciousness and was pronounced dead three hours later. It had been 363 days since Duane's near-fatal overdose in Nashville, when Oakley had pleaded with God to "Please just give him one more year." Duane Allman was twenty-four.

As for the Allman Brothers Band, just like in Gregg's song "Midnight Rider," the road goes on forever—or at least until 2014, when Gregg, Jaimoe, and Butch, the only original members, performed their final show. 1973's *Brothers and Sisters*, the band's first post-Duane LP of all-new studio material, added the outstanding piano player Chuck Leavell to the line up and has several strong moments (including the airy instrumental "Jessica" and the band's single bona fide hit, Betts' "Ramblin' Man"), but it is the only post-Duane album by the band that I own. Without Duane's genius guitar playing and far-sighted vision and gutsy leadership, the band's albums and concerts throughout the succeeding decades are, at best, passionate approximations of the real thing; at worst, the respectful sounds of a tasteful tribute band in all but name.

Gregg and Betts both pursued solo careers of moderate critical and commercial success, and even though, with Duane gone, the two frequently butted heads over the band's sound and direction, every few years they would somehow end up back together as part of the Allman Brothers, because a proven brand name is a lucrative thing to waste. Betts was kicked out of the group in 2000, for the drunken and disruptive behaviour that had been going on for years, Trucks fatally shot himself in 2017, and Gregg died five months later of liver cancer.

Berry Oakley had been the first original Allman Brothers member to exit the brotherhood after Duane's irreplaceable loss. Oakley crashed his motorcycle into a Macon city bus in 1972, one year and thirteen days after Duane's own fatal accident, and only three blocks from where his bandmate met *his* end. He was also twenty-four years old. People close to the band said that Oakley died the same day that Duane did, it just took him longer. You could say the same thing about the Allman Brothers Band.

LEE MAVERS

Music, the greatest good that mortals know,
And all of heaven we have below.
–Addison

Rock can be pop, but pop can never be rock, and pop qua pop has to be pretty great for it to be any good. Sometimes, it can even be perfect. So perfect that its evanescence and even its human maker or makers don't matter. Only the song matters. Perfection isn't exactly abundant in this life, so let us simply be thankful for whatever numinous delights do exist. Even if it only lasts a few minutes and its creator never made anything else as noteworthy. Like "There She Goes" by the La's. Like Lee Mavers, the fugitive composer of "There She Goes."

To Brian Wilson, the perfect pop song could only be the Ronettes' "Be My Baby." For John Peel, it was "Teenage Kicks" by the Undertones. For my friend Mark it has to be Dwight Twilley's "Could Be Love." Everyone has their own favourite pop song and that's as it should be. There's no place for music-critic snobbery when it comes to what particular three minutes or so of musical magic makes time stop and your soul swoon and everything, everywhere, suddenly make sense. "There She Goes" is my favourite pop song. It's also perfect.

Perfect novels and perfect albums are rare because their size and scope thwart perfection. "Sometimes," Horace wrote, "even Homer nods." But a pop song is necessarily short—no more than four minutes, although ideally closer to three. Writing of Nathaniel Hawthorne's tales in his essay "Hawthorne," Edgar Allan Poe claimed, "All high excitements are necessarily transient. Thus a long poem is a paradox." A half-hour version of "Dark Star" can deliver a lot of things—engrossment, prolonged appreciation of the Grateful Dead's inspired instrumental interplay, even mystical intimations—but "high excitement" is not one of them. Like Poe's ultimate tale or poem, the perfect pop song "induces an exaltation of the soul which cannot be long sustained." Poe notes, however, that a "poem *too* brief may produce a vivid, but never an intense or enduring impression. Without a certain continuity of effort—without a certain duration or repetition of purpose—the soul is never deeply moved." This is why the Ramones' "Now I Wanna Sniff Some Glue"—clocking a mere 1:34—while thoroughly hummable and gloriously moronic, can only ever be a minor punk-pop classic.

Perfect pop songs usually include lyrics that aid in its conjuring, but most importantly, do not distract from the song's spell. No matter how literate the lyrics, without a memorable melody and that difficult-to-identify, but absolutely essential, special, aural something, it is no better than mediocre *abab* poetry. The perfect pop song is, foremost, perfect musically, and manages to avoid what Poe calls "The

Heresy of the Didactic": a tale's, a poem's, or a song's "sole arbiter is Taste," he claims. "With the Intellect or with the Conscience, it has only collateral relations. Unless incidentally, it has no concern whatever with Duty or with Truth." How often—particularly for those old enough to remember a pre-Google world—have we loved a song only to discover that from the beginning we've been singing the wrong words? A high school friend of mine swore that the line "the girl with kaleidoscope eyes" in the Beatles' "Lucy in the Sky with Diamonds" was actually "the girl with colitis goes by." He had even constructed an entire theory to bolster his claim, maintaining that the lyric was a wry comment on sexual promiscuity in an era of unfettered free love. Another friend thought that the chorus of one of her favourite Led Zeppelin songs was "Olive, my love"—and not, as it actually is, "all of my love." And it didn't make any difference that what they were both singing was wrong. The psychedelic tenor of the former remained intact, the ode-to-love tone of the latter was entirely undisturbed. The music made the wrong words sound right.

For a pop song to be perfect, originality isn't necessary, just as long as the song in question is unique. All art is cannibalistic—every artist feeds on what was served up before they even knew they were hungry—and popular music is especially so. Although Brian Wilson's debt to Phil Spector and the Ronettes' "Be My Baby" is obvious to anyone who adores the Beach Boys' "Don't Worry Baby" (the opening, unaccompanied drums; both songs' novel use of the melancholic to convey the romantic; the giveaway employment of "Baby" in the title itself), its fingerprint is unique anyway because, regardless of its debt, it's such a great tune. Arcade

Fire's "Sprawl II: Mountains Beyond Mountains" is no less wonderful for so clearly resembling Blondie's "Heart of Glass" because it utilizes the earlier tune to become something else, something independently fine. All art recycles. But really good artists tend to reprocess the work of other really good artists, in turn eventually becoming themselves inspiration for others. "Immature poets imitate," T. S. Eliot wrote. "Mature poets steal."

And Lee Mavers—the La's' singer, songwriter, and guitarist who made a single album nearly four decades ago and has refused to release anything since—knew how to steal. He had to. Otherwise "There She Goes" wouldn't be so powerful, so good, so timeless. So perfect.

Lee Mavers was born in Liverpool in 1962 and was an arty kid who liked to draw and listen to music. Biographical background material about Lee is so scarce, MW Macefield, author of *In Search of The La's: A Secret Liverpool,* spent four years attempting to interview Lee for his book about the band. He eventually got his interview, but without gaining much insight into Lee's pre-La's life.

At eighteen, Lee played bass in a local noise-punk band called Neuklon for a few years. In 1984 Lee joined fellow Liverpudlian Mike Badger's group, the La's (the group's name, denoting both the major-scale *la* note and the common Liverpudlian abbreviation of *lad,* were Badger's ideas), because both shared a passion for the music of Captain Beefheart, then and now one of those secret-handshake artists that act as a potential-friendship litmus test. Initially he didn't sing or even play guitar in the La's but only held down the bass spot. Still,

Badger told Macefield that "I was attracted to Lee because he was just *different*, a different person to the normal people you'd meet. He had a lot of character and he also looked dead cool, which when you're twenty-two means a lot."

It wasn't long before the skinny, steely-eyed boy child with the bowl haircut was regularly bringing in songs that he had written and insisting upon dividing the vocal duties with Badger. Later, Badger told the BBC that Lee "said to me, 'Your time's nearly up in this band.' I was like, 'What? It's not your band, mate!' I said, 'I'm off,' packed my guitar and got on a bus. I was gutted." Pushed or jumped, it doesn't really matter what you call it. The bottom line is that Lee hijacked the band that his friend had started, named, led, and asked him to join because... well, because he'd started writing his own songs and wanted his own band to play them. No one said that carving out your own identity doesn't occasionally require stabbing a friend or two in the back.

Adding another guitarist, Paul Hemmings, the band became an exclusive conduit for Lee's developing musical vision, which, while having nothing to do with Beefheart's fractured blues, was grounded in the same uncompromising iconoclasm that helped the good captain survive nearly two decades adrift on an ocean of ridicule, indifference, and commercial marginalization. In an age of big riffs, bigger hair, and processed, digitized recording values, Lee's tidy, acoustic-kissed, neo–Mersey Beat pop-rock songs were as much of their time as Beefheart's cubist country-blues were of his. Debuting their new, oddly old-sounding songs all over Liverpool, though, the La's newfangled retro music made them one of the most successful club bands in town, and they were soon signed by London-based Go! Discs, a small but happening label that loved the band's unique, out-of-time sound and sent them into a London recording studio to knock out a single.

Whether because Lee was a vigilant, perfectionist purist, incapable of settling for anything less than musical flawlessness; or because he was an obsessive-compulsive contrarian, incapable of letting go of his creations because, if no one heard them (or heard them in a way that Lee deemed substandard) they could never be judged; or whether because of some combination of these two explanations—here's what happened: studio after studio was booked and paid for by Go! Discs, multiple versions of the proposed single ("Way Out") and several other songs were attempted and recorded, and all of them were pronounced unsatisfactory and rejected by Lee. Speaking to Andy Murray of the website Northern Soul in 2017, thirty years after he left the band, Hemmings clearly remains exasperated by the lead La's unrelenting equivocation:

> There's no rhyme or reason to it. I mean, even a simple matter of listening to the demos: Lee would say "that's the wrong demo tape." Well, it's actually the master demo tape. "Yeah, but I prefer this version." OK, so you use that version. "But it's being played through the wrong cassette deck." OK, we'll get this cassette deck. "Yeah, but it's being recorded through the wrong mic." OK, you get this mic. "But that's the wrong coloured lead." OK, you get this coloured lead. You go on and on and on 'til nothing happens.

Somehow a version of the single was wrested from Lee and released in 1987, and if the song itself isn't especially impressive, its overall sound is very distinctive in the context of the times, '60s influenced but still thoroughly contemporary. This was clearly not a work born of nostalgia, but of someone who simply had good taste. "Way Out" only got as high as #86 in the UK charts; Hemmings quit the group not only because of completion-phobia, but because the band was playing the same songs live night after night in an attempt to get "tighter" for recording purposes (although there was no shortage of new ones to be debuted); a new guitarist, Lee's childhood friend John Byrne, was plunked into the recently vacated lead guitar spot; and work commenced on the next proposed single, a relatively recent composition entitled "There She Goes."

A regular part of the early La's' live sets was a song cowritten by Lee and the departed Badger, "Callin' All," and that is what it feels like when the opening jingle-jangle guitar notes (performed by new guitarist Byrne) of "There She Goes" ring out of your speakers: a call to all to listen to *this*. Not that anyone has to be told—with the mirage-like materialization of those first few sparkling notes, it's impossible not to sit up a little straighter and lean your ear a little closer to the speaker. Following a ten-second eternity of this forever-after-ingrained circular electric guitar figure, when the entire band finally joins in—Lee on strummed acoustic, John Power's simple but steady bass, the simpler-than-simple *boom-boom pop, boom-boom pop* drums—it is as though an army of sweet sound had marched through your speakers and taken over your living room. And that's before Lee even sings a single word.

"Sing," however, is such a stale description for what Lee accomplishes, vocally, in "There She Goes," his soaring falsetto getting the goosebumps going before the title of the song is even out of Lee's mouth. It's not all celestial choirboy siren-songing, though; there's also Lee's scrappy Scouse snarl ("the feeling that remai-ai-ai-ains"), Power's pillowy backing vocals, and maybe best of all, the we-all-fall-down swirl of beautiful confusion that is Lee's tetchy testimony in the bridge to how she calls his name, she pulls his train, how no one else can heal his pain. Lee's influences here (conscious or not) are obvious—the sweetly chiming opening Rickenbacker of the Byrds' "Mr Tambourine Man"; Alex Chilton's confused confession of romantic faith in Big Star's "September Gurls"; the tough power-pop push of Todd Rundgren's "Couldn't I Just Tell You"; the Beatles' customary masterful mixture of melody, song structure, and words —but once they're tossed into Lee's magical musical blender, they amount to something far greater than the sum of their already pretty-great parts: "There She Goes" by the La's. In 1988 Lee was once again convinced to release one of the numerous versions of the song that had been recorded, and although it only got as far as #59 on the singles chart, it was mostly met by rapturous critical opinion (and eventually made it to #13 when it was re-released at the time of the appearance of the La's eponymous LP debut in 1990).

Both the group and their label justifiably encouraged, work began on completing the band's first album, with the assistance of another producer (their third so far), Mike Hedges, but once again Lee would not or could not stop recording: different studios, different guitar sounds, different mixes. Even different mixing desks, including the vintage, Abbey Road–employed recording console that Go! Discs magnanimously managed to locate because Lee maintained that contemporary equipment and recording techniques couldn't capture the real-feel warmth of guitars and drums the way that the older equipment did. It almost worked.

Not long afterward, however, Lee changed his mind and decided that the entire album needed to be re-recorded—again—but this time his producer and label had had enough. Subscribing to the You-can't-not-like-it-if-you-never-have-a-chance-to-hear-it theory, Hedges believed that "Mavers didn't want it to be finished.... Things were perfectly good enough, but he started to say things were out of tune when they obviously weren't." Except for the dependable Power on bass, the band lineup changed over again, and *another* producer, Steve Lillywhite, was chosen to get the album finally finished and released (by now Go! Discs had sunk a substantial chunk of change into the band in recording costs alone and were eager to see some return from their investment). The entire LP was re-recorded, Lee again deemed it outstanding and then unacceptable, and relations between the group and their label and amongst the band members themselves reached a nadir. Lee Mavers and his latest collection of La's went home to Liverpool to consider their next move.

In 1990 Go! Discs commissioned Lillywhite to assemble the album for release and even picked a single ("Timeless Melody") to precede it. Released late that year, *The La's*, although greeted warmly by critics and rising to #30 on the UK album chart, was immediately denounced by Lee to anyone in the press who could be bothered to scribble down his spleen. It's hard to understand why. The album does, admittedly, sound slightly of its time—faintly gauzy and a little dry and hard—but not egregiously so, and certainly nothing compared to most of the contemporary competition. The drums even sound like drums.

Although Lee claimed he hated the record, he and the band were compelled to mount their first full-scale European and North American tours to recoup some of the money they owed Go! Discs. On every stop, however, Lee would slag the album, implying how wonderful it would have sounded if only they'd had the right producer, the right mix, the right-coloured lead…During a brief interview of the band by MuchMusic VJ Erica Ehm, before performing "Timeless Melody," an uncomfortable-looking Lee doesn't even do that, mostly just staring angrily at Ehm, while Power patiently attempts to address one inane question after another. Band morale was not, shall we say, high.

And what of the album itself, whether the Mike Hedges edition or the official Steve Lillywhite version or any of the many mixes that have emerged since *The La's* release thirty-five years ago? The bulk of it is pleasant, melodic guitar rock, and while little of it sticks in the ear or hangs around the heart, it is smart, trad-based pop-rock that, retrospectively, sounds a lot like the beginning of the British music industry's early '90s move away from synthesizers and drum machines toward guitar-based bands (hello, Oasis, Blur, Pulp, Suede, et cetera). But, setting aside the wonderfully woozy, neo-psychedelic "Looking Glass," nothing else even comes close to the splendour of "There She Goes." Which isn't the criticism it might seem. That would be like a Christian complaining that Mary and Joseph didn't have twins. "There She Goes" is two and half minutes of pop perfection. To ask for more is simply ignoble.

Eventually, the Liverpudlian elephant crouching in the corner of the room must be acknowledged: perhaps Mavers just didn't have any more great songs in him. It happens. The respective histories of pop and rock and country and blues are filled with one-hit or one-great-song wonders. And they aren't any less wondrous because there's only one of them.

Sixpence None the Richer's "Kiss Me" is as catchy as the flu in February and achingly romantic, but you'll listen in vain for another song half as moving in their entire catalogue. But this is not failure; this is assuredly success. When millions of people can hum your tune and you've provided solace and smiles and even inspiration and hope to innumerable strangers, you and your song are successes.

The rest of the Lee Mavers story is as predictable as it is unfortunate. A couple more years of grouchy, disconsolate touring. More defections (including the loss of the loyal Power, frustrated by the static set lists and lack of meaningful recording dates). And alternating bouts of semi-retirement and briefly reformed versions of the La's, with Lee as the only original member (except for a short 2005 reunion with Power). In 1999 Lee even ended up working again with the dismissed Badger, who was now a sculptor. Badger remembered how Lee insisted that he first learn all of Lee's songs and the appropriate guitar parts:

> I did! (laughs) It got signed off by Lee and let me tell you that's no mean achievement! But then it was like, "When are you going to work on this new song I've got?" but he was like, "No you have to learn this one first." It was becoming obsessive and I just thought, "This isn't working." It was a shame because I had put six months into it.... [But] as an artist you have to have a product; otherwise, you're not really an artist. You can talk about doing things or say I am conceptualizing or there's a reason like that's not the best studio, tape, guitar, amp, time of day, the stars aren't configured right or the weather's wrong. How far do you want to go down that road to make excuses not to do something?

Because he's never left Liverpool, Lee occasionally even runs into old friends, like former La's guitarist Paul Hemmings, who recalls,

> I got the train from London. It was winter, it was freezing cold, and the train caught fire. We had to stop at Milton Keynes and who got off the carriage that was on fire but Lee! It was lovely to see him, it'd been a long time. The train used to take ages then, so I spent the next three and a half hours with him. It turned out he was still re-recording the original album at [the Damned drummer] Rat Scabies' studio. Ten years later, he was still doing exactly the same thing. And I was thinking, how can you possibly do this without being burnt out?

The stop-and-start catalogue of brief reformations and aborted recording and re-recording sessions detailed in *In Search of the La's* is as dispiriting as it is exhausting. On the other hand, Lee's committed non-presence on social media and the internet is as refreshing as it is, perhaps, unsurprising. Neither he nor the band even has a website. Among the most creatively parsimonious of major rock musicians (one LP and a few singles over the course of nearly forty years), Lee is nonetheless biologically prolific, the father of four children. With several "There She Goes" cover versions (including one by Sixpence None the Richer, which resulted in their second biggest hit after "Kiss Me") and its employment in a few films, Lee and his family are able to live on a steady stream of royalties. Lee doesn't perform live anymore, but occasionally an insider will let leak that Lee has written some *amazing* new song, that it is simply *genius*, that it is as good as or better than *anything* he's ever done. But none of them ever is. Good songs, many of them, yes, but…no.

As the cult of Lee Mavers has grown ("Misunderstood mastermind or lazy poseur?"), a market has emerged for all things Lee: a compilation of BBC sessions; a deluxe edition of the La's only album, including the superior Mike Hedges mixes and a few unreleased songs; and, finally—for now—a four-CD box set that contains the original album and everything else, whether studio or live, worth being released. Even the most fanatical Brit Pop follower, however, will be hard pressed to convince him- or herself that these older recordings are worthy of the reverence given to such other legendary unreleased works as the Beach Boys' aborted *Smile* album. The box set does, however, include five versions of "There She Goes." And every one of them is perfect.

DUSTER BENNETT

This crumbling pageant shall devour,
The trumpet shall be heard on high,
The dead shall live, the living die,
And Music shall untune the sky!
–Dryden

He wasn't the greatest at anything. Even the thing he was best at—being a harmonica-blowing, electric-guitar-twanging, bass-drum-thumping, blues-shouting one-man band—had been done before, by Juke Boy Bonner, one of his earliest inspirations. What he did do better than anyone else, before or since, was embody the paradox that was Duster Bennett. An example of independence and integrity in a world in short supply of both, yes, but also a white blues musician in the dying days of the British blues boom and a teetotaling Christian refugee and devoted family man adrift in the sybaritic late-1960s and early '70s. "Opposition brings concord," Heraclitus wrote five hundred years before the birth of Christ. "Out of discord comes the fairest harmony."

Anthony Bennett was born working class and Anglican in 1946 in Welshpool, Powys, Mid Wales, a few miles from the Wales-England border. One of his early teachers, Irene Warne, told Tony's biographer, Martin Celmins (*Duster Bennett: Jumping at Shadows*), that Tony "was a clean and polite boy and very different from the others. But he was also rather nervous and jumping around a lot." Tony and his older sister, Christine, were regular Sunday school attendees, but once she heard the Good News, she became Tony's evangelical conduit to Heaven-or-Hell, saved-or-lost Christianity. Youth doesn't need another reason to feel confused, alienated, or self-conscious, but Tony's newly acquired religious fervour added a heaping dose of Manichaeism to the emotional mix. Childhood friend Melvyn Warren-Smith: "I honestly think that a lot of his dark moods stemmed from the heavy religious thing that his sister drew him into... He had built up this belief system which was so very strict [e.g., no cursing, no alcohol, no sex before marriage] that he would frequently end up beating himself up. And I mean that literally,... thumping himself on his head when things went wrong, or when he felt that he'd stepped over the line." A spiritually oscillating outlook on existence may not make for a tranquil mind or a contented life, but it's not a bad ball and chain for a neophyte blues musician to haul around. How can you sing about being saved if you don't understand sin? Guilt, fear, and redemption are all part of the blues musician's kit bag.

Like approximately twenty billion other future British rock-and-roll and blues-based musicians who came of age in the 1960s—Syd Barrett, Roger Waters, Pete Townshend, Keith Richards, Eric Clapton, Ian Dury, et cetera—Tony enrolled in art school (specifically, the Epsom School of Art) where he majored in playing his guitar and harmonica when he should have been pursuing his studies. In the liner notes to *The Complete Blue Horizon Sessions*, childhood friend, college mate, and future musical collaborator Top Topham recalled that Tony "was never to be seen without a guitar, harmonica or kazoo. I recall that, for many, this obsession operated at close to pest level." One sympathizes with those forced to endure first-hand the missionary zeal of the newly converted, but any young British person at this time with any taste at all—and quite a few with none—were American blues mad. Pink Floyd, for instance, was named after two of Camberwell College of Arts student Syd Barrett's favourite blues musicians, Pink Anderson and Floyd Council.

No matter one's background, however, or how lucky a person may be, in terms of when and where they were born and the education and support (financial and otherwise) they are fortunate enough to receive, every great artist—every great *anything*—is first and foremost a devoted autodidact. The teacher may open the door, but it is up to the student to come inside. Topham marvelled at Tony's musical eclecticism and extraordinary ability to emulate other artists, and he remembered Tony's being never satisfied until he viscerally understood the gnarled and knotty roots of whatever art form interested him:

> Tony explored art and then blues music by learning from the primitives. Here was a talented landscape painter who at first insisted on painting—caveman style—with sharp-

ened sticks and not brushes. And here was a chromatic harmonica player who had taught himself to sight-read Larry Adler classical pieces and yet began studying the blues by listening to jug band music and country blues. It was the feeling he was after.

First the feeling, then the form. They should engrave that over the front doors of every art college and music school.

Tony formed a band while at college, and not surprisingly it was a jug band. Across the Atlantic, nascent versions of the Grateful Dead (Mother McCree's Uptown Jug Champions) and Canned Heat (the Canned Heat Jug Band) were doing the same thing, around the same time, and for much the same reason: it was easier to gather a bunch of people who possessed the rudimentary skills necessary to play jug instruments than it was to assemble a group of musicians capable of handling electric ones (the Dead's youngest member, Bob Weir, started off at the bottom rung of the ladder, sentenced to keep time by blowing into a jug). The other thing Tony did was meet the woman he would spend the rest of his life with, fellow Epsom art student Stella Sutton. She was good-looking, intelligent, and liked the blues—what else could he want? In time, a new college (The Guildford School of Art, where Tony became nearly as passionate about pottery as he was about music) and another jug band (the Hokum Hounds). One day in 1966, at the tail end of a gig with the new jug outfit, he performed by himself (aided by the simultaneous employment of his own bass drum and cymbal, harmonica, and guitar). He was a huge success with the small crowd, probably in part because the average British music fan had never seen anyone perform solo like this before. It wasn't long until Tony Bennett, the amazing one-man blues band, was working the local clubs.

Although it was possible in 1967 to get gigs at London clubs playing nothing but the blues and R&B, making a living at it was another matter, and Tony took a job in a clothing factory. In December he opened up for Peter Green's new band, Fleetwood Mac, and the group's leader and lead guitarist was impressed by the young man's unique set-up and deep feeling (feeling was what Green's own sensitive playing was all about as well). In time, Green told Mike Vernon, the head of the Mac's record label, Blue Horizon, about the newcomer, and after checking out his live show, Vernon returned home suitably impressed. Vernon recalled that "almost instantly, our initial favourable reaction was to turn into massive enthusiasm. Here was a unique performer with unbound energy, personality, charm and unquestionable talent, not only as a musician, but also as a songwriter."

All that was left was the name. The American crooner Tony Bennett was a huge, worldwide star, and although no one was going to confuse the British, blues-belting Tony with the one who had famously left his heart in San Francisco, two Tony Bennetts in the music business was one too many. It was Tony who came up with the new moniker—Duster—in tribute to Elmore James' backing band, the Broomdusters (which James had named after his most well-known tune, "Dust My Broom"). It also sounded pretty cool, which is never a bad thing when you plan on making your living in show business.

~

Duster's Blue Horizon LP debut, *Smiling Like I'm Happy*, was released in the late summer of 1968 (a single, "It's a Man

Down There" b/w "Things Are Changing," preceded it). Most of the album—and the single—distinguishes itself foremost by its irresistible energy and obvious delight in the very act of music making, bright-eyed and bushy-tailed busking British blues-punk with a frown-turned-upside-down face. The in-concert ambience of the record is bolstered by the inclusion of the riotous instrumental "Country Jam," a country blues with some serious giddy-up. It's a hoot, too, to hear Duster's girlfriend, Stella, supplying the harmonizing high notes to "Times Like These." The entire album is an audio snapshot of a great night out at the pub with an exciting—and excited—young performer on stage until well past closing time. Whether covering classics like Juke Boy Bonner's "Life Is a Dirty Deal" or performing his own "Got a Tongue in Your Head," one-man-band Duster infuses everything he plays with an infectious joy, quite an accomplishment considering *Smiling Like I'm Happy* is composed of nothing but blues songs with titles like "Shame, Shame, Shame" and "Worried Mind." It is the responsibility of anyone playing the blues to make it new—to make it personally relevant—which means making the blues make sense to the individual performing it. The music on *Smiling Like I'm Happy* isn't warmed-over Chicago electric blues or bombastic blues-rock à la Cream, but wittily literate, twitchy country blues with a steady beat courtesy of a scrawny guy with Brillo Pad hair in a sweater vest, strumming and blowing and banging and singing his worries away—and ours too. "Energy is Eternal Delight," William Blake, another Englishman with a case of the cosmic blues, wrote. *Smiling Like I'm Happy* is a delight.

That the twenty-two-year-old Duster didn't create an album of immortal songs his first time in the studio is not surprising, but *Smiling Like I'm Happy* does contain two self-penned minor masterpieces, the solo "Jumping at Shadows" and the Fleetwood Mac–abetted "My Love Is Your Love." Although the album's knees-up material suited the agreeably near-shrieking upper register of Duster's voice, slower, quieter songs like these exhibited another side of his vocalizing, revealing a bruised incredulity not yet turned to sour cynicism, but certainly not unaware that, as Duster's old hero Juke Boy Bonner wrote, sometimes it's a struggle just to stay alive.

The simmering-slow "Jumping at Shadows" features an unaccompanied Duster on electric guitar, softly plunking out the truth, and backing it up with a quietly stinging, singing confession that things aren't quite right and he doesn't know why. That it's damn catchy as well—especially for a slow, single-instrument-supported blues song—only helps make its case. For variety's sake (and because labelmate Fleetwood Mac was becoming well known among the blues record–buying British public, and their attachment to Duster's project would raise its public profile), Green, bassist John McVie, and drummer Mick Fleetwood join Duster on a few of *Smiling Like I'm Happy*'s songs, including the aforementioned "My Love Is Your Love." Perhaps a little too similar in sound to Ray Charles' "Lonely Avenue," it is nonetheless a near-hypnotic blues, driven by the insistent guitar figure played by Green at his unmistakably Peter Greenest, slow-burning best.

The new album didn't sell much beyond Britain's small but passionate coterie of blues devotees, but that was okay—reviews were enthusiastic, the size of his live audiences was growing, and in 1969 Stella and he got married. Duster was also becoming a popular session player, he and his harmonica helping out, among others, Champion Jack Dupree (on his *When You Feel the Feeling You Was Feeling,* when the American bluesman was recording in London for Blue Horizon), Chicken Shack, and even returning the favour of Fleetwood Mac's assistance by appearing on the Mac's sophomore LP, *Mr Wonderful.*

While Duster was hanging out with Peter Green and a few others from the band one night, someone brought out a Ouija board and an impromptu seance took place. Even among such a heavy-partying crowd, Duster still managed to avoid the ubiquitous temptations of alcohol, drugs, and groupies but was nonetheless left disturbed by what the others considered nothing more than a fun way to kill a couple of hours. Some people just shouldn't mess around with the dead. That they're only talking to themselves doesn't matter—it only takes one interlocutor for a conversation to turn out badly.

Another single was released ("Raining in My Heart" b/w "Jumpin' for Joy"), and while the A-side was a pleasant '50s pastiche and the flip an exuberant get-on-your feet-and-put-your-hands-together number, lacking only an overcrowded roomful of screaming country-blues fanatics to sweat and sway along, it felt like a bit of a holding pattern. Appropriately, the decision was made to record Duster's next album, *Bright Lights,* in front of a live audience, in an attempt to showcase the dynamism of a Duster Bennett show.

From the honking, hollering, crash-and-smash arrival of opening track "She Lived Her Life Too Fast," you're magically there: the Gin Mill Club at the Angel Hotel, Godalming, Surrey, April 15, 1969. Duster had a fondness for all those too-many-pals, too-many-parties blues laments, and "Bright Lights, Big City" is another in this line, assisted here (and on one other track, "Talk to Me") by, among others, old pal Top Topham on guitar, Peter Green on bass, and Stella on background vocals. There aren't really any highlights on the album, but there aren't any lowlights, either. Whether it's the frantic fun of stomp-along tunes like "Just Like a Fish," "Just Like I Treat You," or "My Babe"; or the slightly soul-inflected slower songs, such as "What a Dream," "I Wonder If You Know (How It Is)," or "Honest I Do," they are all a part of the same deeply pleasurable package. If only one could bottle this sort of elation and energy and soul... Wait a minute, you can: just slip *Bright Lights* into your CD player and voila, instant rock and soul revelry.

As much fun as the live album is, though, there is also a tinge of apprehension once the CD is back in its case and the stage is empty again and the doors of the Gin Mill Club have been locked tight for the night. Duster was clearly more than a live phenomenon—numbers like "Jumping at Shadows" suggested that there was a fine, burgeoning songwriter underneath the rabble-rousing performer—but neither the "Raining in My Heart" single nor the *Bright Lights* album showed much indication of this. Maybe it was because he was so busy playing gigs—his primary source of income—and contributing to other people's records, not only as a harmonica for hire but also as a neophyte producer (four tracks by Lloyd Watson). Songwriting, like any other form of sustained creation, is the product of what V. S. Pritchett, in his essay on Chekhov, "A Doctor," calls a "vegetative temperament"—the ability to let ideas, emotions, and formal properties like structure and sound organically incubate in one's mind, regardless of how busy one is with the miscellaneous demands of day-to-day life. Demands like earning a living for one's family and being a good partner, neither of which are often priorities for many musicians or artists, then or now. But they were to Duster.

Fortunately, like the dedicated mystic, Duster was beginning to develop the necessary ability to be in the world but not of it, and his next single, the cleverly tongue-twistingly titled "I'm Gonna Wind Up Ending Up or I'm Gonna End Up Windin' Up with You" b/w "Rock of Ages Cleft for Me," is the very special end result. The A-side, like "Raining in My Heart," is a faintly '50s-sounding love song, but the similarities end there. Whereas "Raining in My Heart" was sweet but slightly cloying, "I'm Gonna Wind Up" is as freshly exuberant as the brand new love affair it recounts. Duster's convivial harmonica is the dominant instrumental colouring, but it is his happily, hopelessly-in-love voice that puts the song across (although the woodblock percussion could have been placed a little lower in the mix). It is not technically soul music—the harmonica makes sure of that—but it is closer to soul than anything else he had recorded, a sort of backwoods Smokey Robinson number or a British Magic Sam side. It also, according to the liner notes supplied by Duster's wife for the jacket back of the *Justa Duster* compilation, "contains the germs of his future musical expressions and plants them in the blues of this decade." Whatever it was, in other words, this was what Duster's listeners were going to hear a lot more of.

The B-side was no typical throwaway. Clearly inspired by Blind Willie Johnson's "Dark Was the Night," "Rock of Ages" is, like Johnson's classic, just a man, an acoustic guitar, a slide, and some earnest moaning and humming. It is also—to these ears—just as, or maybe even more, moving. "Rock of

Ages Cleft for Me" might have started out as an eighteenth-century Anglican hymn, but Duster's tender, anguished instrumental rendering transcends metaphysical beliefs and religious affiliations. As busy as he worldly was, Duster was learning to save a piece of himself—the best part—to create special moments like these.

And things were about to get much, much busier, because Duster was asked to join John Mayall on an upcoming two-and-a-half-month North American tour, both as a one-man opening act and as a member of headliner Mayall's latest group. Mayall is a justly revered British blues figure, who worked tirelessly to spread the blues gospel—it was his various Bluesbreakers bands, of course, that gave a succession of English guitar players (Eric Clapton, Peter Green, Mick Taylor) a chance to first strut their stuff—but Mayall wasn't in Duster's league, either as a songwriter or as a performer. And although Duster benefitted from the regular paycheque and his first exposure to America and much larger audiences than he was accustomed to, he was still a hired hand principally working to actualize someone else's musical vision. Additionally, Blue Horizon had assembled a compilation for the US market, *Justa Duster,* containing a few cuts from the *Bright Lights* live platter, plus several singles that had never been released outside of the UK. It was an excellent introduction to Duster's work so far—except that it did not appear in American record shops until Duster's US tour with Mayall was nearly over.

Duster's time overseas did have one other benefit: the recording, while in New York, of "I Choose to Sing the Blues," backed by B. B. King's drummer and bass player. The tune, a Ray Charles number, is a saucily strident statement of faith in the blues life, and if Duster's slightly reserved vocal doesn't quite convince, his confident harmonica and the expert chug-a-chug of the rhythm section make it a nice little addition to the Duster canon (if another miss sales-wise). Once back in England, work began on the next LP—what would turn out to be Duster's third and final album on Blue Horizon, *12 db's*.

Two changes are immediately evident. For the first time, all of the tracks are produced by Duster himself, and on several of them he's joined by Top Topham on guitar, as well as a bassist and a drummer. There are still a few one-man-band numbers, but the album's best tunes don't employ the usual guitar-bass-drum-harmonica setup, and most utilize overdubbing. "Sugar Beet" is a pleasantly languid instrumental; "If You Could Hang Your Washing Like You Can Hang Your Lines" is a nasty-nervous, almost folk-rockish lament about the pitfalls of the music business that is catchy enough that, with less vitriolic lyrics, it might have had some chart action; "I Love My Baby" is Duster dipping his toes in blues rock; and "Hill St Rag," a spry instrumental featuring Duster alone on mandolin (along with some foot stomping and clapping), isn't anything unique song-wise, but what is interesting is Duster's attempt to shake things up, to discover some stimulating new sounds in the studio, to keep the blues alive and safe from atrophied orthodoxy (something he would endeavour to do, in a variety of ways, throughout *12 db's*).

Of the band-assisted tracks, "Vitamin Pills" is certainly the most peculiar, a fairly straight twelve-bar blues, distinguished by the same odd, slightly out-of-phase vocal that Dave Edmunds would use to such great effect on his "I Hear You Knocking" hit single. Duster might have had his own hummy hit—which was probably what he was shooting for—

with his crisp country-rock take on the Kinks' "Act Nice and Gentle to Me," but for whatever reason, the public didn't bite (no wonder "If You Could Hang Your Washing Like You Can Hang Your Lines" is a such a sour take on the vagaries of the cold business side of making warm-hearted art). "That Mean Old Look" is an endearingly goofy, bubbly blues; "Slim's Tune" is British dance-hall blues; and "Sweeter Than Sugar" and "On Reconsideration" are Duster inching even closer to soul music, attempting not to get caught up in the straight-blues bag. The only clunker in the bunch is the overly earnest, swathed-in-strings "Woman Without Love." Even here, though, as with all of the other songs on the album, as stylistically different as they are, it still sounds, at root, like the same old busking Duster Bennett. Which leaves "Everyday."

Duster's label boss and former producer Mike Vernon is on record expressing his dissatisfaction with the track. One hopes that Duster's insistence on taking over production duties prejudiced Vernon's opinion (no one likes to hear they're not needed anymore, even when they're not), because "Everyday"—bum vocal notes and the occasional shrill of the harmonium aside—is that rarest of art objects, whether a song, a novel, a poem, a film, or a painting: both utterly original and intensely moving. Instrumentally, it could not be simpler—Duster all alone and lonesome on creaking harmonium—and lyrically, too, it is absolutely unequivocal, Duster confessing in the first line that he wishes that every day could be Christmas day. It's strange, it's touching, it's enough to make an agnostic long for a cup of eggnog and the entire world lit up with gently blinking coloured lights.

Then the blues died. Many—especially those who genuinely loved the music or whose livelihood depended upon it—took this as one more sign of the decline of Western civilization, and they might be right. But just as glam, hard rock, prog rock, and the singer-songwriter movement popped the British blues–boom bubble, so, later on, would pub rock kill off glam and hard rock, just like punk would make what came before it seem obsolete, just like new wave would do the same to punk, just like... You didn't need a subscription to *Rolling Stone* or *New Musical Express* to know which way the wind blew or, as it is written in Ecclesiastes, "Of the making of what is musically fashionable there is no end." Or something like that—Duster would have known the exact quotation. The bottom line was that gigs became harder to get, advances got smaller, and record labels that dealt exclusively in the blues went out of business (including Blue Horizon, in 1971). Of course, there will always be true believers, bless 'em, who continue to play and promote the blues (or any other musical genre outmoded by changing economic conditions and a shifting cultural climate). Junior Kimbrough, for instance, wrote, performed, and recorded scorching country blues into the late 1990s and even opened his own authentic juke joint, Junior's Place, so that he and other musicians would have somewhere to play raunchy, real-deal music. Like Fat Possum, the small independent label he latterly recorded for, though, they are the zealotic exceptions to the rule. Meanwhile, Duster, who believed in the blues as deeply as he did anything, kept on playing and singing.

It is oftentimes easier to espouse *onward and upward*, however, than it is to do it. And after the commercial failure of *12 db's*, after leaving Blue Horizon, after parting ways with his manager, nothing seemed to come easy. He also failed to assemble a satisfactory permanent band—his first—for touring purposes. According to Celmins in *Jumping at Shadows*, one member of the band was let go because, as Duster's wife put it, Duster "realized that they had very different attitudes to everyday things that meant so much to Tony"—which was code for the Bennetts' continuing exasperation with the American piano player's insistence on smoking pot in Duster and Stella's house, a definite chez-Bennett no-no.

It was around this time that, demonstrably depressed, Duster, according to friend and guitarist Keith Randall, "asked a local priest to help him about being possessed by dark forces or a dark spirit," portended, or perhaps even unconsciously precipitated, by Duster's own "Jumping at Shadows" of several years before, with its reference to "going insane" because the devil was getting to him and its being no one's fault but his own. "The priest performed an exorcism ritual and it was such a violent and distressing experience that it almost knocked him to the ground, with the force of what was being released. Duster said that the priest shook intensely and actually almost fell over. However, it worked—Duster felt so anyway." He needed a new record deal and a decent advance more than a priest and an exorcism, but whatever a person requires to get right and keep going is their own soul's business. Duster kept going.

Although he wanted to produce other artists, and Stella and he occasionally talked about becoming full-time potters when they were out of the music business (no Hope-I-Die-Before-I-Get-Old nonsense for them), art—to any real artist—is like being in the mafia: once you're in, you're in for life. Even when all the signs seem to indicate that you and the art you make are no longer required, in a world you are less and less able to recognize.

There was still the occasional session gig (including blowing harp on B. B. King's *In London* LP), still a steady trickle of interest in Duster as a solo performer from the few clubs that continued to book the blues, and even the occasional commercial coup, as when he was chosen to open, one-man-band style, for the reigning boogie-rock kings, Humble Pie. But the greatest satisfactions in his life in the early '70s were the births of his children and his and Stella's decision to leave the city and move to the country (initially near Dorking, eventually to Syerscote). He also acquired a new manager, Philip Roberge, who, unlike the showbiz shysters that Duster lampooned in "If You Could Hang Your Washing Like You Can Hang Your Lines," put his own money where his mouth was and in 1973 financed several recording sessions at various London studios, to put together enough material for Duster's overdue fourth album (*12 db's* had appeared in 1970).

Because it is Duster's final LP, one would like to be unreservedly laudatory, but art doesn't work that way—it either does or does not work. Eventually sold to Toadstool, a small Australian label (after, to Duster's understandable frustration, Roberge struck out in finding a domestic release), 1975's *Fingertips,* as the album was called, sometimes succeeds and sometimes does not, quite often within the same song. The problem is partly the material (where is this album's "Jumping at Shadows" or "Everyday"? Why is Duster covering "Fingertips"?), but even the best songs frequently compete to be heard against an annoyingly punchy horn section, overly busy drumming and guitar fills, and omnipresent background singers. Much of the album is no longer soul-inflected Duster, but Duster doing pro forma soul ("High Ground") and even funk ("Risk It for a Biscuit"). The musicianship itself is fine (Roberge shelled out for some of the best London session players available, including Nicky Hopkins on keyboard), but Duster's dependably warm, amiable voice often seems out of place amidst the sonic clutter.

Fingertips' best tracks are the more straightforward blues numbers—like "I've Got to Be with You Tonight" and "Blue River Rising," where one isn't distracted from Duster's vocals, as with the more conspicuous "soul" numbers—and the harmonica-heavy instrumentals "California Zephyr" and "Gone Gershwin/Summertime." Prior to the album's release, Roberge did find a British label, RAK, to release a single, the A-side being a version of the traditional "Comin' Home," but it wasn't just bad luck that made the 45 a collector's item instead of a hit single. If the booming drums and string section were not distracting enough, the men's choir is ludicrously overripe. Perhaps the most-Duster thing about the entire *Fingertips* project was the album cover, depicting a bearded Duster, leaning in the doorway of his new country cottage, attired in wellingtons, jeans, and a sweater vest.

It is equal parts reassuring and disheartening to learn that, according to Stella Bennett, Duster was demoing new songs that he was extremely pleased with, right up to his death: "The commercial stuff was poppy, which was just a direction he fancied going in for a bit, but it wasn't what he really wanted to do.... He was writing then material which he felt was better than the songs from the *Fingertips* sessions.... They were more serious songs." A few of which, like the moving "My Own

Will," available on the compilation *Bright Lights Big City: The Collectors' Duster Bennett*, bear this claim out, even in rough demo form.

But another album was not to be, and not because by 1976 disco had replaced soul and funk in the music marketplace or because Duster's adored blues was about as anachronistic as a supposed soul singer showing up for an album cover shoot in knee-high rubber boots. On March 26, 1976, returning home late to his wife and three small children from a gig supporting Memphis Slim, Duster was killed in an automobile accident when he fell asleep at the wheel of his van. Backing another musician was not what he had envisioned himself doing at this point in his career, but a gig was a gig, and he needed the money. His wife was pregnant with another child, their fourth. Duster couldn't have been more pleased with the news.

DANNY KIRWAN

Do good by stealth, and blush to find it fame.
–Pope

The legend of Fleetwood Mac goes something like this: in the beginning, there was Peter Green, Gibson Les Paul for hire in John Mayall's mid-'60s Bluesbreakers, a brilliant but psychologically troubled musician who put the Mac together in 1967 (unassumingly naming it after his crack rhythm section of drummer Mick Fleetwood and bassist John McVie) and played some staggeringly good guitar and wrote a bunch of great tunes before having his guitar-god wings clipped by drugs and mental illness. Then, the story goes, the rudderless good ship Mac floundered on the seas of artistic and commercial irrelevancy for a few years in the early '70s before the pop-gold renaissance that came when Lindsey Buckingham and Stevie Nicks joined the group mid-decade.

A legend, H. L. Mencken wrote, is a lie that has attained the dignity of age. Fleetwood Mac's dark ages (1970–74) are the lie that has become rock-and-roll legend, and principally because of the guitar-playing, songwriting, and singing talents of Danny Kirwan, who joined the group in the summer of 1968 as an alarmingly fresh-faced, eighteen-year-old prodigy and was booted from the band four years later for drunken volatility—and by the age of thirty was out of the music business for good and on his way to full-blown alcoholism, debilitating mental illness, and eventual homelessness.

For a former member of a world-famous rock-and-roll band, Danny Kirwan is remarkably little known, both in terms of the biographical details of his life and the wonderful music he created. He is not a legend—he is a mystery. Although he's still waiting for the biography he deserves (I nominate Martin Celmins, Peter Green's biographer and all-round British blues authority), the music, as always, is there for us to listen to. In Celmins' biography of British one-man blues band Duster Bennett, Bennett's wife, Stella, told Celmins, "Everything you want to know about Duster is all there in his music." Maybe not everything—we still need that Danny Kirwan biography or documentary—but musicians do communicate most meaningfully through their music. That's why they're musicians. And whatever else Danny Kirwan was—alcoholic, mentally unstable, homeless, impoverished—he was foremost a musician. Danny Kirwan might be Fleetwood Mac's mystery man, but it is a mystery with a soundtrack that deserves to be heard.

Before any of that, though, yes, Fleetwood Mac *was* Peter Green. The Mac played its first gig, as a four-piece blues band, in August 1967. Sure, the name of the band reflected his admirable anti–rock star attitude, and from the beginning, Jeremy Spencer's Elmore James (and, later, classic rock and roll) replications were a big slice of the Fleetwood Mac live-performance pie. But the much-lauded Green was the lead guitar player, singer, and chief songwriter—and likely the main reason it was so easy for the band to score a record contract almost immediately after its formation. In Steve Graham's 2008 documentary *Peter Green: Man of the World*, Green's former employer, John Mayall—who knew guitar players—opined that "Peter in his prime in the '60s was just without equal." Occasionally—very occasionally—the hype is justified. And in the case of Fleetwood Mac, act 1, it was. Almost.

I own not only the six-CD *Complete Blue Horizon Sessions: 1967–1969* (which contains, among other goodies, three of the four albums released with Green at the helm, plus the double-LP *Blues Jam in Chicago*), but also the complete *Live in Boston* collection, which catches the Green-led Mac at the peak of its latter-day live powers (Green left the band about three months after these early February 1970 gigs were recorded). That said, while the former contains such Green-penned perennials as the Santana-covered "Black Magic Woman" and the transfixing "Albatross," more than a few of the blues covers and blues-based originals, while worth hearing because of Green's sensitive touch and the fluid, expressive tone he coaxes from his six-string, would probably have been more impressive experienced live in some sweaty club on a beery Saturday night. For the most part, I actually prefer the slide-guitar tsunamis Jeremy Spencer unleashes when acting out his Elmore James fixation to Green's more restrained, if always tasteful, trad-blues tributes. (Although a little of Spencer's old-time rock-and-roll pastiches, however uncannily accurate and occasionally amusing, go a long way. Spencer was a potty-mouthed one-man Sha Na Na before there ever was such a thing.) And while the *Live in Boston* material undeniably burns—by this point, Danny had brought another blistering guitar to the mix—sometimes there's more sonic smoke than fire, the overall playing occasionally more furious than focused, the extended jamming (as on the twenty-four-minute, thirty-eight-second "Rattle Snake Shake") too-often riff-reliant and louder than it is alluring. I'm a fan of the bluesy Mac—as a lead guitar player, Green is the anti-hotshot, usually opting for slow and felt as opposed to fast and obvious—but I'm not a fanatic. With *Then Play On*, however, Green's last LP with the group, something had happened that helped transform the band's sound into a much more compelling musical mélange: Danny Kirwan.

The transformation had begun almost immediately after Danny was asked to join the group, a year before work on the album commenced in spring of 1969. (Characteristically, Green liked the idea of adding another musician to share some of the songwriting and performing spotlight.) An adoring Danny used to follow Green around from gig to gig and even helped haul his equipment, and Danny's three-piece blues band, Boilerhouse, opened up for the Mac a few times in London. Green had been impressed enough to befriend the Brixton teenager (born in 1950), who was working in an insurance office at the time, and he tried to find Danny more musically sympathetic band members. When Mick Fleetwood suggested that Danny join their group instead, the cast for Fleetwood Mac, act 2, was set.

Barely legal drinking age when he signed on with Fleetwood Mac, no one could have looked less like a blues-based, incipient rock and roller than Danny. His pencil-thin physique and straw-blond hair, bowl haircut, and big blue eyes inspired Fleetwood's wife, Jenny, to call him Peter Pan. Martin Celmins (*Peter Green: The Authorized Biography*) describes Kirwan at the time of his recruitment by the Mac as looking like a "kidnapped choirboy." Green himself sometimes referred to Danny as "Young Eyes." In retrospect, it is easy to see how, as massively talented as he was, perhaps Danny ran away to join the rock-and-roll circus a little too early.

He might have been an apple-cheeked teenager, but Green himself admitted that the Hank Marvin–inspired, soothing and sighing "Albatross," released as a single in the fall of '68 (and making it all the way to the #1 spot on the UK singles chart), would not have happened without Danny's way with melody and counter-melody (it is, after all, however bewitching, really only a two-chord song). Fleetwood and McVie were willing to go wherever Green's gift steered him, but neither were songwriters. And Spencer, for all he brought to the band's live performances, was such an impersonation specialist he would leave the stage for extended periods during concerts and doesn't even appear on the finished *Then Play On*. Although Green was increasingly open to other influences (while touring America, for example, West Coast bands like the Grateful Dead ignited his passion for free-form jamming), he was a blues disciple from the outset, at one point contemplating moving to Chicago and bashing it out on that city's South Side, where many of his African American idols honed their craft. Danny's influences were a little more eclectic.

Although he was discovered performing in a three-piece blues band, there was a blues boom going on in the UK at the time and plenty of paying work, so that in and of itself isn't especially significant. Danny's mother had a sizeable record collection (she had also been an amateur singer), and he grew up listening to a lot of early twentieth-century jazz guitar (Django Reinhardt being especially important), jazz violin, big band, and hit-parade, lovey-dovey pop, which might help explain why melody, tone, and texture were paramount to him as a guitarist and as a composer. And he *was* a composer; all of the songs he recorded with Fleetwood Mac, including the many moving instrumentals, were meticulously arranged and impeccably performed, a Danny Kirwan hallmark.

Unfortunately, this perfectionism, like all virtues, had its less-appealing side. In the liner notes to the Fleetwood Mac compilation *Before the Beginning: 1968–1970, Live & Demo Sessions*, Boilerhouse bassist Trevor Stevens recalled how "I got used to the idea that [Danny's] pitch was perfect.... It always used to stress him unless [his guitar] was exactly in tune. So I was always passing him the bass to check the tuning before I played to make him happier. Of course, he was still like that with Fleetwood Mac and it used to annoy John McVie no end." In *The Vaudeville Years of Fleetwood Mac: 1968 to 1970* (a compilation of outtakes and live tracks) liner notes, Green is quoted from an interview he gave when Danny and he were both still in the band: "He's neurotic and worries about everything. Whenever he has to be anywhere he gets there about an hour early. He even worries about simple things like catching a bus and bites his nails until they bleed."

Why, though? Why the incessant worry and self-destructive bad habits (which, with time, got significantly worse)? As with many people, musicians or otherwise, their origins might go back to childhood. Clifford Davis, the band's manager during Kirwan's tenure with the group, told Bob Brunning, author of *Fleetwood Mac: Behind the Masks* (and very briefly John McVie's bass-playing predecessor in the band), that "I felt a little sorry for [Kirwan]. His mother had split from his father [when he was an adolescent], and Danny was always trying to find him, and he had a lot of problems with self-confidence and security." And that was *before* Green abruptly quit the band in the summer of 1970 and Danny was thrust into the role of reluctant front man.

The first song Danny recorded with Fleetwood Mac, the instrumental "Jigsaw Blues," the B-side of "Albatross," was a clarinet number, transcribed for guitar, originally recorded by Joe Venuti and Eddie Lang's Blue Five in 1933 (as "Jig Saw Puzzle Blues"). It is just the sort of jaunty, jazzy number that Danny's mother and his missing father might have jitterbugged to, long before their son was born. Pretty esoteric stuff for 1968, when all the cool people knew you weren't supposed to trust anyone over the age of thirty. The rock and rollers who came of age in the mid- to late-'60s had an enormous advantage over subsequent generations of musicians: while the latter tended to find their aesthetic sustenance exclusively in rock and roll, their predecessors were nourished on a variety of pre–rock and roll musical styles and genres. Even when the inspiration was almost exclusively rock or pop, the influence pool was much wider and deeper for the older generation. Glen Matlock, for example, didn't come up with all of those catchy tunes on *Never Mind the Bollocks, Here's the Sex Pistols* by listening to Sham 69 or UK Subs LPs; his teenage record collection was filled with Small Faces, Beatles, and Motown records. A photocopy can provide a convincing likeness, but after enough duplication the uniqueness of the original begins to lighten and fade. Ergo, bands like the Tragically Hip.

Then Play On, Danny's album debut, is a very long one, fourteen tracks and nearly fifty minutes in length in the reconfigured, dual British/American version. Although it was obviously never intended to be Green's final statement, that's what it nonetheless feels like—like he believed he needed to cram in everything he had to say just in case he didn't get a chance to say it later. It is also Danny's coming-out party. Appropriately, then, the album opens with Danny's "Coming Your Way" (the munificent Green ceding the leadoff spot to the newcomer), and that's what it sounds like. The bubbling Afro-Cuban drums (another likely by-product of listening to American West Coast bands like the two-drummer-powered Grateful Dead and the Latin-influenced Santana); Danny's and Green's stinging, call-and-response guitars; Danny's straightforward but slightly menacing vocal; the doomy, near-metal coda: this is hard, spiky rock, the sound of a band *pulling* from the blues, but not being entombed in them. "Closing My Eyes" *is* a Peter Green–penned song, and it's also moody bluesy without being "the blues," the stark instrumentation (just a couple of guitars, including an acoustic, plus a bit of percussion) and meditative, what's-it-all-about? lyrics miles away from the twelve-bar confessionals that the early Mac was known for. It is also a bracing change of pace from the preceding rocker.

"Fighting for Madge" isn't textbook blues, either, but what it is—a few minutes of undistinguished jamming captured in the studio—is not an improvement. Biographers make much of the deleterious effect Green's exposure to drugs (particularly LSD) while touring America had on his mental health; you can say much the same thing about his introduction to full-scale jamming. Like drugs, jamming can be exciting and liberating; it can also be, like drugs, busily empty and boring. Owsley's acid might have helped pickle Green's brain, but the Grateful Dead's free-form musical example didn't do him or his music many favours, either.

Danny's "When You Say" is the ideal tonal corrective: primarily acoustic, melodically unforgettable, and achingly lovelorn in spite of the boy-loves-girl, girl-loves-boy lyrics. Even the *la la la las* in the bridge sound sad. With "Show Biz Blues" we're back in Fleetwood Mac all-blues territory, for the first and last time on *Then Play On*, Green on shrieking bottleneck doing his best Bukka White and wondering if the fans out there really give a damn about him. As affecting as it is to hear his honest bewilderment at the machinations of big-business star building (which was what rock and roll was rapidly becoming by this time), one cannot help but think that if the impressionable Green had never stepped foot in hippie Shangri-La San Francisco he might not have taken it all quite so personally. You can be sure that Bukka didn't.

It is tempting to call Green's instrumental "Underway" "Albatross, Part 2," because of the clouds of phased-out notes that float in with its arrival, but the mesmerizing melody lines Green comes up with, combined with Danny's shimmering harmonic accompaniment, make that diminution impossible. Only three minutes long on the album, live, it could meander for ten or fifteen magnificent minutes, a rare instance of improvisatory success. The nasty, unrelenting riff that announces side-one closer "One Sunny Day" is an additional Danny trademark. On tunes like this, Danny sticks close to the root notes and leans into them—hard—squeezing every iota of sound from each. Another of his acknowledged influences was the Beatles, and it shows—even Danny's rudest rockers are imbued with captivating riffs and instantly memorable melodies. *Wake up one morning, feel good one sunny day*... Nice thought, anyway.

Side 2 opener "Although the Sun is Shining" is another corker courtesy of Danny, the delicate arrangement and subtle vocal harmonies two more musical characteristics he was primarily responsible for introducing into the band's evolving sound. It is also quintessential Danny Kirwan: the very un-rock and roll, crooning vocal, the hints of tremolo and bent notes in his electric guitar playing, the clean, crisp acoustic guitar wafting underneath. Green's "Rattlesnake Shake" has to be in the top five all-time masturbation songs, right up there with Jackson Browne's "Rosie," Lucinda Williams' "Right In Time," the Who's "Pictures of Lily," and Chuck Berry's "My Ding-a-Ling." The hook Green conjures up is as nasty as the wonderfully boorish words he wrote to accompany it. It's also the only Green tune on the album that isn't given over to his increasingly uneasy sense of life's sundry disappointments and dangers. "Without You" may be Danny's song, another beguiling slow-burner with a spooky, echoey atmosphere and dependably forlorn lyrics, but it's Green who impresses most, almost outdoing his idol, B. B. King. His guitar tone throughout is pure liquid smoke. Unfortunately, she—"Madge"—is back with "Searching for Madge," a tedious waste of six minutes of wax on an already-bursting LP.

Thankfully, a double blast of Danny follows. "My Dream" is a bright, buoyant instrumental, and "Like Crying" is harmonized lead guitar lines and tag-team vocals, and bluesy isn't supposed to be this hummable, is it? There's a brief black-and-white YouTube video of an impossibly young-looking Danny and a bemused-seeming Green working through an early arrangement of this song. Things wrap up with "Before the Beginning" in appropriately poignant fashion (between Danny's parade of punctured romances and Green's ongoing metaphysical heebie-jeebies, this is an album heavy on heartbreak and dread). Green, singing over an echoey, eerily minimal arrangement, once again wonders if there's anyone out there who can hear him, if there's anyone who can hear him sing his song. It's the last number on Peter Green's last album with Fleetwood Mac.

Incredibly, maybe the best that Green had to offer was still to come: two final, superlative singles recorded and released not long after the conclusion of the *Then Play On* sessions in a staggering final burst of energy and invention (the manic high heralding the depression that was soon to overwhelm him?). "Oh Well (Part 1)" b/w "Oh Well (Part 2)" manages to be both weird *and* wonderful. The pulverizing, unforgettable riff that announces part 1 (played by Green on dobro), combined with his scorched-earth testifying and Danny's lacerating licks is, somehow, matched for innovation and poignancy by the all-instrumental part 2—the theme to a spaghetti Western as composed by Beethoven—featuring Green on Spanish guitar, drums, and cello and his girlfriend, Sandra Elsdon, on recorder. (Stray member Spencer even gets in on the act and adds some sombre piano.) "The Green Manalishi (with the Two Prong Crown)" b/w "World in

Harmony" is where it all wraps up: one side of throbbing, thundering madness ("The Green Manalishi" was a Green neologism for money and its inherently corrupting powers, an increasing obsession) and one side of soothing sorrow. "World in Harmony" was Green and Danny's sole cowrite and another gentle gem that oozes Danny's way with melody and melancholy.

By the end of May 1970 it was all over: Green announced his departure from the band he started and named, as well as his decision to henceforth divide his time between giving away his money to the poor, playing jam-centric, free-of-charge concerts, and rolling with the cosmic flow. (In reality, he descended into a pit of drug-abetted mental illness from which he never really returned.) Those were the official reasons why Green quit the group.

Unofficially, Danny might have had something to do with it. Adding to Danny's mystery is the fact that no television interviews and only three print interviews with him exist. It's as if he's compelled to converse with posterity almost exclusively though his music. In one of the print interviews, though, for *Guitar Magazine* in 1997, with the indefatigable Martin Celmins, Danny obliquely states that although Green and he connected creatively, they didn't get on too well personally. In *The Vaudeville Years* liner notes, band roadie Dennis Keane contends that Danny's attitude toward Green changed with the enormous success of "Albatross" (a #1 hit). When he first met Danny, Bob Brunning thought him "painfully shy and polite" and "in awe of everyone in the band and even people like me," who were only tangentially connected to the group. Empowered by the band's commercial triumph and the accompanying attention and adoration, however (the blond, teenage Danny had no shortage of female admirers), Danny grew more confident and began to assert his independence. Which is understandable—he *was* still a teenager; that *is* what teenagers do. Which, in the case of the Fleetwood Mac family, meant that the emboldened child began to lock horns with his fellow guitar-playing head of the house. If sons are to become men, sooner or later they must symbolically kill their fathers. Peter Green was Danny's substitute father. *Then Play On* engineer Martin Birch: "Danny and Pete began to clash a bit. More so Danny with Pete than Pete with Danny.... Sometimes Danny tried to bully Pete—he would go right up to him with his guitar and say something like 'I want' and play something on his guitar."

After Green's exit the surviving members embarked on what was to become Fleetwood Mac, act 3. In *Play On: Now, Then, and Fleetwood Mac; The Autobiography*, Mick Fleetwood recalled, "Losing Peter was like taking a rudder out of a sailing boat. As a band, we were still afloat, but we were drifting, with no map and no land in sight." Fleetwood, the band's unofficial overseer of all things practical, decided that what the devastated group needed was to get out of London and head to the country and clear their heads and live together with their partners and kids and practice together and write together and come together as who they were musically going to be next. The band rented an old house in rural Hampshire and lived there for six months, where they pieced together their next album, *Kiln House*, named after their bucolic retreat.

In his *other* autobiography, *Fleetwood: My Life and Adventures with Fleetwood Mac* (if you've been in a group for more than fifty years, I suppose you're entitled to more than one memoir), Fleetwood remembered how, post–Peter Green, "Not only did Jeremy and Danny not want to front the band...the entire band had a terrible case of nerves.... We were leaning on Jeremy to emerge from behind his persona and write about his life. Same with Danny, who now had the burden of replacing the Green God as lead guitarist." Danny might have hastened Green's departure in his understandable need for self-affirmation, but being an essentially "shy and quiet" sort, even at his happiest and healthiest, he was not ideal front-man material. An excellent songwriter and a captivating singer and player, Danny preferred to be by himself or spend time alone with his girlfriend or record demos on his own.

Martin Birch also noted how, during the *Then Play On* sessions, "Danny was always very keen on Peter listening to his tracks. Danny would say, 'I'd like Peter to hear this.' And Peter would say, 'Well if you like it then that's fine with me.' I often got the impression that Danny was looking for Peter's approval." One hesitates to psychoanalyze why people behaved the way they did more than half a century ago, but it is impossible not to see Peter Green's desertion of Fleetwood Mac impacting Danny just a little bit more than it did the other abandoned Macs because of the trauma incurred when his birth father went AWOL when he was growing up in Brixton. You probably don't need Freud for this one.

Perhaps not surprisingly, then, Danny, only twenty years old when promoted to head Mac, began to drink more and more heavily and to exhibit the sort of petulant, problematic behaviour that would eventually contribute to his ouster from the group. Increasingly, Danny seemed to be either aloof or antagonistic. In *Peter Green: The Authorized Biography*, Fleetwood's then wife, Jenny Boyd, recalled how, initially, "Danny was like a son: he used to come and have supper with Mick and me a lot.... He was like a little Peter Pan. Once Peter had left and they were all rehearsing at Kiln House, it was pretty stressful because they didn't know if they could make it as Fleetwood Mac on their own. Danny suddenly started having these total outbursts and tantrums that had no grounding to them at all—a side of him would just kick in and be totally inappropriate to the situation."

Deprived of Green's leadership and songs and the distinctive sound of his guitar, 1970's *Kiln House* shouldn't have worked—and it didn't, not entirely. One man down, Spencer was obliged to do more than learn a new Elmore James cover or come up with a clever Big Bopper parody; indeed, his own "This Is the Rock" has the honour of kicking off the album. As heartening as it was to have everybody on board and paddling in the same direction, though, the fact remains that Spencer was a very derivative songwriter. "This Is the Rock" is pretty much what it says: an echo-laden, neo-rockabilly state of the hep-cat union that, because it was 1970 and not 1958, is more agreeable nostalgia than a statement of rockin' purpose (although Danny's *wha do wha* background vocals are a Roaring Twenties treat). Spencer's other songwriting efforts range from the dreadful ('50s country pastiche "Blood on the Floor," which sounds like a morbidly depressed Conway Twitty with a bad hangover) to the pleasantly inconsequential (the Everly Brothers takeoff "One Together," which is, admittedly, difficult to get out of your head). His covers (a snarling take on Fats Waller's "Honey Hush"—here renamed "Hi Ho Silver" and featuring some fiery guitar from

Danny and Spencer's fiendish vocal; the Buddy Holly tribute "Buddy's Song"; and a faithful version of Donnie Brook's 1961 pop hit "Mission Bell") are fun filler.

"Station Man," however, cowritten by Danny, Spencer, and McVie (part of the homegrown charm of the album is how even the nonwriters in the band felt compelled to pitch in with a line or a lick), is a chugging triumph. It rumbles out of the station with Danny's voice up front, but is buttressed by the husky-sweet harmonies of McVie's new wife, former Chicken Shack singer and keyboardist Christine McVie (née Perfect), who would officially join the band as a full-time member soon after *Kiln House*'s completion. Their shared vocals *ooze* longing and unidentified doom. Spencer could have earned his co-credit just for the neat little slide run he uses to punctuate several of the vocal lines. It is a rare instance of his using his bottleneck prowess to adorn a non-straight-up-blues number, an encouraging development. Fleetwood lays down an infectious offbeat rhythm (similar to the one he would later employ on mega-hit "Go Your Own Way"), and the guitars, throughout, sound huge. Danny is everywhere, on overdubbed lead and rhythm guitar frequently as engrossing as the solos. There are even some engaging tempo changes and a few crunchy power chords during the bridge when Danny wails about that never-arriving train that is Fleetwood Mac's very own Godot.

If Christine McVie had not been enlisted as a fifth band member, Fleetwood Mac might have scraped through making *Kiln House* (it's only a little more than half an hour long), but would have probably eventually gone the way of most groups who lose a crucial member. McVie not only honeyed up the harmonies; her electric keyboard and acoustic piano added new colours to the group's musical palette. And when she began to place her own tunes on subsequent albums (beginning with two good ones on *Kiln House*'s follow-up, *Future Games*), not only was Green's songwriting absence slightly ameliorated, but McVie's singer-songwriter inclination added another musical mode to the Mac attack. Of course, there is such a thing as too much of a good thing: by the time Buckingham and Nicks joined the band five years later, sensitive singer-songwriters were essentially *all* that the band was, Lindsey Buckingham-is-a-pop-music-genius believers to the contrary.

The remaining three songs are all Danny Kirwan originals, and each one is a winner and indicative of the conspicuously non-blues, non–progressive rock (à la *Then Play On*), post–Peter Green direction the band was now travelling. Danny's vocals tend to be either tender or tough-talking aggressive, and "Jewel Eyed Judy" is a bit of both and all the better for it. Subject matter–wise, Danny usually confined himself to love songs (just like in all those old records of his mother's that he grew up on), but how he sings his words is what makes them work, as here, alternately untailored and tortured. Musically, it sounds a bit like Badfinger really rocking out, but with better, more interesting musicians. In the verses, Danny recalls an old flame and idly wonders whether she could still love him; on the raging chorus, complemented by some screaming, stabbing electric guitar (at times it sounds as if Danny is strangling his instrument), he implores her to come back.

Playing live, he often looks as if he *is* strangling his guitar. A frighteningly intense performer in spite of his scarecrow physique, whatever was going down in the music seemed to be going down inside him as well. In a short interview in the booklet accompanying *The Complete Blue Horizon Sessions: 1967–1969* box set, Green claims he more than once witnessed Danny crying while playing on stage. And in the multiartist anthology *Something Inside of Me (Unreleased Masters & Demos from the British Blues Years: 1963–1976)*—a necessary purchase for Kirwanophiles because it includes the crudely recorded, five-song acetate Boilerhouse laid down just before Danny departed for Fleetwood Mac—Trevor Stevens, Boilerhouse's bassist, also recalls that "Danny used to weep when he played. It was extraordinary how he got into the playing when he played in minor keys.... People used to say that the faces he pulled was an act, but it wasn't. He was just so moved." Danny wasn't much of a lyricist—his words mostly stay out of the way of the music and get the job done, although they are rarely memorable—but the sounds he made with his melodies and his guitar usually tell us all we need to know about what he's thinking and feeling. Most of Danny's songs, even the happy ones, are written and performed in the key of melancholy. *Gorgeous* melancholy. Lots of people are sad. Not many people make lasting art out of it.

"Earl Gray" is a short instrumental, of which Kirwan was a master (recall that his first-released Fleetwood Mac song was a '30s-style guitar tune). Brian Wilson called his own songs "pocket symphonies"; Kirwan's instrumentals could be dubbed "pocket sonatas" for their austere beauty. And although his McCartney-worthy melodies are never less than elevating, he always manages to throw in a minor-key chord changeup every once in a while, to keep charming from becoming cloying. Check out the "Earl Gray" demo, "Farewell," on the odds-and-sods *Vaudeville Years* collection; it's mainly just Kirwan strumming an acoustic guitar and *la la la la*ing where the lead guitar is supposed to go, but it might be even more moving than the finished cut. Fleetwood's joyful bashing and newcomer Christine McVie's energetic work on electric keyboard underlies "Tell Me All the Things You Do," a crushing rocker with twitchy lead guitar (another Danny Kirwan attribute) and some absolutely evil wah-wah thrown in to seal the deal. *Kiln House* might be an overall failure as an album; as a blueprint for the new sound of Fleetwood Mac and a showcase for Danny's developing gifts, however, it is an undeniable triumph.

"Dragonfly" b/w "The Purple Dancer," released not long after *Kiln House*, is a miniature masterpiece, a superlative A-side/B-side distillation of everything that Danny did so wonderfully well—in addition to what, if they had stayed together, Fleetwood Mac, act 3, could have gone on to accomplish. The difficulty in attempting to describe "Dragonfly" is that clichés make sense. It's ethereal. It's dreamy. It's sublime. *Sublime—really?* Really. Kirwan borrowed its lyrics from a 1927 W. H. Davies poem, "The Dragonfly," and its Blakean close-up of a dragonfly ("the king of flies" with "his opal crown") and momentary but mesmerizing visit to the poet's garden ("a fleeting visit, all too brief") is the perfect lyrical correlative to the dreamy, floating music Danny conjures up. Almost every Danny Kirwan composition is distinguished by something beyond the ordinary emanating from his guitar, but the shimmering, simmering, arpeggio-seasoned stew he cooks up here is, well, sublime. If a label is absolutely necessary, call it psychedelic folk-rock. Which was probably why it flopped as a single. It was 1971, after all, and psychedelia was as much yesterday's news as love beads and tie-dye.

"The Purple Dancer" may pale in comparison, but only because "Dragonfly" is such a dazzling kaleidoscopic wonder. It's another cowrite, credited to Danny, Fleetwood, and John McVie, but Spencer adds some sighing slide to the B-side's mix and even spits out a few verses in his typically brash fashion—the only time he and Kirwan sang on the same track. It works. Their alternately unhurried (Danny) and unhinged (Spencer) dual delivery makes for an enriching vocal tandem that boded well for the band's future. (Christine McVie's sorrowful sighs on the outro only improves the vocal blend.) Fleetwood provides a funky stutter-step rhythm during Spencer's turns at the microphone, and the main melody, reminiscent of the Grateful Dead's "St Stephen," keeps coming back to you long afterward, a pleasantly repeating melodic echo.

~

One day, while the band was on tour in early 1971 promoting *Kiln House*, Spencer stepped out of the hotel in Los Angeles and never returned. The band located him a few days later, a freshly anointed member of the Children of God religious sect, who announced he had no intention of returning to the group or the sinful world of rock and roll (incredibly, fifty-plus years later, he is still a member), and Fleetwood Mac, act 3, was over. The group had several weeks of concert dates already booked and faced possible financial ruin if they were cancelled (Spencer's on-stage presence and importance had increased significantly with Peter Green's departure), so manager Clifford Davis put in a long-distance phone call to plead with Green to hop on a plane and save his former band's hide. Decent fellow that he was, if increasingly musically directionless and mentally unbalanced, Green agreed to help out, but only if, instead of its usual set list, the band simply jammed for the couple of hours it was contracted to be on stage.

Unfortunately, Green's desire to jam wasn't always matched by his capacity to move beyond the locked-in limits of the blues or bluesy rock, and Danny's passion was for well-structured songs, not free-form jamming. Worse, Danny, if still uncomfortable in his role as lead Mac (live, his murmured onstage announcements often sound like apologies), apparently resented his former mentor's reappearance. Green's friend, conga player Nigel Watson, who Green had insisted also be part of the short-lived band, recalled, "Once they got into the tour, Peter began to take the leading role for the whole gig, which annoyed Danny Kirwan, who felt overshadowed." Fathers: can't live with 'em, can't live without 'em.

Returning home, the group embarked upon act 4 by hiring American Bob Welch as Spencer's replacement. The band members' various comings and goings were enough for their record label to feel compelled to include a rundown of who was out and who was in on the back cover of their next LP, *Future Games*. Welch's first impressions of Danny were to prove regrettably prescient. Danny, he said, was

> a nice kid, but a little bit paranoid, a little bit disturbed. I would go up to his room and really try to work with him, to be open with him, but he would always take things I said wrongly. I thought it was just me, but as I got to know the rest of the band, they'd say, 'Oh yes, Danny, a little... strange.' He'd play something, and I'd say, 'That's kinda nice,' and he'd say, 'KIND OF NICE? YOU MEAN YOU DON'T LIKE IT?' He would take offence for *no* reason.

The move to add Welch to the band made sense, in a way. A journeyman musician who played dependable guitar and was an okay singer and a prolific writer, he also seemed unlikely to quit the band for religious reasons any time soon, which the group had been having a little trouble with lately. But something was undeniably lost with Spencer's exit. There is no question that, compared to Welch, Spencer was a limited musician and songwriter, and Welch's across-the-board competence insured that the band was rarely ever less than professional. But the loss of Spencer's fiery slide playing and raunchy rock-and-roll irreverence and deep connection to the group's hard-core blues beginnings nudged Fleetwood Mac toward a less interesting brand of mainstream rock. Everything comes with a price, even professionalism.

Future Games leads off with Danny's billowy, mainly acoustic "Woman of a Thousand Years" (the sole percussion is provided by Fleetwood tapping a wooden block or banging on a bongo), which is about as far from the rock-and-roll mainstream circa 1971 as you can get. Although there's a woman in the title, the song is not of the typical "she loves me/she loves me not" variety, and Danny comes up with some of his best, most evocative—and atypical—lyrics. Like Robert Hunter or Gene Clark or Bob Dylan, this time Danny forgoes his customary straightforward lyrical method and instead uses words like a visual artist employs colour, not worried about literal meaning so much as finding the right lyrical tone and texture and feel. It is also more than seven minutes long and sounds like a forgotten, foggy dream, definitely not your typical LP leadoff track.

Record labels at this time had not yet entirely figured out that selling rock-and-roll music is no different from selling anything else—find out what people want and then give it to them until they want something else, then give them that—and they were still allowing musicians to be artists and their albums to be art. It would not be long before they would insist that something like Christine McVie's "Morning Rain," which appears next, be front and center as track number one. It is a charging, piano-driven track that emphasizes what McVie does best: well-structured, catchy love songs (Danny also contributes some snarling wah-wah). There are usually a couple of them on every subsequent Fleetwood Mac album, most of which are never less than pleasant and some of which are better than others and some of which, like later gems "You Make Loving Fun" and "Over My Head," are great.

"What a Shame" is appropriately titled. An instrumental, cowritten by the entire band, it is an abrasive, honking mess (the saxophone duties are handled by Christine McVie's brother), reportedly recorded because Reprise, the band's label, rejected the seven-song version of the album the group submitted and demanded that they go back into the studio and cut another tune. One can only hope that it was intended to be what it sounds like: a four-minute *fuck you* to the grumpy grownups in charge.

New guy Welch gets his turn in the spotlight with the title tune, "Future Games," which closes side 1 and *strains* for hipness. It, too, is emblematic of its composer's strengths and weaknesses. Granted, the lyrics are pretty lousy—nothing sounds less like poetry than someone attempting to sound poetic—and everything is just a little too tidy and smooth, but Welch does have an undeniable way with a melody, and the occasional jazziness of his guitar is a nice bright addition to the band's musical palette. "Future Games" wouldn't have sounded out of place on dawn-of-the-decade, late-night FM radio, right between a long number off Yes' debut album and the new Moody Blues single.

Side-2 opener "Sands of Time" is quintessential Danny, nervous nirvana with an emboldening, ascending chorus and nearly eight minutes of his captivatingly jittery guitar (which is wonderfully complemented by McVie's throbbing, blobby bass). I have no idea what it's about, which is one of the reasons why it's such a wonderful tune, Danny again wisely eschewing words depicting romantic woes and wows in favour of nonrepresentational images and enigmatic asides. It doesn't matter what it's about—you know what it *feels* like. It feels like the sound of time running out of time. It feels like the centuries collapsing into one another and turning, for a moment, into eternity.

"Sometimes," written in the then-fashionable country-rock mould, is another Danny song that helps give *Future Games* its agreeably mellow consistency ("What a Shame" and Welch's other offering, the pallid R&B number "Lay It All Down," excepted). "Sometimes" might have a bit of twang to it—and lyrically, is a little too reminiscent of "Jewel Eyed Judy" from the previous LP—but with its yearning lead vocal and charming *la de dah* background vocals and its irresistible chorus performed in a piercing falsetto, it is still unmistakably a Danny Kirwan song; just as album closer "Show Me a Smile" is archetypal Christine McVie: sweet but not syrupy, it is unquestionably lightweight, but contributes to the record's low-key appeal.

The same band was back for 1972's *Bare Trees*. Since the release of *Future Games*, Danny married his girlfriend, Claire Morris, who soon after gave birth to a son, Dominic. When not enduring the strain of touring—always an ordeal for the perpetually anxious, physically frail Danny—he seems to have spent much of his time writing, demoing new songs, drinking too much, and alienating his bandmates. Danny was head of the Mac family now, and his skinny shoulders were sagging under the weight. "Liberty means responsibility," George Bernard Shaw wrote in *Man and Superman*. "That is why most men dread it." Or silently resent it. By this point, Mick Fleetwood recalled, Danny "was a walking time bomb.... It was a major event to ask him for a cigarette."

Like all of the Mac's albums with him on board, *Bare Trees* contains the good, the not-so-good, and the great. Christine McVie's two numbers fall under the first category: "Homeward Bound" (uninspired title notwithstanding) is a solid soft-rocker and "Spare Me a Little of Your Love" sounds like Carole King meets Aretha Franklin, and that's not a bad thing. Welch is responsible for the album's nadir, but also one of its highlights. "The Ghost" is dominated by an annoying flute and is the kind of paint-by-numbers pop that Welch could seemingly crank out at will, which he did for much of his subsequent solo career. But give the man credit: for every hundred tunes like "The Ghost," he also managed to create some first-rate pop-craft, and here it is "Sentimental Lady." He later cut a glossier version of the tune as a solo artist and scored a top-ten hit with it, but the version recorded for *Bare Trees* is superior. It still has the same scrumptious chorus and the long-lingering main melody, but it is rooted in crackling acoustic guitars and McVie's atmospheric electric-keyboard and organ work and doesn't overdo the background vocals. Anyone who cannot enjoy "Sentimental Lady" is either hearing impaired or a pop-hating pedant.

Danny contributes five songs to *Bare Trees*, three more than either Welch or McVie. In spite of the stresses of touring and the increased drinking (compounded by the emaciated musician's disinclination to eat), Danny was always writing new songs, right up until he stopped composing entirely and devoted himself full-time to alcohol and forgetting. Leadoff track "Child of Mine" is a typically tight, chugging rocker, with pledge-of-commitment words addressed to his infant son (he avows never to leave him, like his own father did—a promise, unfortunately, that Danny couldn't keep), but whose lyrically incongruous chorus, with its corny exhortation to *K-k-k-keep that soul beat rockin'*, comes across as commercially contrived as anything Welch ever wrote. Maybe Danny and the rest of the band were feeling the pressure from their label to come up with something for the radio. If so, this wasn't it.

Danny quickly recovers with "Sunny Side of Heaven," another stunning instrumental that, if it was not so gorgeous, might seem trifling, but which is sanctified by its soothing melody and the crashing chord changes in the chorus. The title track is also a Danny number. Like "Child of Mine," it is impossible to dismiss entirely because of the propulsive electric guitars—and the staccato chorus illustrates just how much effort and invention went into even lesser Kirwan songs—but it seems a little too eager to please. When artists try to ingratiate, they usually just grate.

The rumbling, raging, electric squall produced by Danny's wah-wah pedal at the outset of "Danny's Chant" is the antithesis of ingratiating, is a gloriously offensive prelude to a lyricless but not voiceless, white noise–wrought melodic triumph. Yes, Danny is content to chant *nah nah nah nah nah nah nah nah nahs* instead of singing words that represent anything, but he was always a better music- and mood-maker than wordsmith; and the surging melody and committed instrumental performance from the entire band (Fleetwood is clearly having a ball attacking his cymbals on the catchy chorus) make it an odd, but oddly moving success. It would be an ideal choice for a hip soccer team's club anthem.

Although on the record McVie's "Spare Me a Little of Your Love" appears between "Danny's Chant" and "Dust," considering together the final two numbers Danny Kirwan recorded with Fleetwood Mac seems appropriate. As outlandishly urgent as "Danny's Chant" is, "Dust" is creakily introspective, the near-murmured musings on mortality carried along by one of Danny's most affecting melodies. The words were once again borrowed from an early twentieth-century British poet, this time the first two stanzas of Rupert Brooke's poem "Dust." The song's chorus, with its simple, repeated *When we are dust, When we are dust!* is desolation made musically enchanting. Along with "Dragonfly," it is a career highlight. They are the only two times Danny appropriated a poet's words for his own, and he should have done it more often. Robert Hunter's lyrics are a pivotal part of why Jerry Garcia's music is so good, and neither Billie Holiday nor Frank Sinatra wrote their own lyrics, either, with zero loss to their standing as musical artists.

"Dust" was Danny's final word with Fleetwood Mac. Although his work in the studio remained incontestably first-rate, Danny had become even more reliant on alcohol by this point, prone to tetchiness and tantrums, and "impossible to work with," according to Welch. "I'd say, 'Mick, he's become such a pain in the arse, the guy doesn't show up to rehearsals, he's embarrassing, he's paranoid, we've spent five hours dealing with him." The tension reached its boiling point while the band was on tour promoting *Bare Trees*. Mick Fleetwood:

> On that long tour in 1972 [Danny] was quite volatile and intent upon rubbing everyone the wrong way.... It all exploded one steamy night in August. For weeks Bob and Danny had been grating on each other. Bob would get mad and I'd have to put myself out to cover for Danny, who would simply withdraw into his own world.... That night there was a row over Bob getting his guitar in tune; it was something tiny, but it touched off a spark. Suddenly, Danny got up, went to the lavatory, and bashed his head on the wall. Five minutes to show time, and there's blood everywhere. Danny then grabbed his precious Les Paul guitar and bashed it to bits in the lavatory.... Back in the dressing room he started throwing things. Outside the place was packed to the rafters with hundreds of kids. Danny yelled, "I'm not going on."

Drunkenness and violence and antisocial behaviour are not necessarily firing offences in the world of rock and roll; refusing to go on stage, on the other hand, and leaving your undermanned bandmates (Danny was the lead guitar player and sang a significant portion of the songs) to scuffle and suffer on their own, is. That night, back at the hotel, Danny was kicked out of the band. Adding to the misery of the moment, Fleetwood claimed that Danny had no inkling—absolutely none at all—that his behaviour had become such a problem. Which, in retrospect, is probably more troubling than the behaviour itself.

~

Danny was together enough to release three, successively less interesting, solo albums over the next seven years, the best, by far, being the first, 1975's *Second Chapter.* The title track, "Falling In Love with You," "Silver Streams," and, especially, "Cascades" are all cinches for inclusion on any sort of Danny Kirwan best-of. It is legitimate to wonder how he and his management (Clifford Davis, ex–Fleetwood Mac manager) managed to secure a record contract, given Danny's increasingly erratic personality. But Danny was, after all, the former lead-guitar-playing front man in a high-profile rock-and-roll band; plus, most of the songs he was writing now probably seemed ideal for the changing nature of radio. If, post–Peter Green, the move had been away from the blues and blues-rock towards rootsy rock and roll and mellifluous singer-songwriter material, post–Fleetwood Mac, the shift was from melodic rock and tasteful ballads toward soft rock and AM-radio ear candy. Other late-'60s/early-'70s rock-and-roll survivors made the transition to easy-listening success (old inspiration Paul McCartney had topped the charts in 1973 with the saccharine-and-strings "My Love"), so why not him? For Danny, though, the transition in musical styles was not solely about fitting in with changing market trends.

Danny had always been a musical Zelig. Not only did he possess an admirable openness toward different kinds of music, but also he was temperamentally an anxious, insecure individual, whose nebulous personality could easily accommodate a variety of musical masks. Discovered playing in a three-piece blues band à la Cream (the tastemakers of the time), the music he made in his early Fleetwood Mac days was predominantly the bluesy rock that main Mac Peter Green was gravitating toward (he even indulged Green's increasing predilection for jamming, never one of Danny's passions or strengths). Post-Green, the albums *Kiln House, Future Games,* and *Bare Trees,* plus the "Dragonfly" b/w "The Purple Dancer" single, all testify to Danny's ability to craft exquisite guitar-based instrumentals ("Earl Gray," "Sunny Side of Heaven"), tough rockers ("Jewel Eyed Judy", "Bare Trees"), moody musical tone-poems ("Woman of a Thousand Years" and "Sands of Time"), folk-rock ("Dust"), country-rock ("Sometimes"), and even soothing psychedelia ("Dragonfly"). Soft rock, which became one of the biggest-selling genres in contemporary music by the mid-'70s, was what radio and record buyers increasingly wanted, and Danny easily obliged. It was also probably where some of his deepest musical roots lay: the early twentieth-century hit-parade music he discovered by way of his mother's record collection, which bear many of the same compositional elements—simple love songs with strong melodies and lush production touches—of Danny's post–Fleetwood Mac career.

Second Chapter was released three years after *Bare Trees,* the last time the public had heard any new Danny Kirwan music. Three years between releases in the context of the popular music industry of the 1960s and '70s was a long time. Only a few years earlier, Creedence Clearwater Revival had released three albums—*Creedence Clearwater Revival, Bayou Country*, and *Green River*—in 1969 alone. Always a prolific writer (several excellent Fleetwood Mac numbers, such as "Like It Like That" and "Open the Door," were performed live but never recorded in the studio), there were twelve fresh tunes on Danny's solo debut. An ex–Chicken Shack bass player and a few other second-tier veterans of various British blues-rock outfits filled out the band Danny took into the studio, and veteran engineer Martin Rushent (who had engineered Fleetwood Mac's *Future Games*) handled the production duties.

The second chapter of Danny's career begins with "Ram Jam City," kick-up-your-heels Celtic rock with a fiddle and clippity-clop percussion and, of course, a catchy chorus. The Ram Jam Club was a popular Brixton music venue back in the long-gone days of the late 1960s, when everyone was young and music and getting laid were all that mattered, and seeing the sun come up was as common as believing that music and getting laid were all that would ever matter. It's a knees-up, anomalous opener to an album dominated by gentle, antediluvian love songs. It is also one of the few tunes on the LP not embellished by strings or horns. "Odds and Ends" doesn't feature any violins, but it does have a tuba and a clarinet solo. It evokes flat caps and bowler hats and bobbed-hair flappers and innocent romantic uncertainties. It is all so resolutely cheery, both musically and word-wise, it's almost disconcerting, as if Danny is trying to sing himself into a different world, one much simpler, safer, and easier to comprehend. "Hot Summer Day" has much the same effect, the swelling strings only emphasizing its anachronistic nature, although buried underneath is a memorable tune imbued with that characteristic Danny Kirwan melancholic tug. The remaining songs on side 1—"Mary Jane," "Skip a Dee Doo," and "Love Can Always Bring You Happiness"—are as insipid as their titles. Each one is so wispy-wimpy, at times Danny sounds like Gilbert O'Sullivan at his bijou feeblest. It is as though Danny, only in his mid-twenties, was regressing all the way back to the simple pop tunes of his mother's youth, succumbing to the moon-in-June-with-a-melody allure of all those flimsy but fun old favourites buried in the grooves of her revered record collection.

Side 2 opens with the title track, which is *very* Beatlesque and snugly soulful and has lyrics that, if still of the predictable lovelorn variety, at least don't sound as if they were made up on the spot. The track is best heard, though, on the *Ram Jam City* compilation that appeared on the small Mooncrest Records label in 2000, which excises the violins and the saxophone and does a good job overall of decluttering most of *Second Chapter*'s best cuts. The violins almost work with "Lovely Days," supporting rather than smothering a very pretty melody. "Falling In Love with You" is the only time on the album Danny rocks out, his twangy electric guitar at the forefront of the mix for a change; it sounds like a hot hybrid of *Everybody Knows This Is Nowhere*–era Crazy Horse and early Grin, and one only wishes that there was more of it. "Silver Streams" almost transcends the clichéd lyrics and 101 Strings (and flute and French horn), because of the unforgettable melody and the inventive guitar sounds Danny cajoles from his instrument, another Danny Kirwan songwriting characteristic unfortunately lacking throughout much of his solo career. *Second Chapter* wraps up with "Cascades," which might be the LP's highpoint. Almost entirely acoustic (once again, the string-scoured version on *Ram Jam City* is the one to hear), sorrowful yet somehow still emboldening, it has a surging chorus and lyrics that don't rely on easy rhymes and hackneyed romantic sentiments. *Second Chapter* was released the same year that his old band brought out their first offering with Lindsey Buckingham and Stevie Nicks on board, *Fleetwood Mac*. Guess which one sold better? (The band's follow-up, 1977's *Rumours*, didn't do too badly in the marketplace, either.)

Instead of putting a band together and promoting his new LP, Danny drank a lot, separated from his wife, and did what he said he would never do, in his song "Child of Mine": absent himself from his young son's life. Which probably induced him to drink even more. *Midnight in San Juan* (1976) and the abominably titled *Hello There Big Boy!* (1979) followed *Second Chapter*, and if you listen hard enough, Danny's still in there somewhere (the vulnerable voice, the tasteful guitar, the glorious gloom), but it is all so slight—the paint-by-number lyrics, the frequently listless playing, the unimaginative production (provided this time by manager Clifford Davis). The absence of a genuine creative partnership in the studio is one of the reasons why Danny's solo albums were not what they could have been. The musicians were all hired hands, not artistically invested band members, and his manager, the guy who handled the bills and talked to the lawyers, was not necessarily the best counsel for musical decisions. This, regrettably, is what happens to people who don't play well with others. Danny was solo, now, in more ways than one.

Concluding that what was needed was not better tunes or different players (more British blues-rock and rock-and-roll journeymen) but, instead, the whir of a primitive synthesizer running through several numbers, the *Midnight in San Juan* and *Hello There Big Boy!* brain trust also added big background vocals to the mix, in an attempt to prop up a couple of less-than-compelling collections of songs. *Midnight in San Juan* features two instrumentals, previously a Danny Kirwan trademark. But instead of Danny's guitar setting the tone, it is a sirening synthesizer that provides the principal coloration. "Midnight in San Juan," for example, sounds like a mid-'70s TV cop show theme song. Danny doesn't even play lead guitar on two cuts ("Gettin' the Feelin'" and "You"). It's like going to dinner at the home of a world-class chef and ordering out for pizza.

Danny's final two solo albums contain fewer and fewer original compositions and more and more covers. The two best cuts on *Midnight in San Juan,* in fact, are "Look Around You," which was written by another latterly dismissed Mac, Dave Walker, and an unexpectedly unfussy, reggaefied version of the Beatles' "Let It Be." *Hello There Big Boy!* contains only five Danny originals (one of which, "Only You," is a ten-year-old, unrecorded Fleetwood Mac number that replaces Danny's searing guitar with rooty-toot horns, and another, "Caroline," was cowritten with manager/producer Clifford Davis). Most of the other songs were provided by the various musicians who played on the record, who probably had visions of fat royalty checks dancing in their heads. If so, they were surely disappointed, because none of Danny's three solo LPs were heard by many people. It didn't help that he continued to refuse to go on the road to publicize his new material and appeared content to get by on the occasional small Fleetwood Mac royalty payment and, eventually, social assistance checks.

It is believed that, after spending several years hibernating in a basement-apartment hidey-hole and enduring a spell of homelessness, Danny eventually ended up in a London men's shelter, where he self-medicated away the days with endless cans of ale and didn't like to talk about the past. The only interviews he did over the last forty or so years of his life are two very brief ones he agreed to do in 1993 (for the *Evening Standard* and the *Independent*) and the aforementioned interview with Celmins in the July 1997 edition of *Guitar Magazine* ("A Rare Encounter with Danny Kirwan"); after coming across Danny sitting on a Covent Garden bench one day in 1992, Celmins kept in contact and developed enough of a relationship with the ordinarily reclusive ex-Mac to get him to agree to a short interview.

Danny, Celmins writes, "was happy to do this interview in his room at the hostel in South London although fatigue set in quickly as the number of empty [beer] cans built up." When Celmins asks the now forty-seven-year-old Kirwan what it was like to join Fleetwood Mac at eighteen, Danny answers, as if still slightly stunned by his meteoric ascension to rock-star status, that it was as if one minute he was just standing around, and then the next there were television cameras everywhere. "Nowadays," Celmins adds, "he rarely touches a guitar." If the teenaged Danny had not departed his mother's basement apartment in Brixton for Fleetwood

Mac fame and fortune, he might not have ended up in a London men's hostel. He also probably would not have written and recorded all of the wonderful music by which he's remembered and revered today.

There were other occasional sightings, as when Mick Fleetwood tracked down Danny's phone number in 1979, when the mega-massive Fleetwood Mac stopped in London while touring the world behind its new album, *Tusk* (the same year that Danny's forgettable last LP, *Hello There Big Boy!*, was also released). Fleetwood: "In due course he showed up at the hotel... looking grubby and very unwashed. It was heartbreaking. He'd lived with us at Benifols [where *Kiln House* was recorded], the kids loved him, and he'd been a good looking chap. Now he looked derelict. He told us he had worms, and that he'd slept on a park bench the night before." When Danny declined Fleetwood's invitation to accompany him to the band's sold-out gig at Wembley Stadium, "I tried to give him a hug," Fleetwood remembered. "'No', he said. 'Don't do that. I don't want to be touched.' I got on the bus and never saw him again."

Danny stopped writing and making music around the same time that the sessions for his final solo album wrapped up in 1979. Although he was divorced and didn't see his son often, his ex-wife would look in on him from time to time, and there was still the occasional get-together. In the early 2000s, Jeremy Spencer, who hadn't had any contact with Danny since 1978, saw him again "when my wife and I met him, his ex-wife Claire, and their son Dominic for lunch in London. It was pleasant enough, even though he was in his own world."

The last forty years of Danny's life were mostly spent in his own world, which usually meant drinking on a park bench or in one of the many small furnished rooms he inhabited or in the pub. Pubs are important to the British, so important that George Orwell wrote an essay ("The Moon Under Water") describing his perfect public house. As noted, there are no extant interviews with Danny captured on tape, but there is a very short (1:45), very moving video that someone posted to YouTube, which utilizes stop-action technology and a few photographs taken of Danny in a pub to create the illusion that we're witnessing a typically timid-looking, pint-sipping, grinning and grimacing Danny, drinking the heart out of just one more useless, dirty London afternoon. His straw-coloured hair is thinning a little on top but is long in the back, and there are dark rings under his watery eyes. He has a three-day shadow (shocking, considering how baby-faced he appeared in his musical prime) and is wearing a shabby, old brown suit jacket. Danny's public house of choice looks to be far from perfect—there are dusty potted plants on the windowsill, and you just know that the tables are slightly sticky and smell like spilt beer, and the bathroom probably reeks of urine—and Danny fits right in among the other decaying alcoholics and assorted barflies and ordinary day drinkers. When, just as he's leaving the pub, the animation makes it appear as if Danny is shyly smiling goodbye to the viewer, the cavernous crow's feet around his eyes and mouth, formerly unimaginable, are deep and earned and wrong.

Bob Brunning wrote in *Fleetwood Mac: Behind the Masks* of the last time that he saw Danny, twenty-nine years before his death from pneumonia in 2018, aged sixty-eight:

Wanting to interview him for my book in 1989, I tracked him down to the St Mango Community Hostel for the homeless in London's Soho. I wrote to him in advance, and checked with the warden that my visit would not be uncomfortable for him, or embarrass him. He shuffled out of his room, still slim, but puffy-cheeked and highly agitated. He couldn't talk to me coherently. He simply patted his stomach, continually repeating, "Can't help you, Bob, too much stress, you know, too much stress." Our encounter lasted about a minute.

I wonder if he had his mother's old records in his room.

NICK DRAKE

Sweet bird that shunn'st the noise of folly,
Most musical, most melancholy!
–Milton

Make no mistake: Nick Drake is famous. His songs appear in major motion pictures. His music is widely available, particularly for an artist who released only three exceptionally poor-selling LPs in his lifetime. His name is on the lips of anyone who considers themself culturally cool. He is the John Keats of contemporary popular music: brilliant, ignored, and dead at twenty-six virtually unknown and underappreciated. That he both believed himself entitled to widespread recognition and respect, and yet was partly responsible for the overwhelming absence of either of these things, is equally undeniable—as is the depression that shadowed and eventually swallowed him. That is the tragedy of Nick Drake; the triumph is his music.

His parents were quintessential early twentieth-century British colonials who met and married abroad. His father worked for the Bombay Burmah Trading Corporation, while his mother's father was an English employee of the Indian civil service. Nick was born in 1948 in Rangoon (his only sibling, a sister, Gabrielle, arrived four years earlier), just before the young Drake family returned to England, where his father secured a position in the private sector with a large engineering firm. Before long, the Drakes were ensconced in a suitably upscale house in leafy, secluded Far Leys, just outside Birmingham. "House" is a relative term—the Drake estate comprised acres of untouched English countryside, and the house itself was large enough that it was necessary to employ a full-time servant. Nick's sister has claimed that theirs was an idyllic childhood and that their mother and father, while of another time, were devoted parents as well as interesting, vibrant individuals.

Like many wives of successful men at this time, Nick's mother was the family's civilizing overseer, and she played the piano, led the family in singalongs, and even composed her own songs. It is old news that most art is produced by the sons and daughters of the middle class—the greatest gift a neophyte artist can receive is lots and lots of free time to explore, to emulate, to idle, to obsess—and the Drakes were extremely generous benefactors (Gabrielle became a well-known stage, television, and film actor). His mother's ubiquitous song-making made Nick's earliest attempts at composition natural and normal. Nick's sister told biographer Richard Morton Jack (*Nick Drake: The Life*) that "Nick was composing songs at a very early age. When he was three or four, two of his great passions were cowboys and food. I can remember two songs he wrote then—one was about a cowboy in a book called *Cowboy Small*. 'Oh Cowboy Small, Oh Cowboy Small/All the other cowboys call Cowboy Small.' The other was about celery and tomatoes." Nick understood early that, whether it's cowboys and celery or the black dog of depression, you write about what you know.

Nick's high school friends—naturally, he attended the same exclusive institution, Marlborough College, as his father and grandfather before him—remember a tall, thin, quiet, but well-liked young man more interested in solo sports, like running, than team sports such as soccer or rugby. Nick's long silences and passivity (in relation to everything but music) didn't begin with his latter-day depression, but were already evident in high school. Classmate Andy Murison remembered Nick as "bright, but he had an ethereal, distracted air. Other than his enjoyment of music, he showed no evidence of energy at all. I don't think he ever started a conversation." Another high school friend, Mick Way, described Nick as "a taciturn, reserved chap, friendly enough, but [who] always kept something back, so he wasn't easy to get close to."

While at Marlborough, Nick played the piano, saxophone, and guitar, and his musical tastes extended beyond the obligatory Dylan and Donovan fixations to include plenty of classical, jazz, blues, and homegrown, highly individual acoustic pickers like the nonstandard-tuning, string-snapping, acoustic-guitar genius Bert Jansch. Nick could usually be found practicing his instruments instead of studying. Some people thrive on freedom's open seas; others drift or drown. Nick kept his feet dry and practiced a lot and listened to a lot of records.

Which is likely why his high school academic record was poor enough that he needed extra, expensive cramming to sneak into Cambridge's Fitzwilliam College, one of the antique university's newer, less exclusive enclaves. Upon his acceptance, the college expressed concern about Nick's poor showing in French, and Nick's father promptly wrote back to the academic authorities to assure them that his son would be attending the Université de Provence Aix-Marseille for six months—where Nick, joined by a couple of friends who were also fortunate enough to have parents willing to cover the cost, spent virtually no time attending lectures or studying and a lot of time smoking hash, taking his first acid trip, and playing guitar. When he returned to England he went down to Cambridge, and, as before, the self-styled curriculum was light on reading and writing and attending lectures and heavy on weed and wine and practicing the guitar and soaking up the supernal sounds of 1967.

Nick played the acoustic guitar almost exclusively at this point, and though *Songs of Leonard Cohen*, *Fred Neil*, *Tim Hardin 2*, and Tim Buckley's *Goodbye and Hello* were just the sort of literate, melancholic, classical- and jazz-tinged folk music he himself would eventually record, no one as musically attuned as Nick could have been uninspired by the more-electric side of the musical revolution of that celebrated year, which saw the release of, among other seminal LPs, *Sgt. Pepper's Lonely Hearts Club Band*, *Are You Experienced?*, *Axis: Bold as Love*, *Days of Future Passed*, *Sunshine Superman*, *The Pipers at the Gates of Dawn*, *The Notorious Byrd Brothers*, *Disraeli Gears*, *The Velvet Underground and Nico*, *The Doors*, *Moby Grape*, *Freak Out!*, *Surrealistic Pillow*, and *Mr Fantasy*. Ostensibly studying English literature while at Cambridge, Nick might have been familiar with Wordsworth's famous lines from *The Prelude,* "Bliss was it in that dawn to be alive,/But to be young was very heaven!"

Cambridge friend Iain Dunn recalled a Nick who "was very conscious of the way he looked. How he appeared to other people was all part of that . . . slight image-building that was going on. The velvet jacket, the Cuban-heel boots." And even much later, during his long, final depression, when he was disinclined to bathe or cut his fingernails, contact lenses—which, according to his sister in *Nick Drake: Remembered for a While,* his father bought for him because Nick had a "phobia about wearing glasses." This "image-building," according to Dunn, was not relegated to the clothes and shoes he wore:

> He was very nice. Incredibly nice. But quite . . . I think "detached" is probably the word. Not remote. . . . I wasn't quite sure if this was a conscious image that he was developing, or whether it was just the way he was. And I think in the end, I came to the conclusion that it was a bit of both. I think he quite liked the idea of there being an air of mystique about himself. But I think he was also genuinely, incredibly shy, and found himself to be quite remote from other people.

Somehow Nick got himself invited, along with several others—including both professionals, like Fairport Convention, and unknown amateurs, like himself, most of whom are long forgotten—to participate in a nearly week-long concert benefit at London's prestigious Roadhouse (Joe Boyd, Nick's producer, believes it was anti–Vietnam War in nature). Ashley Hutchings, Fairport Convention's bass player, spotted the unknown singer-songwriter, introduced himself, and secured Nick's phone number and, according to Boyd, in his memoir *White Bicycles: Making Music in the 1960s*, "Ashley handed me his phone number, saying, 'You ought to call this guy, he's pretty interesting.'" When someone says an artist or a work of art is "interesting," it usually means one of two things: either the person or object is so insignificant or incomprehensible that it is a handy, mollifying euphemism, or it is used to signify that the individual or piece of art really is not like anybody or anything else. Boyd could tell which kind of "interesting" Hutchings meant. After getting in touch with Nick and listening to the brief demo tape he had put together (in the small music room of the parental home at Far Leys), Boyd offered Nick the full package: not only a chance to record an LP for Fairport's own label, Island, but also the opportunity to sign managerial and publishing contracts with Boyd's recently formed company, Witchseason. If writing weekly essays for his tutors on *The Canterbury Tales* and *Piers Plowman* wasn't particularly appealing before, now, the fall of 1968, it seemed entirely pointless. Nick was going to be a star.

~

Although he would not officially withdraw from university until the fall of 1969 (disappointing his mother and enraging his father), much of Nick's energy over the next year was consumed with commuting back and forth between Cambridge and London to record his first album, *Five Leaves Left*. In the late '60s, twelve months was an unusually long time to spend recording an album and preparing it for release, but because Nick had no band, sympathetic players had to be found and complementary arrangements needed to be worked out. Strings were in—Boyd acknowledges in *White Bicycles* that John Simon's use of strings on *Songs of Leonard Cohen* was his model—and Richard Hewson, who had scored the orchestral arrangement of Mary Hopkin's recent worldwide smash, "Those Were the Days," was brought on board. Nick made his increasingly uneasy feelings about Hewson's bland, middlebrow arranging known, and eventually his Cambridge friend Robert Kirby would get the nod to write the bulk of the string arrangements.

That Nick's songs sound best unembellished, and certainly without the cinematic sweep of violins or the moribund bubbling of cellos, is clear from listening to *Five Leaves Left*'s opening track, "Time Has Told Me." Anchored, as most of the album's songs are, in the warm, woody sound of Nick's deftly plucked acoustic guitar and his consistently quirky chord changes (Nick rarely merely *strums*), the only accompaniment it requires is Danny Thompson's supple bass, the occasional twang of Island labelmate Richard Thompson's tasty electric guitar, and Paul Harris' sparse piano. It's English folk-rock, essentially—meaning there isn't any rock, only mid-tempo rolling—the perfect platform for most of Nick's songs, which never raise their voice, let alone get up and do the boogaloo.

Nick is no two-chord folkie, though; even a song as straightforward as this has its jazzy wrinkle. When Nick sings of leaving behind the things that aren't who he really is, the notes ascend and almost allow him release before inevitably falling back into minor-chord murk and a more measured rhythm. This austere yet rich sound echoes the song's deceptively simple lyrics, which employ nature imagery and contemplation of the changing seasons in place of evoking other people or noteworthy experiences or events. Especially in his later work, his lyrics are often minimal to the point of near-incomprehensiblity, relying less on linearity and logic and more on association and repetition. Song lyrics are not poems, and Nick's are no more amenable to being read as such (in spite of the occasional misguided academic attempt to do so). But once they are allied to sympathetic sounds, and the responsibility for keeping them moving and grooving is left to the music, the Blakean simplicity of Nick's words cannot but impress. He may not have graduated, but he did study English literature at Cambridge University.

Nick's voice, whether singing the words to "Time Has Told Me" or any of *Five Leaves Left*'s ten tracks, is English bone china–fragile and barely-there breathy; it is also unhurried and almost conversational, as opposed to the usual declamatory manner of most performers (even holding on to his British, patrician accent, at a time when most English performers—Ray Davis and a few others excepted—sang "accent-less"—that is, like Americans). There is a perspicacious patience to Nick's vocal delivery, a purposeful plainness, that seems to imply that he knows—even if the listener does not—that he is speaking of life's most important things, and that a subject as weighty and elusive as this is too important to risk getting mired in the artificiality of artiness. Nick never raises his voice; his expert phrasing means he doesn't have to.

If "Time Has Told Me" is wearily stoical, "River Man" is a metaphysical whodunit (or is it who-is-it?), the river man of the song's title either a reclusive wise man, a metaphor for death, or some especially good pot. That Nick was a heavy cannabis user is suggested by the title of his first album—it refers to the warning label inside a pack of Rizla rolling papers, most dope smokers' skin of choice at the time. Whatever the words of "River Man" mean to you, its drifting, misty music ensures that you're right. It is the one instance on *Five Leaves Left* when the orchestration (buttressed by Nick's always interesting guitar playing) works unequivocally well (it is also the only piece not arranged by Robert Kirby; veteran arranger Harry Robinson supplied the restrained string charts). It's a gently spooky sound, and one ideally suited for the story of the wayward, enigmatic Betty and her endless, gloomy searching. With "Three Hours," it's back to Nick and his fluttering, Spanish-style fingerpicking, and another moody, wonderfully opaque piece of songcraft. If the words confuse you, sing them—then they'll make sense. "Way to Blue" is an attractive piece of alternating minor/major-chord soul-searching (Nick's chording, metaphorically speaking, often lets the sun peek in, only to always, eventually, pull the drapes closed), but the heavy-handed strings sound like something from a BBC World War II documentary. "Day Is Done" suffers from the same sort of ornate arrangement, but the song is so good—so characteristically Nick Drakian good—it almost doesn't matter. That Nick could compose a song about the entropy of existence while still a teenager is beyond precocious; that it manages to avoid self-pity and achieve a bruised universality is remarkable. Feeling sorry for yourself doesn't equal art; compelling the listener to experience—to confront, even to embrace—the fragility of life, does. "'Cello Song" is dominated by the instrument invoked in its title (played by Clare Lowther), and the effect is occasionally ominous, but never overblown. Nick fingerpicks a pleasant pattern on his guitar, the bass and congas keep it lively, and when Nick hums along with the Middle Eastern–tinged cello lines during the song's fadeout, it has the effect of a full orchestra.

The less-is-more aesthetic has disappeared again by the time we get to "The Thoughts of Mary Jane," however, one of the prettiest melodies Nick ever came up with. Another tale of another lost, nomadic soul (or about the pleasantly disorientating effects of marijuana—it really doesn't matter which), the overall effect—soothing mystification—is like that of a lot of Nick's work: intriguingly anomalous. Unfortunately, the LP version is burdened by not only a morass of strings, but a persistent flute, which aims for ethereality but manages only to sound frothy. The outtake available on the posthumous *Time of No Reply* compilation, featuring just Nick's acoustic guitar and Richard Thompson's restive electric, is the one to listen to. Nick's atypical chord changes and muted vocals and wistful words are plenty precious enough—they don't require the pasted-on solemnity of violins or the manufactured jollity of flutes. "Man in a Shed" is a jaunty (for Nick), jazzy little tune with fun (but, being Nick, far from frivolous) lyrics about one more dreamy recluse spending his days hiding away from what the rest of us call reality. Aided only by bass and piano, its simplicity and surprising geniality are a refreshing change of pace (in an era when LPs were carefully structured entities and not just collections of songs to be streamed or downloaded).

"Fruit Tree" is another shrewd mini-disquisition on worldly weariness and the vicissitudes of fame, but again, the strings smother when they should simply support, the overall effect twee instead of tragic. Concluding track "Saturday Sun" is the only time on *Five Leaves Left* that Nick plays piano, and his unhurried, jazzy tinkling is an ideal vehicle for his archetypal take on happiness' heartbreaking but inescapable ephemerality. For every Saturday night, there is always a Sunday morning waiting in the wings, ready to transform Saturday's amiable sun into Sunday's cold rain. Other than Nick on piano and Danny Thompson's breathy bass and some rudimentary percussion, the main instrumental colouring comes from the overdubbed vibraphone, courtesy of Tristan Fry, and it works wonderfully, the after-hours, feet-up-and-tie-undone-for-the-day feel of the tune made manifest in the paradoxically iridescent but discernibly fatigued and hungover tones of Fry's instrument. It is Joe Boyd's most impressive moment as *Five Leaves Left*'s producer, and more of this sort of jazzy accompaniment would have served the songs well. As would the inclusion of the session outtake "Time of No Reply," another song about fame's capricious nature, which is superior to several songs on the LP; perhaps Boyd or Nick thought that two songs with "time" in the title would be one too many.

Five Leaves Left appeared in the fall of 1969, when it was time for Nick to hit the road and make some converts. Except that he didn't. He managed a brief, three-song BBC radio session and several shows opening up for labelmates Fairport Convention (who were supporting their own new album, the superb, Joe Boyd–produced *Unhalfbricking*), but it was quickly apparent that Nick was *not* a natural performer. Which, given his lack of gigging experience and inherent introversion and reserve, should not have been surprising. Playing in a studio, which Nick had no trouble doing, you're performing for yourself and posterity. Playing for university friends while everyone sits around passing the pipe or in front of a classy concert crowd, like at the Royal Festival Hall, where audience etiquette tends to ensure patience, politeness, and a minimum of yahooness, Nick was okay, if a little uneasy, and never one to "work the crowd." Plopped down on a plywood pub stage in front of fifty-or-so beer-guzzling, chain-smoking, chat-chat-chatting people, however, many of whom had never heard of Nick or his music, but who were drawn out on a rainy autumn evening by the prospect of a long night of suds and singalong folk songs, he was lost. On the one hand, Nick's intense interiority help make his songs the depthful, melancholic delights they are; on the other, it also curtailed his ability to put those same delightful songs in other people's ears. "A man's character is his fate," Heraclitus wrote.

One attendee at an early gig recalled that Nick "didn't introduce any of [his songs]; he didn't say a word all evening. It was actually quite painful to watch." Speaking to biographer Trevor Dann (*Darker Than the Deepest Sea: The Search for Nick Drake*), singer-songwriter Ralph McTell, who made his living working the same folk-club circuit, recalled a gig Nick and he played together at Ewell Technical College: "Nick was monosyllabic.... He was very shy. He did the first set and something awful must have happened. He was doing his song, 'Fruit Tree,' and walked off halfway through it. Just left the stage." McTell did not see or hear what that "something awful" was, but it is safe to assume that it was nothing more than a noisy, indifferent audience or a misbehaving sound system. And how ironic that Nick packed it in during the performance of this particular song, which so eloquently laments how true fame is never achieved until the artist is dead in the ground.

Stage fright is one thing, but not bothering to show up for media spots and behaving as if the world owes you a listenership simply because your record is very good is another. Muff Winwood, who was Island's A&R manager when *Five Leaves Left* was released (and a former member of the hard-working Spencer Davis Group, who in its heyday lived in the clubs, and one of whose compilation albums was the self-explanatorily titled *Eight Gigs a Week*) remembers "waking Nick up at his grotty flat in Notting Hill. I had to make friends with the bloke downstairs to let me in. Nick used to stay up 'til six smoking dope and then my job was to get him out of his stinky bed." It didn't always work: "I lost count of the number of TV sessions and radio sessions we missed because he was so untogether. It was totally frustrating. He was a complete pain in the arse, drove me up the wall."

Reviews of *Five Leaves Left* were either ecstatic or nonexistent, and album sales were reportedly in the low single-digit thousands, but Island, to their considerable credit, wanted another album, and Joe Boyd was again tapped to produce it. This is as good a time as any to mention how much I admire the majority of Joe Boyd's production work—for his long labours with Fairport Convention alone, he (and engineer John Wood, whose name on the back of any LP always ensures a clean, crisp-sounding disc) should be awarded A1 musical-overseer status. But in making Nick's next album, 1970's *Bryter Layter*, it is as though much of Boyd's usually reliable sense of subtly and suitability temporarily abandoned him.

To begin with—*three* instrumentals? "Introduction" does possess a windy, wide-screen appeal, and all three contain a kernel of melodious interest—how could they not? Nick wrote them and employed his usual superlative fingerpicking—but the title track and album-closer "Sunday" are both sunk by the orchestral glop that Boyd and Kirby piled over them, as well as by the silly flute that periodically pokes its nose in. They sound like posh background music.

This time out Nick benefitted not only from Richard Thompson's subtle electric guitar (alas, only on the LP's second track, "Hazey Jane II"), but also from Thompson's fellow-Fairporters Simon Pegg on bass and Dave Mattacks on drums, and all three make for a great Nick Drake–as-folk-rocker backing group. "Hazey Jane II" is a brisk (for Nick), deceptively upbeat tune with lyrical lines that sometimes go on so long that Nick has to rush to get in all he has to say. Nick might only be strumming his acoustic on this one, but, being Nick, he keeps it fresh by throwing in a few unexpected vocal falsetto twists. It's not exactly radio friendly—which is what was probably hoped for—because Nick's furtive vocals and world-wary lyrics were not going to push any of the competition off the charts; but it is also more than a playful piece of eccentric pop craft, an indication that Nick did not have to stay stuck in morose folksinger mode all the time. He might not have been able to rock out, but it is clear that with the right musicians, he could have rolled along nicely, at least once in a while. Regrettably, the prominent, punchy horns that were added to the Fairport-plus-Nick basic track sound like they were lifted off a Tijuana Brass record.

"At the Chime of a City Clock" is urbanized Nick, the boy from the bucolic village, out on his own and using his sensitive antennae to illuminate London's big-city downs, but the yearning melody is compromised by the alto sax, which might have been added to bestow a bit of big-city feeling, but only succeeds in cheapening an otherwise lovely, understated track. If there had to be a saxophone—or a flute—why not from someone like Island labelmate Chris Wood, whose atmospheric smudges of sound bejewel so many wonderful Traffic tunes? "One of These Things First" is a pleasantly busy little think piece on the eternal theme of what-if, distinguished by the long note Nick holds when he sings of how "I could have been..." It only seems like filler because Nick is such a superlative songwriter. "Hazey Jane I" is a languidly lovely peek into the soul of another of Nick's tragically ambivalent outcasts who curse where they come from and feel like a relic of something long gone. The minimalist string arrangement isn't necessary, but as on the previous LP's "River Man," it doesn't detract either. The orchestral offence that is inflicted upon "Fly," however, is a crime against truth and beauty. A delicately sliding chord pattern is all that's necessary to endow Nick's measured ode to human limitation and insignificance with all the tonal swathing it requires, but that does not stop its disastrous interment in strings and cello. Skip the *Bryter Layter* version and go directly to the demo included on *Time of No Reply*. "Poor Boy" is the nadir of Nick's recording career, a snappy, cocktail-jazz rumination on the poor boy (Nick?) who can't stop feeling sorry for himself. The Holiday Inn–lounge saxophone is back again, and although I'm sure they were intended to be self-mockingly ironic, the two female background singers who occasionally shriek the chorus are about as welcome as a mariachi band at a funeral.

Then there is "Northern Sky," one of Nick's most beguiling compositions. His darker stuff, like much of the material to follow on the next album, *Pink Moon*, is undeniably beautiful, but "Northern Sky" is nothing less than euphoria made manifest in song. The subject—sudden entrancement, illumination, beatitude, whatever term you choose to use—is blissfully echoed in guest John Cale's roomy arrangement, which features his piano, sturdy organ, and charming celeste. It is as bliss-kissed as Nick ever got in song, and Cale's arrangement and perceptive playing are a sky-opening invitation to meet him there. In *White Bicycles*, Boyd recalls that Cale, recently kicked out of the Velvet Underground and fresh off producing the Stooges' classic first LP, was in London to aid in the recording of fellow-fired-Velvet Nico's new record. After Boyd played Cale some *Bryter Layter* rough mixes, Cale demanded,

> Who the fuck *is* this guy? I have to meet him, where is he? I mean, where is he *right now*? I rang Nick and told him that John Cale would be over in half an hour. Nick said, "Oh, uh, OK." I wrote out Nick's address, John grabbed it, and ran down the stairs. The next morning I had a call from Cale. "We're going to need a pickup for the viola, an amp, a Fender bass and a bass amp, a celeste and a Hammond B-3 organ. This afternoon." I had scheduled a mix on another project that day but Cale had decided it was time to record "Northern Sky" and "Fly" [unfortunately, Cale's attractive viola and harpsichord work were buried on the latter underneath the overdubbed orchestral avalanche]. They arrived together, John with a wild look in his eyes and Nick trailing behind.

Cale's immediate appreciation of Nick's music, combined with his production brilliance and—maybe most importantly—his *up and at 'em, get 'er done yesterday* energy and enthusiasm, were just what Nick needed, particularly later when his discouragement and depression deepened. It was their only collaboration. The next time Nick entered a recording studio, he would insist on working without a producer.

Bryter Layter's reception was similar to that of the first album, and Nick's state of mind at this point can be gauged by his encounter with a sympathetic journalist, Jerry Gilbert (it may have been the sole interview Nick gave over the course of his entire career):

> I'd love to say that there was this huge charisma that came with him when he walked in the room, but there was absolutely not—just a chap with his head down, stooped, very shy, very self-effacing, not wanting to talk much about himself, really uneasy. I don't remember what he was wearing—he had long hair, which he played with all the time.... Normally in an interview there's a bit of chat before and after the tape was rolling, but there was none of that with Nick.

Worldly indifference is not a bad attribute for an artist to have, but if you're not going to occasionally capitulate to the commercial side of music making and learn to practice the ancient art of *yakkety yak* for the sake of your songs, you had better be prepared to hit the club circuit and preach your music to the people, one gig at a time. Which, of course, Nick was also unwilling to do. In Gilbert's *Sounds* interview, Nick states that he would have done more gigs if he had enjoyed them more. Most people don't have the luxury of only going to work when they suspect they'll enjoy it. There is art, and then there is the business of art. Each makes its own demands and offers its own rewards. To reap the latter, however, you first need to bear the costs of the former. When it came to the business part, Nick did not. Yet Robert Kirby remembered that when it was apparent that *Bryter Layter* was not going to sell any more than *Five Leaves Left*, Nick "took that like being hit in the stomach by Mike Tyson. I think that that really did knock him back a long way."

It was around this time that Joe Boyd relocated to the US to take a job with Warner Brothers. Boyd had not only been Nick's producer, but also his manager and the individual whose small company looked after his publishing. Even more importantly, he was Nick's in-house champion at Island, the one who, despite lousy sales and general indifference, had never wavered in his belief in Nick's musical vision. And now he was gone.

Nick reluctantly moved back home. He stopped writing songs. At his parents' instigation, he saw a psychiatrist. He began taking antidepressants, which he loathed (for fear they would smother his creativity) and would frequently stop taking. He spent some time in a mental health facility. It rankled him to have to live under his parents' roof (according to his father's journal, often appearing uncivil, uncommunicative, and downright rude), but felt incapable any longer of living on his own. As for friends, John Martyn, whose "Solid Air" is the best musical tribute Nick could have wished for, told his own biographer, John Neil Munro, "Nicky was nobody's friend, really. He was a very solitary figure. He didn't set out to be solitary but he just ended up that way.... He became so withdrawn that it was very difficult to be in the room with him.... It was a very black space that he was in." What was once, at worst, aloofness was now approaching despair.

But depression is rarely a clear cause-and-effect affair. The commercial failure of his music undoubtedly contributed to

Nicks's worsening state—how could it not? Joe Boyd recalls in *White Bicycles* one episode when, during a trip back to Britain, he met up with Nick, and "his hair was greasy, his hands dirty, his clothes rumpled. More unnervingly he was angry. I had told him he was a genius, and others had concurred. So, he demanded, why wasn't he famous and rich?" Nick's perception that Boyd, among others, had abandoned him certainly did not improve Nick's mental health, either. Some have hypothesized that Nick's prodigious drug consumption (mostly pot and hash) disastrously exacerbated his characteristic lethargy and inherent introversion, which cannabis can certainly do. Others have speculated that Nick was homosexual (certainly, no one seems to remember him getting laid, let alone having a girlfriend), and that, as he grew older, his chronic despondency was tied to his repressed sexuality. Who knows where our happiness goes? Bottom line: Nick was an increasingly bitter, obviously depressed young man.

~

Beauty can never be depressing. Dark, unnerving, melancholic—but never depressing, because depression, by its very nature, *depresses*; it shuts down the avenues of engagement and appreciation and wonder. *Pink Moon*, Nick's last album, released in 1972, is exceptionally dark, unnerving, and melancholic, but its immaculately sculptured magnificence generates awe in the listener, not despair. It ignites one's appetite for existence, not extinguishes it. That it was completed at a time when no one knew Nick was even composing new songs (and was so depressed that, at one point, he contemplated electroshock therapy) is a testament to his commitment to his muse. *Pink Moon* is only a little over twenty-eight minutes long, an ideal length for a collection of such intensely desolate, densely packed songs. Also ideal is the LP's instrumentation: Nick and an acoustic guitar (and on the title track, a few seconds of overdubbed piano). Bare truths, bare sounds.

Opener "Pink Moon" may be strummed, but it is a brilliant piece of strumming, and not just because the end result is a startlingly lovely melody. Nick employs his usual unusual blend of major and minor chords, as well as alternating light-and-heavy fingertip pressure as applied to the strings (he didn't use a pick) to create an entire world of mournful shade and light in two minutes, flat. Nick's lyrics, like his everyday interlocutions, had by this time compressed, concentrated, hardened (like Yeats' later poems), becoming more like the anguished utterances of a brooding, emotionally bruised recluse. "Pink Moon" is about the omnipotent, indifferent, inescapable spectre of oblivion. Although Nick had listened to and liked and even played some blues covers when he was younger, his music (like Richard Thompson's) is principally bereft of any of the twelve-bar clichés of the genre, but "Pink Moon" could have been written by Blind Willie Johnson, if he had studied the works of William Blake and grown up in the English countryside.

Things don't let up with "Place to Be," another steadily strummed lament for lost strength and abandoned hope. When Nick sings about being weaker than the palest blue, it is almost as if you're not sure he's going to make it to the end of the lyric, such is the fragile timbre of his voice. "Road" is a craftily constructed (the melody is plucked out on the lower notes), two-verse, broken prayer, composed of eight chiselled lines, one of which Nick repeats four times, for emphasis (the one about needing a road to see him through). Like several songs on the album, it is over in just under two minutes and it could not have gone on any longer. "Which Will" is prettily plucked and gorgeously impenetrable and reminds one of Townes Van Zandt's oft-repeated ambition to write a song so good that no one understands it, not even him. Side 1 of the original vinyl concludes with the brief instrumental "Horn" (1:19), a call to the faithful who aren't listening. The loneliness evoked by Nick's spare, chary playing is chilling.

"Things Behind the Sun" is an older song, but it fits in seamlessly with the newer material: exhausted, ominous, but oddly comforting in its bleak beauty. After noting above that Nick rarely played anything resembling straight blues or with a predictable tempo, we nonetheless come to "Know," a strangled blues song for the wordlessly mystified. Over an undeviating, almost abrasively repetitive pattern of notes, for two minutes and twenty-three seconds, Nick sings the same four, short, plaintive lines, when he is not humming along to the unrelenting rhythm of his guitar. It is minimalism taken to the maximum. Of course Nick wrote a song called "Parasite." Another rolling, hypnotic number, it features Nick in the apt role of urban outsider, the big-city horror show of T. S. Eliot's metropolitan wasteland, tied to an appealing major-chord hook, when Nick sings of being the always-observing, never-participating parasite. (Well, that's one way of looking at being an artist…) "Free Ride" is no such thing: a briskly picked, gently biting indictment of burnished superficiality. Penultimate track "Harvest Breed" is, like "Road" and "Know," extremely short (just one minute) and lyrically succinct, but no less powerful for its brevity—it is Nick talking himself into accepting his imminent annihilation. It is also as desolately pretty as it is portentous. "From the Morning" is nothing less than a benediction. For all of the sorrow and unease that *Pink Moon* has mined to make its magic, Nick leaves us with the splendour of dewy dawn and benevolent nightfall and a wish that all Earth's creatures partake of the simple earthy joys he himself has been denied. It is a prayer.

The story goes that Nick went into the studio with just engineer John Wood, knocked out the album's eleven songs, live, over the course of a couple of nights (the only overdub was the memorable snatch of piano on "Pink Moon"), and dropped if off at Island Records' reception desk with the explanation that this was his new album. Not quite—he handed the tape directly to Island president Chris Blackwell. It was released in 1972, and not surprisingly, Nick's dark valentine to the world went largely unheard. If the other two albums didn't sell, what were the odds that the all-acoustic, all-anguish *Pink Moon* would do the commercial trick? Additionally, as Island Records' managing director David Betteridge recalled, by 1972, "We were busy with Cat Stevens, Roxy Music, Bob Marley and goodness knows who else, and Nick was never a priority for us. I think the perception was that he'd had his shot, and he just got put out to pasture."

After *Pink Moon*'s release and swift disappearance, and several gloomy months avoiding his parents at home and his friends in London, Nick thought that maybe a straight job was his best chance of regaining some mental equilibrium. His delighted father secured him a position working with the computer arm of his own company, but Nick quit after a few days. He would snap at his parents (Nick's mother Molly recalls, in the documentary *A Skin Too Few*, "He said once, 'I don't like it at home, but I can't bear it anywhere else'"), hibernate in his bedroom, and ignore his friends; or, if he did drop in on one of them unannounced, he would sit impassively with a cup of tea or a joint and stare at his shoes for hours, before leaving as suddenly as he had arrived, sometimes slipping away without saying goodbye or anyone even noticing. How desperate was he for something purposeful to do, to be somewhere he belonged? He contemplated *joining the army*, and even got as far as securing an interview with a recruiting officer before sensibly backing out.

"Just before he died he looked like Howard Hughes," Linda Thompson, wife and singing partner of Richard Thompson, recalled. "There was this beautiful boy with the milky white, almost see-through skin, who always took great care of his hands and fingernails, and now he was dirty and unkempt and his nails were too long to play the guitar." But not so long that he couldn't try. What else was there to do? Just because no one is listening doesn't mean we still don't need to talk. And Nick's way of communicating with the world was through song, so sometime in early 1974 he went back into the studio with, once again, just engineer John Wood behind the glass, and recorded his last five songs, four of which would not be released until five years after his death, and the fifth not for three decades. Boyd professed his shock at Nick's sudden inability to play and sing at the same time, but results are what matter, not how they are achieved.

"Voice from the Mountain" is a triple play: numinous, luminous, stupendous. Utilizing his unnerving falsetto, Nick sings of unfamiliar voices, peculiar sounds, and their mysterious arrival and departure, just like the gods we have forgotten to listen for. For someone whose writing is so insular and introspective, Nick's songs are largely free of the obviously autobiographical, but one cannot help but hear "Rider on the Wheel" and "Hanging on a Star" and think of Nick's conversation with Boyd about his inexplicable anonymity. The former song is pluckily persistent, the latter droopingly accusatory; both are muffled wails of incomprehension and anger. "Tow the Line" is only so-so, but it is still archetypical Nick—the ruffled chords, the sombre vocals, the opaque lyrics—and would have made a nicely innocuous second-side cut. Ideally, it would have come before the jolt of "Black Eyed Dog," as harrowing a three minutes and twenty seconds as you will ever spend with your headphones on. The black-eyed dog that sits outside Nick's door and calls his name is depression and death, of course, but what elevates the terror even further is, by tune's end, Nick's wearied acquiescence to his fate. The battered notes Nick manages to coax from his guitar are funeral music. His own.

Nick Drake died November 25, 1974, at home, in his childhood bedroom, of an overdose of the pills he had been prescribed by a psychiatrist to combat his depression. Opinions differ as to whether the overdose was purposeful or accidental. Either way, it was probably inevitable. He wouldn't live to see his songs used in a Volkswagen television commercial and in Hollywood films and his popularity soar to unimaginable, uber-hipster heights. No matter: the music remains. And now it rises. And it is everywhere.

MUDDY WATERS

He best can pity who has felt the woe
–Gay

It's not a good idea to disagree with Lowell George. Little Feat's principal singer, chief songwriter, and lead guitar player may have made a brilliant mess of his short life, but when it came to music, Lowell knew what he was talking about. Performing his own "Apolitical Blues" in concert with the Feat in the mid-'70s (available on the posthumous, two-CD, live *Ripe Tomatos*, vol. 1, *Ripe Recordings, 1971–2001*), however, when he's heard to mutter, just before taking off on a typically scorching solo, "Howlin' Wolf invented rock and roll," he was only mostly right. Sure, as Muddy Waters sang, "The blues had a baby and they named it rock and roll," and the Wolf was certainly there at its conception, but if anybody in the blues business had a right to see their name listed under "Father" on the birth certificate, Muddy was the guy.

And not only because the first real rock and roller, Chuck Berry, when asked by an interviewer to name his greatest musical inspiration, immediately replied, "Definitely Muddy. His sound! That's what I played before 'Maybellene'—before I turned pro, I guess you call it." And not because one of the biggest rock-and-roll bands, ever, named itself after one of his songs. When the Mississippi-born and -raised Muddy moved to Chicago in 1943 and traded in his acoustic guitar for an electric because he couldn't be heard over the drinking-and-dancing din of the audience, he was not the first blues musician to plug in and turn it up (T-Bone Walker beat him to it), but he was certainly the one who made the country blues rattle and shake and rock and roll all over.

Before he was Muddy Waters he was McKinley Morganfield, born in 1913 in the Mississippi Delta and destined to work away his years in the cotton fields, just as his father and his grandfather had done before him. His mother died when he was three years old, and—his father already having left home to start another family—he was taken in by his maternal grandmother. She not only raised him but nicknamed him "Muddy," for his propensity to play in the Delta's ubiquitous rivers and water basins. (He wouldn't become "Muddy Waters" until he made it to Chicago and added the "Waters," because it was too-good a show-business name to pass up.) Muddy moved with his grandmother to Stovall, Mississippi, where relatives worked on the enormous Stovall plantation, which had a reputation for being, as far as plantations went, a decent-enough place to work. Decent, maybe, but hardly desirable. Children too young to carry a cotton sack (usually under ten) were never too young to work, becoming, for example, water boys, who would roam the dusty, burning fields all day with their thirst-slaking jug. Work, sleep, repeat; and so it has been, and so it shall be.

But not for Muddy. School may not have been mandatory (he left when he was about eight years old), but church was, and like most pioneering blues and rock-and-roll artists, white and Black, the Baptist church was where he first learned to sing and shout and testify. The blues is gospel with a beat, its subject matter suffering instead of salvation. His grandmother had a phonograph player, and the teenage Muddy was soon buying or borrowing country-blues 78s by performers like Blind Lemon Jefferson, Son House, and Charlie Patton. Before long, he was figuring out how to make a harmonica and a homemade acoustic guitar sound like what he heard coming out of the record player. He eventually became good enough to perform at the Saturday-night fish fries held on the plantation, working until sunrise for food, booze, and maybe seventy-five cents, and later, to play the occasional juke joint. It was at one of these that he heard Son House preaching the blues on bottleneck guitar. Although Muddy later maintained that his talent was one part his own, one part Robert Johnson, and one part Son House, the latter was the biggest influence, even showing the young Muddy how to build his own bottleneck and teaching him how to alter his guitar to open tunings. The mature, electric Muddy Waters music does not sound much like Son House's guttural, slam-bang acoustic blues, but the best teachers show us foremost how to be and think and sound like ourselves.

Muddy got married in 1932 and fathered a child (by another woman) a couple of years later, but for the rest of us, the most significant thing that happened around this time was his purchase of a brand new Sears, Roebuck acoustic guitar for the astronomical price of eleven dollars (when the average labourer made about fifty cents day). In an interview he gave much later, Muddy claimed he had decided when he was a child to become either a preacher, a baseball player, or a musician—anything other than working the fields—and his new guitar was testament that Sunday sermons and double plays were now in his past. When some of the same people he had been playing with around Clarksdale began to migrate to Memphis and Chicago, Muddy was tempted to try his luck at making music his sole source of employment (even spending some time scouting the scene in St Louis), but between what he heard from the urban exiles about country blues being yesterday's news in the big cities and his love for his aging grandmother, Muddy chose to stay in rural Mississippi. If Muddy wouldn't come to the city, the city would have to come to him. Which it did, in the form of Alan Lomax and his tape recorder.

In the summer of 1941, the Library of Congress funded a field-recording trip intended to capture for posterity the regional "folk" music (e.g., "country blues") of, among other places, the Mississippi Delta. Asking around for singers who sounded like Robert Johnson, Alan Lomax and his colleague, Fisk University professor and folklorist John Work, kept hearing the name "Muddy" and eventually tracked down the nearly thirty-year-old, full-time agricultural worker and occasional musician. After finally convincing Muddy that he wasn't a government agent attempting to entrap him (Muddy ran his own after-hours place for a while and even bootlegged a little), Lomax coaxed Muddy to perform a few songs for his bulky recorder, in return for twenty dollars and two copies of the result. What Lomax and Fisk heard (available on *The Complete Plantation Recordings*) was authentic country blues, complete with stinging slide-guitar accents learned directly from the already legendary Son House. Aside from the assured acoustic guitar work and the straightforward appeal of some of the songs (the "I Feel Like Going Home" and "I Can't Be Satisfied" prototypes "Country Blues" and "I Be's Troubled"), what is most conspicuous about Muddy's first recorded music is his warm, resonant voice. It's the blues, all right, songs of loneliness, loss, and sorrow—and lust—but, unlike Robert Johnson or Son House, who sound utterly *submerged* in their sorrow, damned denizens of purgatorial-grade despair (which, of course, is part of their appeal), Muddy sounds like he's suffering but still getting by, his songs a manifestation of spiritual catharsis rather than weary capitulation.

Subsequent visits by Lomax managed to get not only a few more Muddy solo sides on tape, but also several tunes performed with the Son Sims Four, a string band, which included a violinist and a mandolin player (much like the Mississippi Sheiks, a group Muddy said he once walked ten miles to hear play). Though not as impressive as his solo tracks, these group recordings are nonetheless revelatory for the country-and-western (as opposed to country-blues) character of tunes like bluegrass great Bill Monroe's "Be Honest with Me" and "Deep in the Heart of Texas." Slightly anomalous sounding—Muddy Waters and violin?—and rhythmically underwhelming, they are still a good reminder that the blues aren't any colour but blue.

Lomax had mailed Muddy his promised two copies of the indigenous African American blues anthology he had finally assembled, including two songs ("Country Blues" and "I Be's Troubled") by Muddy, and the latter had his picture taken, outfitted in his best suit, proudly holding the LP for the camera (the photo is on the cover of *The Complete Plantation Recordings*). Newly remarried (without bothering to get divorced from his last wife—like father, like son), that summer, his thirtieth, Muddy asked his employer for a raise and was told he could work for what he had always earned or find himself another job. In Robert Gordon's definitive *Can't Be Satisfied: The Life and Times of Muddy Waters*, friend Myles Long remembered how Muddy "pulled under a shade tree to rest. I don't know what he [and his boss] was fighting about, but I saw Muddy start to walking.... I didn't see him [again] until he come back with his band from Chicago."

~

Good-paying, wartime factory work was in abundance in northern industrial cities like Chicago, and Muddy almost immediately got a job in a paper plant, earning per week about a sixth of what he would have made all year on the plantation (and in just eight hours a day, not the twelve he toiled in the fields). Musically, though, things were not going as well, jazz-influenced jump blues being the music du jour of the clubs, and Muddy's "old-time blues" apparently a thing of the rural past. Muddy told an interviewer that people would mock him for continuing to play the straight blues—what he always referred to as "deep blues"—derisively referring to it as "sharecropper music." There were plenty of other factory-working African Americans with pockets full of money to spend on Friday and Saturday nights, and what they wanted was to drink and dance and flirt and have fun—*not* listen to some guy up on stage plucking an acoustic guitar and singing about how down-and-out he was. So Muddy played the only places he could: house parties. Even then, he told another interviewer, he often had to perform for not much more than food and whiskey. The main thing, he said, was to be heard. For the blues to be heard.

The alone-with-his-guitar (*à* la Robert Johnson or Son House) era was clearly over, and Muddy knew he needed to get a group together if he wanted to secure gigs. By good fortune, he was introduced to a friend of a friend, guitarist Jimmy Rogers. Also of the Delta and also raised by his grandmother, Rogers was also making good money working a factory job but had not given up on playing the formative music of his—and Muddy's—youth. Talking to interviewer John Anthony Brisbin, Rogers recalled how "I understood what Muddy was tryin' to do, because I was acquainted with the style that he was comin' into [electric blues]. I could help him out to fill in. I could fit into what he was doin'.... We'd rehearse all the time. That's all we would do"—that, and work forty hours a week, plus overtime, at their respective jobs—"just lay around and practice, run through songs and build songs and sounds and tones."

Aided by a rotating cast of drummers, bassists, and harmonica players, Muddy and Rogers worked their way up from playing rent and house parties (in addition to appearing at the Maxwell Street Market, a popular performance spot on weekend afternoons) to the occasional tavern gig on Chicago's predominantly Black South Side. It was around this time that Muddy started exclusively using an electric guitar, principally because, as noted, an acoustic wasn't loud enough to keep the party going. An amplified guitar doesn't lie, and although Muddy was confident in his slide playing, Rogers and a new friend, Claude "Blue Smitty" Smith, worked with him to improve his technique.

They must have done a pretty good job, because a couple of producers took an interest in the newly electric band's leader, aided by the encouragement of Big Bill Broonzy, who was not only the first person that Muddy saw play electric guitar, but who also talked up the younger man's talents around town. And while the result of the initial session was fairly anemic (ragtime piano and busy horns of a bygone epoch immediately undercutting Muddy's efforts), the second, for Columbia Records, while a little saccharine song-wise, showed the development of what Muddy et al. were up to live: loud, propulsive city music with plenty of back-country soul. It was all a little too raw for Columbia, however, and the results were not released for more than two decades. Adding to his disappointment, his grandmother died in 1946, although she did leave him enough money in her will for him to put a down payment on his first car, an invaluable acquisition for a busy big-city musician.

It was at the Maxwell Street Market that Rogers heard Little Walter, who, though only a teenager, was blowing harp with his own band. The other members of the group, Rogers recalled, were pedestrian, but Walter was special, someone who would almost single-handedly elevate the harmonica to the status of featured instrument. People tend to focus on Little Walter's celebrated microphone-cupping method of blowing and his insistence upon having his own amplifier so he could be heard alongside the rest of the band (combined with his experiments with distortion and echo), but who came first at this or that really only matters to historians. Walter is still listened to today (and if you want to play the harmonica, he is *compulsory* listening) because he compelled his instrument to leap and loop and laugh and go places no other harmonica had gone before, his fascination with jump-blues saxophonists imbuing his playing with an undeniable swing. He was also an unruly alcoholic who would die at thirty-eight from injuries suffered in a street fight. But once he joined Muddy and Rogers, the first great electric-blues band was in place. They called themselves the Headhunters, because wherever they plugged in, the three of them would cut down any other band in the joint. There are no participation awards in art. You either cut or get cut. The Muddy Waters band cut.

Artists have a not-undeserved reputation for not being generous when it comes to other artists—if one's career is a stock that is either rising or falling, why give a competing artist a leg up, if one day they might use your head as a ladder rung?—but Muddy, who would go on to promote the work of, among others, Howlin' Wolf, Buddy Guy, and his own band members Little Walter and Otis Spann, was by most accounts a genuinely munificent man. Maybe one of the reasons for Muddy's rare magnanimity was the help that he himself received coming up in Chicago in the '40s, not only from the aforementioned Big Bill Broonzy, but also from Sunnyland Slim, who encouraged the Chess brothers, part-owners and overseers of a new record label, Aristocrat, to give his friend and colleague Muddy Waters a shot at cutting a few sides.

The tunes that Muddy made for the neophyte label in the fall of 1947 were recorded without his regular band because, ironically, Aristocrat wanted a more stripped-down, country-blues sound. Aristocrat's idea of country blues was an odd one, though, and the piano player and saxophonist they had booked ensured that neither the Chess brothers nor Muddy were pleased with the result. Another session several months later, in the spring of 1948, was going much the same way when Muddy suggested that he cut a tune on his own, aided only by his electric guitar and the bass player booked for the session, Ernest "Big" Crawford. One immediately recalls the initially unproductive, but eventually triumphant, culture-changing auditions of Little Richard with Specialty and Elvis Presley with Sun that were belatedly saved by the respective artists' frustrated appeal to just let them do what they wanted to do—just once—damn the doomed commerciality of whatever got recorded.

What got recorded that day in April, 1948, was "I Can't Be Satisfied" and "I Feel Like Going Home," both featuring, for the first time on record, Muddy playing bottleneck on his electric guitar, the searing, sensual expression of existential exasperation and out-and-out horniness translating into an utterly anomalous band sound that was so frugally raw—just guitar, bass, and a single vocal—yet so abundantly full. Leonard Chess is reported to have uttered to his girlfriend in the recording booth, "What the hell is he singing?" but Chess pressed three thousand copies of the single, and they were all gone by the next day. By the following week the Chess brothers were big Muddy Waters fans. They weren't the only ones. Muddy recalled how, coming home one warm summer night from a gig (which, with the success of his record, were much more plentiful and better attended), he heard one of his songs through an open apartment window. Muddy said he was scared—for a moment, he thought maybe he had died and gone to heaven.

Things were good—he had even met the woman he would spend much of the rest of his life with, Geneva Wade, although this never stopped him from seeing other women, particularly younger ones (one of his songs *was* called "She's Nineteen Years Old")—but they could have been better. Muddy still worked five days a week (now delivering venetian blinds around town) while playing the clubs at night, and although they were packing them in wherever they performed, Leonard Chess still would not allow him to bring his own group into the recording studio. From Aristocrat's point of view, why meddle with what was clearly working (i.e., selling)? Several Muddy Waters singles followed his first release, pairing him once again with "Big" Crawford on bass (best of all, "Train Fare Blues"), but Muddy wanted to hear on record what the people at Chicago's blues bars, like the Zanzibar and the Du Drop Lounge, were hearing every weekend: a tight, explosive *band*.

So eager were they to get something down on tape, in early 1950 the group recorded several songs for another small Chicago label, Parkway, the entire band's first time together in a recording studio. The standout result by far was "Rollin' and Tumblin'," a combination field chant and one long, loud, menacing group hum with everybody joining in, Leroy Foster's chugging drums, Little Walter's wild harmonica, and Muddy's rude bottleneck making for a frightening slice of electrified Delta derangement. Although the song was credited to the Baby Face Leroy Trio and not to Muddy Waters, Aristocrat was livid and insisted that Muddy return to its studio and re-record the song, which he did, once again, with only Crawford on bass. The Aristocrat version is sparser, shorter, and less emotionally stirring, though still another excellent early Muddy Waters cut—as was another Muddy "original" recorded at the same session, "Rollin' Stone."

How original some of Muddy's "originals" are depends upon one's idea of originality. "Rollin' Stone," for example, is essentially Robert Petway's "Catfish Blues," made more musically Muddy—made electric—and with certain lines deleted and certain new ones added, including some that would end up being recycled in "Mannish Boy," which would not appear for another five years. Today, we would call it "stealing" or "plagiarism," but the early to mid-twentieth-century blues musicians regularly borrowed aspects of earlier songs to make new ones. It wasn't just Muddy: the line in the song about the narrator wishing he was a catfish was one that Petway himself filched from another, older song.

The Chess brothers, Phil and Leonard, had bought out their other partners and renamed Aristocrat; the Chess Records 45s that quickly followed benefitted from Chess' decision to finally allow more than just Muddy and a bass player to perform on his records—probably because Jimmy Rogers had had a hit with a nearly full-band version of "That's All Right," a tune recorded at the end of one of Muddy's sessions. Even though they only add Little Walter to the mix (and occasionally the exceptional jazz-influenced drummer Elgin Evans), "Louisiana Blues," "Long Distance Call," "Honey Bee," "She Moves Me," and "Still a Fool" swing like none of Muddy's previous songs had—like no blues songs had before—partly because Evans was such an expert timekeeper, who could always be counted on to sublimely serve the song, but principally because Little Walter often played the harmonica like a horn, imbuing Muddy's songs with a slippery sophistication that, combined with Muddy's dark hollow wail and the cold sting of his bottleneck guitar, made for a new kind of blues.

New and commercially successful: each successive single was a hit on the R&B charts, which likely led to Chess' further capitulation in allowing Jimmy Rogers to add his electric rhythm guitar to Muddy's new songs, giving the band a beefier, even more rhythmically locomotive-like sound. When pianist Otis Spann—like Little Walter, another instrumental innovator—joined the group in 1952, the nonstop, free-flowing filigrees and ornate runs of his right hand anchored in the rock-solid timekeeping of his left, the classic Muddy Waters sound—the sound of contemporary urban blues at its finest—was set.

Another distinguishing feature of the group was that Little Walter, Rogers, and Spann were all able singers. Spann in particular had a deep, distinctively genial, instantly engaging voice that would help set apart the many fine solo albums he recorded while a member of Muddy's band, the best being *The Blues Is Where It's At*, with Muddy guesting on electric guitar. With two electric guitars, electric bass, piano, amplified harmonica, and drums, the Muddy Waters band was also louder than anybody else around (remember: rock and roll had not been invented yet), but this wasn't merely Blue Cheer with the blues—Muddy's band could be as silky smooth as a brand-new twenty-dollar handkerchief ("I Just Want to Make Love to You"), as randy as an in-heat Rottweiler on a short leash ("I'm Ready"), or as marvellously spooky as "(I'm Your) Hoochie Coochie Man."

Even when he lost bandmembers along the way (Little Walter had a hit in 1952 with "Juke," the band's instrumental theme song, and left to lead his own band, although he still played on many of Muddy's recording sessions; Henry "Pot" Strong took over on harp only to be murdered by his wife; Junior Wells came on board and was promptly drafted into the US Army; James Cotton took over for Wells, before he, too, exited to form his own group; Rogers left to start a solo career; Spann stayed around the longest, until 1968, a couple of years before his death from liver cancer), Muddy kept right on playing the Chicago clubs as much as he wanted—sometimes seven days a week by this point—occasionally venturing out of town on short tours, and recording more enduring electric-blues songs. *Muddy Waters* blues songs.

Increasingly, the best of these Muddy Waters songs were written by Willie Dixon, the mammoth bassist who worked for Chess as a studio musician, producer, and songwriter. "I Just Want to Make Love to You," "I'm Ready," "(I'm Your) Hoochie Coochie Man," "Young Fashioned Ways," "You Shook Me," "You Need Love," "The Same Thing," "Mannish Boy," and "I Love the Life I Live, I Live the Life I Love," aren't necessarily "better" songs than those Muddy wrote during these years, approximately 1954–64 (e.g., "Trouble No More," "My Home Is in the Delta," and "You Can't Lose What You Never Had"), but they tend to be a bit catchier and more traditionally structured (with well-defined verses and choruses), which are a couple of reasons why the songs Dixon composed, not only for Muddy, but for Howlin' Wolf, Bo Diddley, Otis Rush, and even Little Walter, among others, have been the basis for so many latter-day rock-and-roll covers (Cream's version of "Spoonful," the Doors' take on "Back Door Man," the Rolling Stones' first hit, "Little Red Rooster," J. Geils' rendition of "Dead Presidents," and the Meat Puppets' skewed rendering of "I Just Want to Make Love to You," to name only a few). Like Muddy and almost every other mid-twentieth-century blues artist, Dixon knew how to recycle bits and pieces of old songs in the public domain and transform them into something new and noteworthy, but this does not make him any less of a songwriting genius. Theoretically, anyone could have put this old line with that old bit of melody and tacked on something new and slapped his or her name on it, but how come Willie Dixon was the one who did it over and over again? Everything seems easy and obvious after someone else has already done it. Muddy might have been the star of the show, but he was extremely fortunate to have such a superlative supporting cast of musicians and one of the century's greatest songwriters helping him shine.

The sun can't shine all the time, though, and when Muddy wasn't gigging around Chicago or touring or recording hit singles, he liked to enjoy his success in typical laid-back Muddy fashion, hanging around the house he had bought—his first—watching baseball in the afternoon in his underwear, cooking and eating and sipping a little champagne (after his doctor warned him off whiskey), keeping an eye on the kids (his, Geneva's, and various grandchildren), and when he felt like they needed it, taking the band downstairs to his basement and working on whatever warranted their attention. Once he was sufficiently rested up, he also liked to chase women. It wasn't just a song title: Muddy really did love the life he lived and live the life he loved.

Ironically, it was Muddy who suggested to a young fan in 1955 that he approach Chess Records about an audition. More than that: when Leonard Chess played back what the kid recorded, it didn't make sense, Chess couldn't see any commercial value in it at all. Muddy could. And told him so. And when Chuck Berry's "Maybellene" soared to the top of the charts, Chess was in the burgeoning rock-and-roll business. Leonard Chess: "The big beat"—which, even more pivotally, was also a speeded-up beat—"the big cars, and young love. It was a trend and we jumped on it." It was only fair. Muddy's electric blues had swept away the old stuff, and now rock and roll was sweeping away the electric blues. To everything there is a season, and this season it was rock and roll. Cotton: "There were weekends that we couldn't get jobs. Me and Muddy would get in the station wagon and drive around and listen to rock and roll. We wouldn't go in the clubs, just listen to what's going on." What was *not* going on was the blues.

Some blues musicians, like Jimmy Rogers, struggled and eventually left the music business (although he was active again many years later), but Muddy kept at it. What else was he going to do? Ask for his old job back at the venetian-blind company? So he toured England, for instance, when domestic concert opportunities were dwindling. The Brits had fallen hard for the blues at around the same time that rock and roll was on the ascent in America. Although his records were not easy to acquire, Muddy was greeted as a living legend when he and Spann made their first foray overseas, because the blues knows no borders. Back home, when Muddy was invited to perform at the 1960 Newport Jazz Festival, it turned out that not all of America was besotted by rock and roll—Muddy and his band were a big hit, although something was inevitably lost when performing before a large outdoor audience in the late afternoon. Sex and death and dancing are nighttime things, and better understood and explored in small, sweaty, overcrowded clubs.

Additionally, another segment of white America had become infatuated with...wait for it...country blues, Muddy's formative first love. Accordingly, the release in 1964 of the album *Folk Singer*, a first-rate collection of Muddy unplugged, and the re-release of several of his most country blues–based Aristocrat and early Chess sides in the form of *The Real Folk Blues* (1965) and *More Real Folk Blues* (1967). Some might view these albums as melancholic reminders of electric blues' increasing obsolescence, but better these knowledgeable nods to the past than what was to follow: Muddy with horns—lots and lots of horns (1967's *Brass and the Blues*); Muddy painted psychedelic purple (*Electric Mud* and *After the Rain*, from 1968 and 1969, respectively); rock-and-roll star–abetted jam sessions (1969's *Fathers and Sons* and *The London Muddy Waters Sessions*, from 1971). The title of the novelty single "The Muddy Waters Twist" says it all.

Much like how the urban jump blues was preferred by African American audiences of the 1940s who viewed country blues as "old-fashioned," in the 1960s soul and funk and even rock and roll were the new sounds that made Muddy's brand of electric blues passé. When blues clubs began to open up in Chicago's non-Black parts of town and Muddy started to land gigs at primarily white college campuses, the blues had turned, if not entirely, then predominantly, pasty. It was primarily white people, like the nascent Rolling Stones, who carried the torch forward for electric blues. Keith Richards: "When we started the Rolling Stones, we were just little kids, right? We felt we had some of the licks down, but our aim was to turn other people on to Muddy Waters." Imitation isn't the sincerest form of flattery—proselytizing is.

It still wasn't enough to put Muddy back in the spotlight or in the charts. But even a bad car accident, while on the road with his band, and his wife Geneva's death from cancer in 1973 could not stop Muddy entirely. He continued to tour—often overseas, where his popularity remained undiminished—although by this point, the sixty-year-old Muddy's shows had become mostly professional affairs, more akin to an evening out at a contemporary Chicago blues bar like Kingston Mines, where the music is of museum quality and enjoyable but predictable, than to the long-gone drunk and disorderly, potentially beatific, if sometimes dangerous, nights at the Zanzibar or the Du Drop Lounge. That said, 1973's *Can't Get No Grindin'* was a slight return to form, a surprisingly vigorous electric-blues album. And while mellower and more acoustically textured, 1975's Levon Helm–produced *Woodstock Album* was also an honest attempt to help Muddy connect with a contemporary audience. When Woodstock, New York, bestowed the key to the town upon him, however, the writing was on the wall. When they start naming streets after you or handing over a key to the city—when you are safe and respectable and venerable—your time as an artist is usually up.

Life brims with small ironies, and in Muddy's career there is perhaps none greater than Johnny Winter, a white, albino, blues-based rock and roller providing the opportunity and encouragement necessary for Muddy to record not only a genuinely great, pure blues LP at the age of sixty-three, but his greatest (most of his classic songs were initially only available as 45s). Set up with his own Blue Sky imprint by

CBS Records, Winter produced *Hard Again* just like they did back in the 1950s: everybody playing together, a minimum of overdubs, and with the emphasis on emotion and excitement. Winter: "What I really wanted to do as a producer was to make Muddy feel comfortable and make his music sound as good as it used to. I felt that the real, raw blues and some early nasty rock and roll hadn't been recorded right since recording techniques had gotten too good for that kind of music."

The result is a gloriously stinky, sex-suffused, hard-driving affair, composed of a few remakes of older songs and some perfectly decent new ones, although it is not the songwriting that caused Waters to exclaim at one point during the three days he spent in the studio, "My pee pee is hard again!" (hence the album's title). This is Muddy's adored deep blues goosed and guided by a rabid rock-and-roll spirit, Muddy's touring band (plus old pal Jimmy Rogers) and Winter wham-banging out one gleefully anarchic take after another. This isn't music to listen to—it's music to dance to, to sing along with, to play while fucking. Listen to the between-song, profanity-laced laughter: even the musicians sound surprised that the music is so hot and heavy, something that could not be said about much of Muddy's music for a long time.

There were a couple of reunions with Winter (*I'm Ready* in 1978 and *King Bee* three years later) that, while supremely solid, lack the special spark of the first Blue Sky release (either could have been dubbed *Almost Hard Again*). There was his remarriage in 1979 at age sixty-six to twenty-five-year-old Marvas Jean Brooks (they'd met when she was nineteen). Then there was the cancer diagnosis and the heart failure that led to his death in 1983. If the blues wasn't dead before, it sure was now.

Just like, around the same time, rock and roll, the brand-new baby begot by Muddy's electric blues, suffered its own noisy death rattle with the last gasp of 4/4 rebellion that was punk and post-punk. So it goes, ashes to ashes, dust to dust.

Prove me wrong. Put some Muddy Waters on and turn it up. Turn it up loud.

NOTES

INTRODUCTION

10 *To endeavour to work*: Jonathan Swift, *The Works of Jonathan Swift, In Two Volumes, Volume One* (Bell and Daldy, 1896), 836.

11 *This is where the soul*: James Segrest and Mark Hoffman, *Moanin' at Midnight: The Life and Times of Howlin' Wolf* (Thunder's Mouth Press, 2005), 83.

ALEX CHILTON

28 *Alex really loved his cocktails*: Holly George-Warren, *A Man Called Destruction: The Life and Music of Alex Chilton; From Box Tops to Big Star to Backdoor Man* (Viking, 2014), 131.

28 *[Alex] wanted it to be*: George-Warren, *A Man Called Destruction*, 132.

29 *one of the most exciting nights*: Rich Tupica, *There Was a Light: The Cosmic History of Chris Bell and the Rise of Big Star* (Permuted Press, 2020), 210.

33 *there was absolutely nobody*: George-Warren, *A Man Called Destruction*, 159.

33 *eating…fried mushrooms*: George-Warren, *A Man Called Destruction*, 157.

34 *If the fool would persist*: William Blake, *Blake: Complete Writings; With Variant Readings*, ed. Geoffrey Keynes (Oxford University Press, 1971), 151.

35 *Alex set the tone*: Rob Jovanovic, *Big Star: The Short Life, Painful Death, and Unexpected Resurrection of the Kings of Power Pop* (Chicago Review Press, 2004), 151.

35 *Fry made the mistake*: Jovanovic, *Big Star*, 158–59.

36 *We would record*: Tupica, *There Was a Light*, 265.

37 *Karen Berg [a friend*: Jovanovic, *Big Star*, 161.

38 *The record was about*: George-Warren, *A Man Called Destruction*, 179.

38 *It was just chaos*: George-Warren, *A Man Called Destruction*, 184.

38 *Alex was using a*: George-Warren, *A Man Called Destruction*, 185.

JAMES BOOKER

49 *His music teacher used*: Earl King, quoted in liner notes to James Booker, *Spiders on the Keys*, recorded live at the Maple Leaf Bar, New Orleans, Louisiana, 1977–1982, produced by Scott Billington and John Parsons, Rounder 2119, 1993, compact disc.

55 *I did see Booker*: Lily Keber, dir., *Bayou Maharajah* (Mairzy Doats Productions, 2013), DVD.

56 *[Booker] wouldn't learn any*: John Kahn, interview with Blair Jackson from his website The Cutting Room Floor, http://www.blairjackson.com/TheCuttingRoomFloorIntro.html (site defunct).

57 *James would call my house*: Keber, *Bayou Maharajah*.

NICO

65 *Life was a bore*: Susanne Ofteringer, dir., *Nico: Icon* (Fox Lorber, 1995), DVD.

66 *I had no intention*: Clinton Heylin, *From the Velvets to the Voidoids: The Birth of American Punk Rock*, updated edition (Chicago Review Press, 2005), 22.

66 *The whole time the album*: Victor Bockris and Gerard Malanga, *Up-Tight: The Story of the Velvet Underground* (Omnibus Press, 1996), 49.

70 *That was the affair*: Legs McNeil and Gillian McCain, *Please Kill Me: The Uncensored Oral History of Punk* (Penguin, 1996), 30.

75 *she didn't do any drugs*: Joe Ambrose, *Gimme Danger: The Story of Iggy Pop* (Omnibus Press, 2004), 71.

THE STAPLE SINGERS

86 *Grandma says, 'Oh, you*: Greg Kot, *I'll Take You There: Mavis Staples, the Staple Singers, and the March Up Freedom's Highway* (Scribner, 2014), 20–21.

90 *In order for one's*: Gustave Flaubert, *The Letters of Gustave Flaubert: 1857–1880*, ed. and trans. Francis Steegmuller (Belknap, 1982), 5.

92 *They would take a break*: Kot, *I'll Take You There*, 57.

93 *is capable of being*: John Keats, in *The Norton Anthology of English Literature*, ed. M.H. Abrams, et. al. (W.W. Norton, 1975), 1894.

94 *I was always like*: Kot, *I'll Take You There*, 84.

CAPTAIN BEEFHEART

102 *He would wash his hair*: Mike Barnes, *Captain Beefheart: The Biography* (Omnibus Press, 2000), 22.

104 *would say, 'Play a high note*: Barnes, *Captain Beefheart*, 78.

108 *I could see that Ry*: John "Drumbo" French, *Beefheart: Through the Eyes of Magic* (Proper Music Publishing, 2010), 213.

113 *the first indication of*: Bill Harkleroad, with Billy James, *Lunar Notes: Zoot Horn Rollo's Captain Beefheart Experience* (Gonzo Multimedia, 2000), 23.

115 *Dear Jim: Ms. arrived*: Richard Ellman, *James Joyce* (Oxford University Press, 1965), 596–97.

115 *I've put in so many*: Ellman, *James Joyce*, 535.

118 *When we weren't rehearsing*: Harkleroad, *Lunar Notes*, 33.

HANDSOME NED

137 *There was this whole*: Michael Barclay, "The Lonesome Ballads of Handsome Ned and Jr Gone Wild," *Exclaim*, Nov. 17, 2016.

139 *He had an amazing voice*: Barclay, "Lonesome Ballads."

141 *Nobody likes to say it*: Michael Barclay, Ian A. D. Jack, and Jason Schneider, *Have Not Been the Same: The CanRock Renaissance, 1985–1995*, (ECW, 2001), 396.

DUANE ALLMAN

146 *He drove the damn*: Alan Paul, *One Way Out: The Inside History of the Allman Brothers Band* (St. Martin's Press, 2014), 2.

146 *Duane knew he lived*: Paul, *One Way Out*, 37.

147 *always believed. He kept*: Gregg Allman, with Alan Light, *My Cross to Bear* (William Morrow, 2012), 64.

149 *he said, "Man that record*: Allman, *My Cross*, 90.

152 *Duane played bottleneck guitar*: Randy Poe, *Skydog: The Duane Allman Story* (Backbeat Books, 2006), 79.

154 *They got this white*: Poe, *Skydog*, 94–95.

157 *One day we were jamming*: Paul, *One Way Out*, 21.

160 *We went all the way*: Scott Freeman, *Midnight Riders: The Story of the Allman Brothers Band* (Little, Brown, 1995), 61.

161 *Duane had listened to*: Paul, *One Way Out*, 61.

163 *one night the Macon police*: Poe, *Skydog*, 208.

168 *One night in the summer*: Paul, *One Way Out*, 135–36.

LEE MAVERS

172 *"Sometimes," Horace wrote*: Abby Osborne Russell, *An English Paraphrase of Horace's Art of Poetry* (W.R. Jenkins, 1896), 70.

174 *Immature poets imitate*: George Williamson, *A Reader's Guide to T. S. Eliot: A Poem-by-Poem Analysis* (Syracuse University Press, 1998), 37.

179 *Mavers didn't want it*: MW Macefield, *In Search of the La's: A Secret Liverpool*, 2nd ed. (Helter Skelter Publishing, 2012), 72.

181 *I did! (laughs) It got*: Mike Badger, interview, Conwy, [Wales,] Nov. 2019, *@_The_Las* (blog), updated Sep. 4, 2020, https://thelasblogs.wordpress.com/2020/09/04/mike-badger-interview-conwy-november-2019/.

182 *I got the train from London*: Macefield, *In Search*, 84.

DUSTER BENNETT

184 *Opposition brings concord*: Quoted in "Heraclitus," in *The Presocratics*, ed. by Philip Wheelwright (Bobbs-Merrill, 1960), 77.

185 *I honestly think that*: Martin Celmins, *Duster Bennett: Jumping at Shadows* (JetMartin, 2007), 32.

186 *Tony explored art and*: Celmins, *Duster Bennett*, 43.

188 *almost instantly, our initial*: Mike Vernon, liner notes to Duster Bennett, *The Complete Blue Horizon Sessions*, produced by Mike Vernon and Duster Bennett, Blue Horizon 518517-2, 2005, 2 compact discs.

189 *Energy is Eternal Delight*: William Blake, *Blake: Complete Writings; With Variant Readings*, ed. Geoffrey Keynes (Oxford University Press, 1971), 149.

198 *asked a local priest*: Celmins, *Duster Bennett*, 99.

200 *The commercial stuff was poppy*: Stella Bennett, liner notes to Duster Bennett, *Fingertips*, reissue with bonus tracks, Castle Music CMRCD-711, 2003, compact disc.

DANNY KIRWAN

203 *Everything you want to know*: Martin Celmins, *Duster Bennett: Jumping at Shadows* (JetMartin, 2007), 191.

213 *painfully shy and polite*: Martin Celmins, liner notes, *The Vaudeville Years of Fleetwood Mac: 1968 to 1970*, Receiver Records RDPCD 14, 1998, 2 compact discs.

214 *Danny and Pete began*: Celmins, *Vaudeville Years*.

215 *Danny was always very keen*: Celmins, *Vaudeville Years*.

222 *Once they got into the tour*: Martin Celmins, *Peter Green: The Authorized Biography* (Sanctuary, 2003), 156.

222 *a nice kid, but*: Bob Brunning, *Fleetwood Mac: Behind the Masks* (New English Library, 1990), 39.

226 *was a walking time bomb*: Mick Fleetwood, *Fleetwood: My Life and Adventures in Fleetwood Mac* (William Morrow, 1990), 108.

229 *impossible to work with*: Brunning, *Fleetwood Mac*, 38.

229 *On that long tour*: Fleetwood, *My Life*, 107.

237 *In due course he showed*: Fleetwood, *My Life*, 233–34.

237 *when my wife and I*: Henry Yates, "Then Play On: The Story of Fleetwood Mac Guitarist Danny Kirwan," *MusicRadar*, Oct. 24, 2018, https://www.musicradar.com/news/then-play-on-the-story-of-fleetwood-mac-guitarist-danny-kirwan.

NICK DRAKE

242 *bright, but he had*: Richard Morton Jack, *Nick Drake: The Life* (Hachette Books, 2023), 41–42.

244 *was very conscious of the way*: Patrick Humphries, *Nick Drake: The Biography* (Bloomsbury, 1997), 67. Ellipsis in original.

244 *He was very nice*: Humphries, *Nick Drake*, 66. Ellipses in original.

251 *A man's character is*: Jonathan Barnes, *Early Greek Philosophy* (Penguin, 1987), 124.

251 *didn't introduce any of*: Jack, *Nick Drake*, 135.

252 *waking Nick up at his*: Trevor Dann, *Darker than the Deepest Sea: The Search for Nick Drake* (Da Capo Press, 2006), 136.

256 *I'd love to say*: Jack, *Nick Drake*, 119–20.

257 *took that like being hit*: Dann, *Deepest Sea*, 164–65.

257 *Nicky was nobody's friend*: John Neil Munro, *Some People Are Crazy: The John Martyn Story* (Polygon, 2010), 104–15.

261 *We were busy with Cat*: Jack, *Nick Drake*, 459.

262 *Just before he died*: Dann, *Deepest Sea*, 180.

MUDDY WATERS

265 *Definitely Muddy. His sound!*: Sandra B. Tooze, *Muddy Waters: The Mojo Man* (ECW, 1997), 136.

270 *I understood what Muddy*: John Anthony Brisbin, "Jimmy Rogers," in *Rollin' and Tumblin': The Postwar Blues Guitarists*, ed. Jas Obrecht (Miller Freeman Books, 2000), 134.

279 *The big beat*: Robert Gordon, *Can't Be Satisfied: The Life and Times of Muddy Waters* (Back Bay Books, 2002), 146.

279 *There were weekends that we*: Gordon, *Can't Be Satisfied*, 147.

280 *When we started the Rolling Stones*: B. R. Sharma, *The Death of Art* (University Press of America, 2006), 12.

282 *What I really wanted*: Charles Shaar Murray, "Muddy Waters: Life After Chess," *Classic Rock*, Aug. 16, 2016, https://www.loudersound.com/features/muddy-waters-life-after-chess.

RAY ROBERTSON is the author of nine novels, six collections of nonfiction, and a book of poetry. His work has been translated into several languages. He contributed the liner notes to three Grateful Dead archival releases: *Dave's Picks #45*, the *Here Comes Sunshine 1973* boxed set, and the *From the Mars Hotel* 50th Anniversary Deluxe Edition. Born and raised in Chatham, Ontario, he lives in Toronto.